A Spectrum of Faith

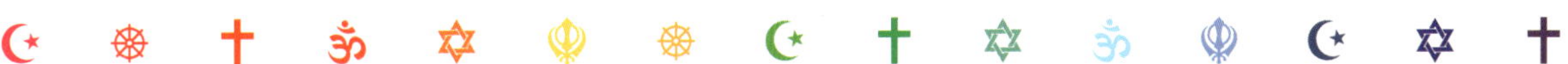

RELIGIONS OF THE WORLD
IN AMERICA'S HEARTLAND

To the people of Greater Des Moines
and their diverse religious communities.

A Spectrum of Faith

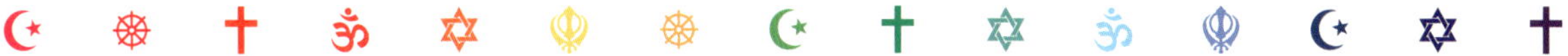

RELIGIONS OF THE WORLD
IN AMERICA'S HEARTLAND

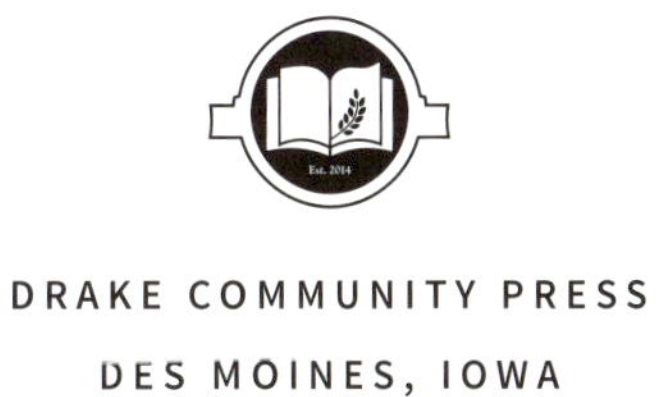

DRAKE COMMUNITY PRESS
DES MOINES, IOWA

EDITORS' NOTE

We have tried our best to employ the most common transliterations of foreign terms, to italicize foreign terms unless they are common in English, and to leave out diacritical marks unless the community has requested them.

Published by
Drake Community Press
2507 University Avenue
Des Moines, Iowa 50311

Printed and bound in the USA

Library of Congress Control Number: 2017935999
ISBN: 978-0-692-85515-7
First Edition

Additional information can be found at
www.drakecommunitypress.org/

Table of Contents

Foreword

Eboo Patel

One of the most enduring symbols of the United States is "the city on a hill." The phrase is from the Bible, specifically the famed Sermon on the Mount, where Jesus tells his listeners: "You are the light of the world. A city that is set on a hill cannot be hidden."

The words come to America aboard the ship Arbella, uttered by John Winthrop in a speech called *A Model of Christian Charity*: "We must always consider, that we shall be as a city upon a hill—the eyes of all people are upon us."

The line suggests many things that Americans believe deeply, notably that our nation is an opportunity to build unique communities, and that we do this not just for ourselves but also to inspire people around the world.

Winthrop, of course, did not intend to include the indigenous people of this continent upon which he arrived in his idea of harmonious community. And he did not consider the African slaves who were arriving in different ships, including many Muslims, part of the city either.

But future American leaders would widen our understanding of this "city upon a hill" and not only include them but note that they were fellow architects of the American possibility.

Before assuming his duties as President, John F. Kennedy used the image in an address where he spoke of "the common threads woven by the Pilgrim and the Puritan, the fisherman and the farmer, the Yankee and the immigrant."

And President Ronald Reagan offered a powerful description in his Farewell Address, stating that he saw this city as "God-blessed, and teeming with people of all kinds living in harmony and peace ... And there had to be city walls, the walls had doors and the doors were open to anyone with the will and heart to get here."

President Barack Obama, when he was still a U.S. Senator, picked up where Reagan left off and gave his own understanding of the city on a hill in his commencement address at the University of Massachusetts at Boston: "I look out at a sea of faces that are African-American and Hispanic-American and Asian-American and Arab-American. I see students that have come here from 100 different countries, believing like those first settlers that they too could find a home in this City on a Hill—that they too could find success in this unlikeliest of place."

Speaking of unlikely places, you hold in your hands a beautiful collection of photos and essays of the City on a Hill that is Des Moines, Iowa. For people from Des Moines, it is no surprise to you that your neighbors are Muslims and Buddhists and Hindus and Christians of all varieties. You have been making food and music and friendships together for years. For those less familiar with Des Moines—including the Chicagoan writing this essay—I look through these pages with admiration, seeing in what you have built something that I believe cities all over the United States and the world should seek to emulate.

I see here the common threads that Kennedy spoke about, the sea of diverse faces that Obama saw at that commencement ceremony and the harmony and peace that President Reagan described. I see beauty and possibility and a new America emerging, one that is stronger than ever before.

And I am more confident than I ever was that this nation is sacred, and that we make it holy by who we welcome and how we relate to each other.

Thank you, Des Moines, for building a city worth setting upon a hill.

Introduction

Tim Knepper

If this project has a remote origin in time, it surrounds my 2002 move to the state of Iowa. Having arrived from the "big city" of Boston, I was astounded by the teeming diversity of religion in a state that I had previously considered "flat" in so many ways. To this day, I remain astounded not only by this diversity itself but also by how little Iowans know about it. One goal of this book is simply to make Iowans more aware of the rich diversity of religion in their state and how that diversity is a function of Iowa's rich history of welcoming refugees and immigrants.

If this project has a more recent genesis in time, it involves my serendipitous meeting of "our" photographer, Bob Blanchard. In the fall of 2014, I wrote an op-ed for the *Des Moines Register* on the dedication of a forty-foot statue of the Vietnamese Buddhist bodhisattva of compassion, Quan Âm. Bob read that op-ed, attended the dedication, and took pictures of it. Later, he contacted me asking if I could introduce him to more religious communities in Des Moines. I said, I have a better idea—let's write a "picture book" about the "religions of Des Moines."

Our early work in the project—my words and Bob's photos—focused on the lived practices and spatial transformations of Des Moines' refugee and immigrant religions. Although rewarding, it was also slow going, in part because we could never quite imagine the final form of the project. It wasn't until the project was picked up by the Drake Community Press that it came together through the creative input of Carol Spaulding-Kruse and her team of student editors. We owe Carol and her students a debt of gratitude, not to mention years of our lives.

Most of the content for this book was generated in the Spring 2016 semester. Fifteen of my religion students immersed themselves in fifteen religious communities. There, they learned that religion is lived in ways that often elude textbooks and go beyond beliefs. Their writing does not pretend to be encyclopedic or even really objective—rather, it reflects their encounters of lived religion. We also owe a debt of gratitude not only to these students but to the religious communities who warmly welcomed them. Many friendships were established and deepened.

Why our book contains only these fifteen sites of worship is an issue that tormented us throughout the life of the project. In many cases, I was simply drawing on previously established friendships and connections. But we felt we needed criteria other than that. So it was decided that each religion would have no more than three representatives, since there are three main branches of both Judaism and Christianity. It was also decided that every religion in the book would be represented by at least two sites of worship, since religions are internally diverse. Given the preponderance of Abrahamic religion in Des Moines, it made sense to include three communities each from Judaism, Christianity, and Islam. And given the fact that there are only two established organizations each for the Asian religions of Hinduism and Sikhism (at least to our knowledge!), we decided that we would also only include two Buddhist communities, one representing the Southeast Asian branch of Theravada, the other representing the East Asian branch of Mahayana.

Still, it pains us that more of Des Moines' religious diversity didn't make it into the book. If we take solace in anything, it is that, as Bob puts it, this is only volume one! As our Muslim friends would say, *Inshallah* (God willing).

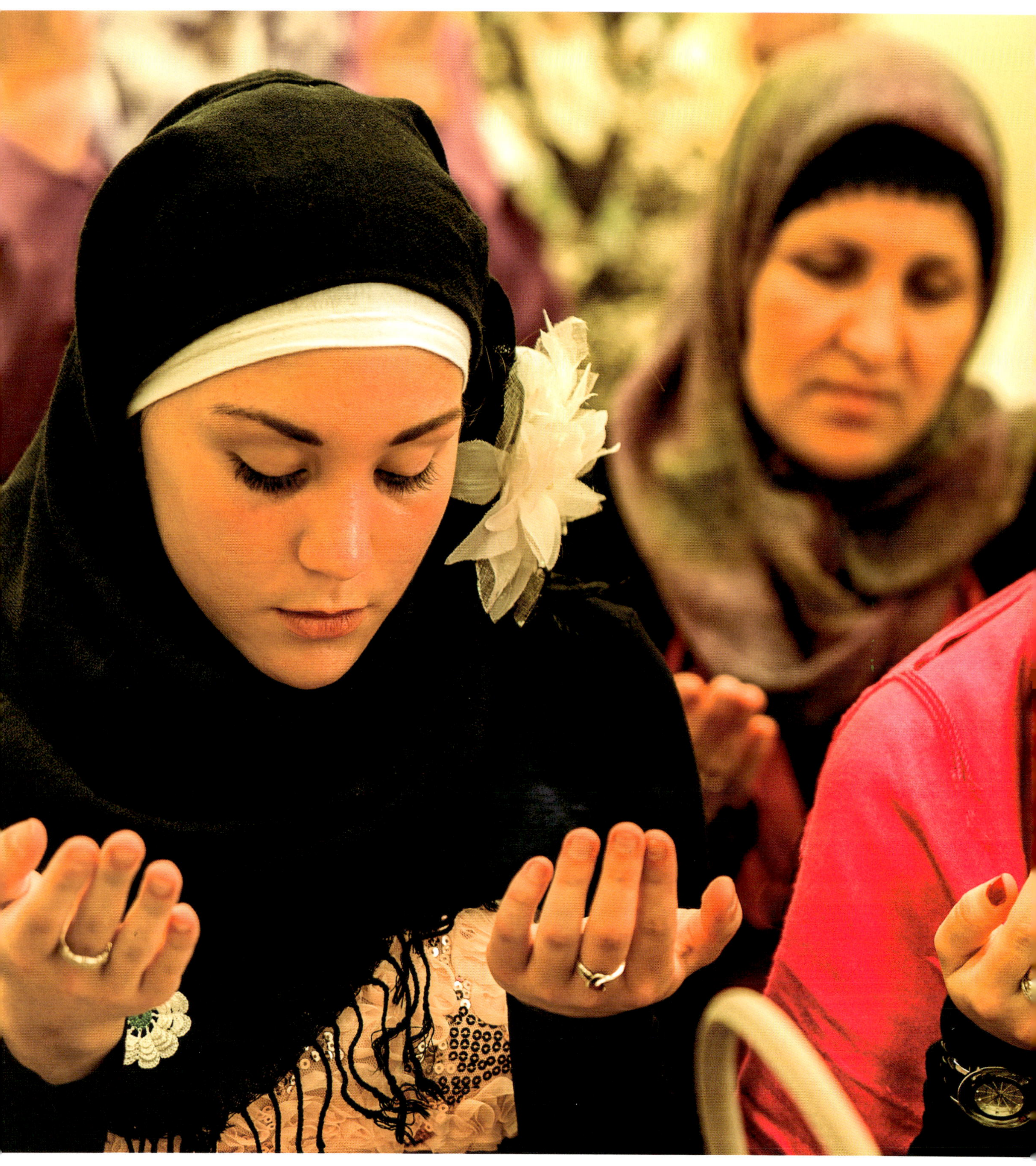

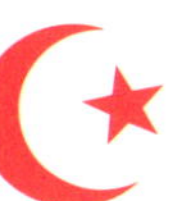

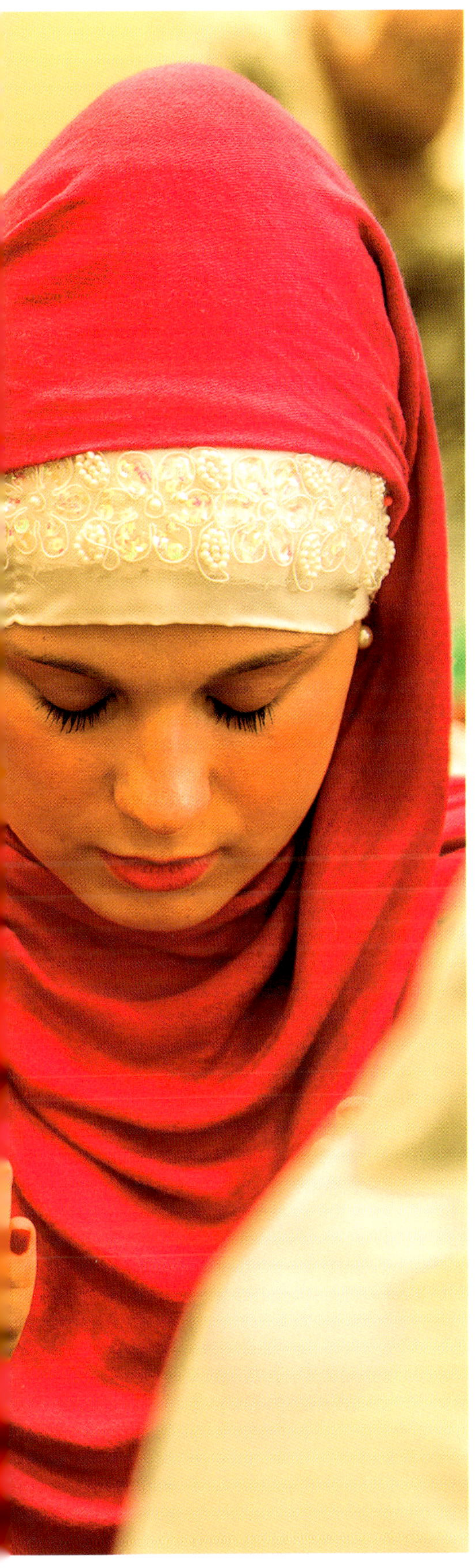

Ezan: Islamic and Education Center

Matthew Becke

IDENTITY Rising from the sidewalk of a busy street in Des Moines, a large white marquee displays in bold letters "Ezan: Islamic and Education Center." The word *ezan* translates to "call to prayer"—the recitation of holy words heralding the prayer conducted by Muslims five distinct times every day. These daily prayers are one of the "Five Pillars" of Islamic faith and highlight the spiritual dedication of Muslims at Ezan. Yet the description is hardly exhaustive. Educators, police officers, doctors, business owners, and even beekeepers comprise the members of Ezan. They are brothers and sisters. They are families raising young children. They are elders and leaders guiding the faithful.

And they are refugees.

The people of this community share a painful history as victims of genocide, a history that has shaped the lives of every one of them. Bosnia, Croatia, and Serbia were once amongst a communist conglomerate of nationalities known as Yugoslavia, which formed after the Second World War. But war broke out as these individual countries began to declare their independence and make claims on specific lands. In the former Yugoslavia, the ruling Communist Party strictly

Adijana Dizdarevic (left) and Lejla Mehmedovoc (right) performing supplication (*du'a*) after one of the daily payers (*salat*)

enforced secular attitudes in society and in the schools, which meant that "Muslim" became an ethnic, as opposed to a religious, affiliation in the eyes of the State. Denied professional opportunity, and politically side-lined as second-class citizens, Muslims in Bosnia-Herzogovina—over half of Bosnia-Herzogovina's population—soon became targets of Serbian paramilitary forces.

Despite—or perhaps because of—this hardship, the unflinching gratitude Ezan members hold for their lives in the United States stands out clearly. I have yet to meet a member of Ezan who did not express praise for their host country. The people of Ezan have worked hard to overcome a painful history that is never far from their thoughts. They have stifled the urge to remain mournful and instead have transformed their tragedy into a chance to grow as individuals, as devout Muslims, and together as a community in their adopted homeland. Here, Muslim identity is a point of pride, not a badge of inferiority. Here, the people of Ezan have the chance to thrive.

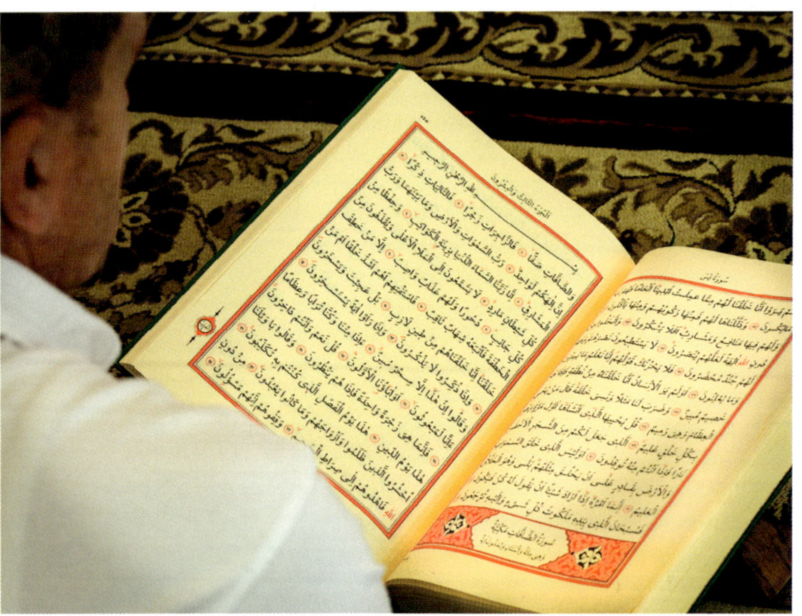

Sefik Tursunovic reading the Qur'an before the call to prayer

When Dzana Memic was only three years old, her family was forced to flee Serbian aggression in the region of Banja Luka. From Germany, her family moved to Des Moines where she grew up. "I was afraid that by learning the English language, I would slowly start to forget my native tongue," says Dzana, "even though I spoke Bosnian with my parents and relatives on a daily basis." Now, at age 21, Dzana is working on her Masters Degree in Health Administration. As she puts it, "I realized that I could have the best of both worlds by taking pride in my Bosnian roots while growing and succeeding in the American lifestyle." She sings in the Bosnian women's choir at Ezan. And she teaches religious education to Ezan children every weekend, helping to educate the next generation of Bosnian Americans.

"When I first covered," says Dzana, referring to her hijab, the head covering worn by many Muslim women, "it was on my 18th birthday, and I was in Turkey. Of course in Turkey, that's how most women are. It's usual for them. When I came back—at the time I was working at a bank—and I didn't know if…I understood that they accepted diversity, but I didn't know if they took it to that extent of me showing my religion in the way I do. Thankfully…they were accepting of it and they enjoy seeing it." It's been three years, with no negative reactions from the larger community thus far.

Warm acceptance from their neighbors and citizens of Des Moines has been the norm for members of Ezan. Against a backdrop of rampant slandering of Islam by much of the American media, Iowa has offered hospitality, not hostility. At the same time, assimilation is not the refugees' goal. Their way of life was taken from them; that's not easy for most native-born Americans to understand. They seek to strike the right balance between integrating into life in the United States and preserving what remains of their Bosnian origins. They hope to enrich Iowa's cultural heritage through sharing of their religious and cultural practices. But for the members of Ezan, preserving that heritage is not just a matter of cultural pride: it's survival.

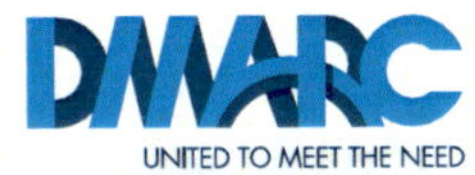

DMARC Food Pantry Network

Des Moines Area Religious Council | 1435 Mulberry Street | Des Moines, IA 50309 | 515.277.6969 | dmarcunited.org

Working together to meet basic human needs for the greater Des Moines community.

The DMARC Food Pantry Network, established in 1976, consists of 13 partner pantry sites, 13 Mobile Food Pantry sites, two food warehouses, and numerous community partners. It is the largest and oldest food pantry system in Iowa. Pantry sites are located in West Des Moines, Ankeny, Johnston, Clive and Urbandale, with eight sites in Des Moines.

Once per calendar month, families can receive a free, three-day supply of nutritionally balanced food. It's not enough for us to just fill stomachs, we want to provide nourishing food to those we serve. Families can also receive additional 'Anytime Items' every day at pantries. DMARC serves 16,000-17,000 individuals every month—60% of whom are children, youth and older adults.

How You Can Help

Donate Funds

DMARC works with a number of food wholesalers to find the best deals. With our purchasing power, we are able to buy anywhere from 2-6 times the amount of food you could in the grocery store with the same dollar. So, if you want to do more with your dollar, consider donating funds to our Food Pantry Network!

Donate Food

In-kind food donations through food drives and our Red Barrel program are still very important to DMARC's work. When donating food, please use our "Most Needed Items" list (reverse) to make sure you're donating items that meet our healthy food guidelines. And if you're not sure about something, look for items to donate that are low in sugar, fat and salt.

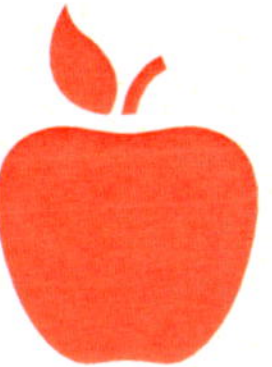

Volunteer

We have all sorts of volunteer opportunities for both groups and individuals! Visit www.dmarcunited.org/volunteer for more details on how you can contribute your time and talents.

Interfaith Opportunitites

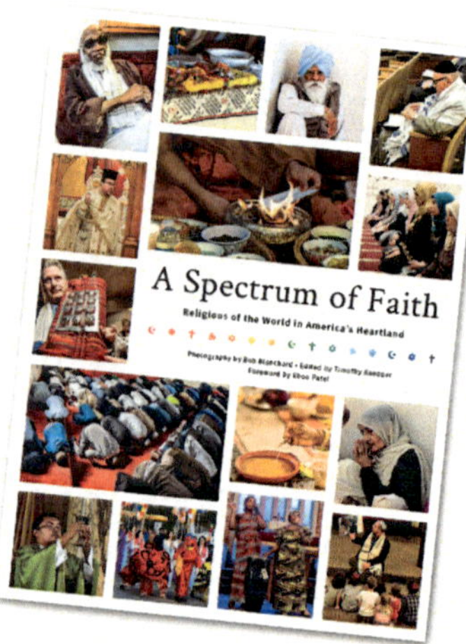

A Spectrum of Faith

A Spectrum of Faith: Religions of the World in America's Heartland invites readers on a vivid journey through words and pictures into the diverse religious communities of greater Des Moines. The book is a joint product of Drake Community Press, The Comparison Project, photographer Bob Blanchard, and DMARC. All proceeds from the book support the DMARC Food Pantry Network.

dmarcunited.org/book/

Meet My Religious Neighbor

Meet My Religious Neighbor is an ongoing series of open houses hosted by The Comparison Project in places of worship in the greater Des Moines area. Each open house generally occurs on the first weekend of the month.

comparisonproject.wp.drake.edu/ meet-my-religious-neighbor/

The Comparison Project Lectures

The Comparison Project (TCP) at Drake University hosts an annual interfaith lecture and dialogue series. The theme for 2017-2019 is "Miracles."

comparisonproject.wp.drake.edu

Interfaith Dialogue

DMARC organizes interfaith dialogue and panels for groups and congregations. For more information on hosting a dialogue, contact Rev. Sarah Trone Garriott at **stronegarriott@dmarcunited.org**.

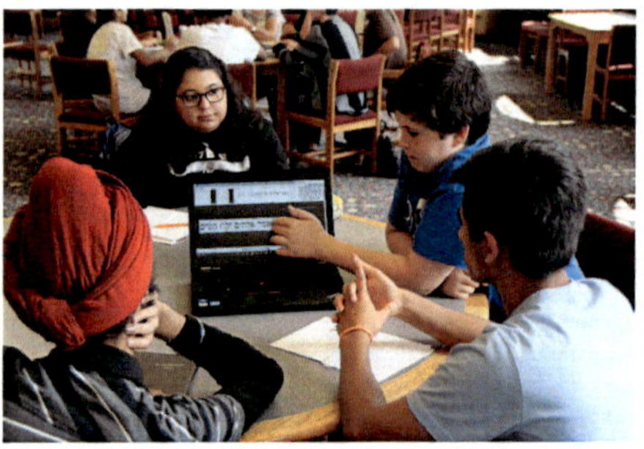

Interfaith Youth Leadership Camp

DMARC and TCP co-host an annual Interfaith Youth Leadership Camp. High school students representing a diverse array of religious traditions create and share a digital story about a personally meaningful faith experience, visit various religious communities in Greater Des Moines, and discuss the principles and practices of interfaith leadership.

iowainterfaithexchange.com/ youthcamp

LEARN MORE:

dmarcunited.org/services/interfaith

comparisonproject.wp.drake.edu

Peace. Prosperity. Acceptance. These are values that the community of Ezan attributes to the Islamic faith. The violence linked to Islam and so often highlighted in our news is far from the reality being lived by this or most Muslim communities. Thankful for the opportunities given and hopeful about the future, the members of Ezan wish to offer their lives as proof that Islam is, at its core, a religion of peace.

HISTORY "It was like a chain reaction," Dzana's father, Rasim Memic, says of the arrival of the first Bosnians in Des Moines, who had come from war prisons. "We didn't have very many options. Back home, everything was destroyed. We are lucky the USA accepted us, and we are more than glad to be here," Memic said. Once established, those first families began to reach out to cousins, friends, parents, and siblings either already in the U.S. or still in Bosnia to come join them. This chain reaction also produced their leader.

In 2009, a young man named Nijaz paid a visit to his cousin in West Des Moines. He had recently completed a Bachelor's degree in Islamic Studies at the University of Sarajevo when he heard about a new mosque in Des Moines that was looking for an imam, or spiritual leader. Ezan invited Nijaz to take on the position. Only 24 years old and, at the time, still residing in Bosnia, Nijaz accepted the opportunity, secured a visa, and began a two-year trial period as the leader of Ezan. Like so many others in his community, Nijaz has welcomed Iowa into his heart and has chosen this location to begin his own family.

"I feel the need to mention," adds Nijaz, "that we Bosnian Americans came from a multi-ethnic and multi-religious country. We used to live in a diverse society." During the war, Bosnians were attacked by those who didn't want to live in a society like that. While some people had left Bosnia before the violence reached its heights, other members were not so lucky. Life became even harder for those who survived the war. Almost everyone at Ezan lost someone they loved. Mosques and homes were destroyed. Muslims endured systematic rape, torture, and the horrors of concentration camps. The world they knew was shelled into oblivion. Even now, mass graves are still found throughout the region, with over one thousand people still listed as missing. In the end, ethnic cleansing had displaced over 3 million people.

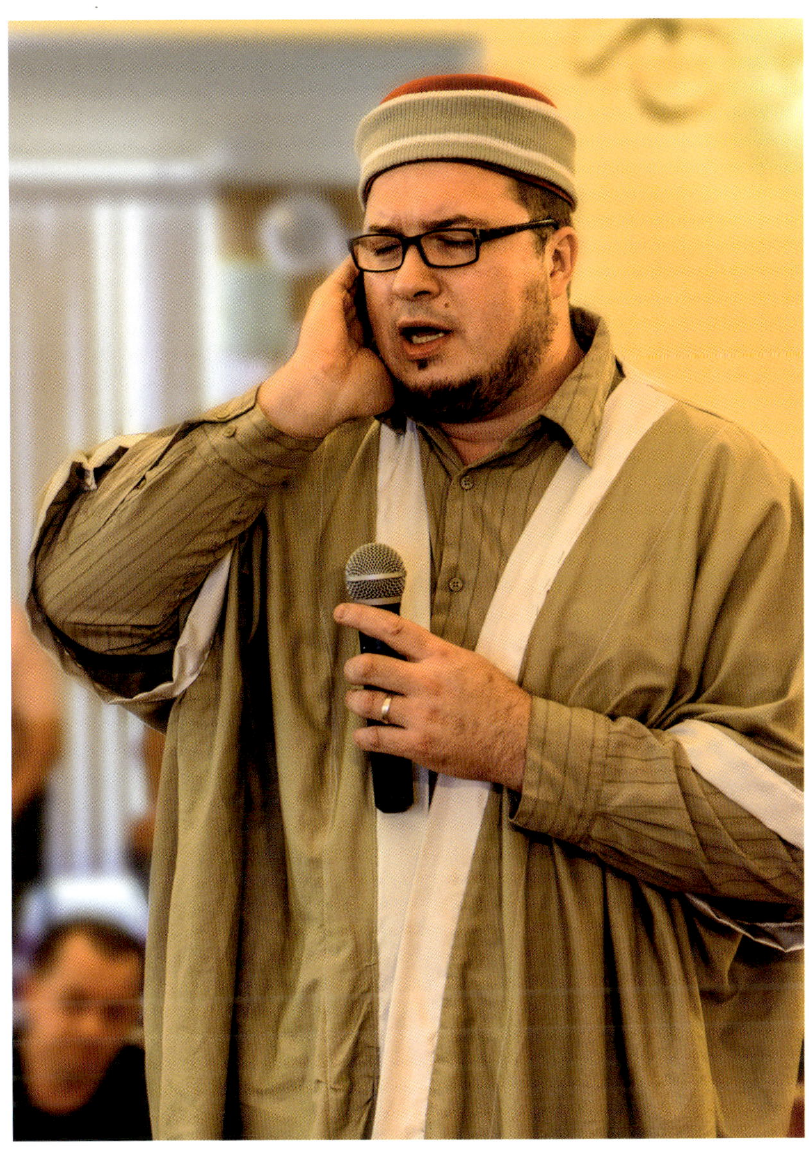

Ezan's muezzin, Nermin Sehovic, issuing the call to prayer

In 1992, the first Bosnian family came to the city of Des Moines, offered refuge by the United States government. And many families followed. Most of the Bosnian refugees who came to the United States after the war did not speak English. They arrived with only a few pieces of luggage.

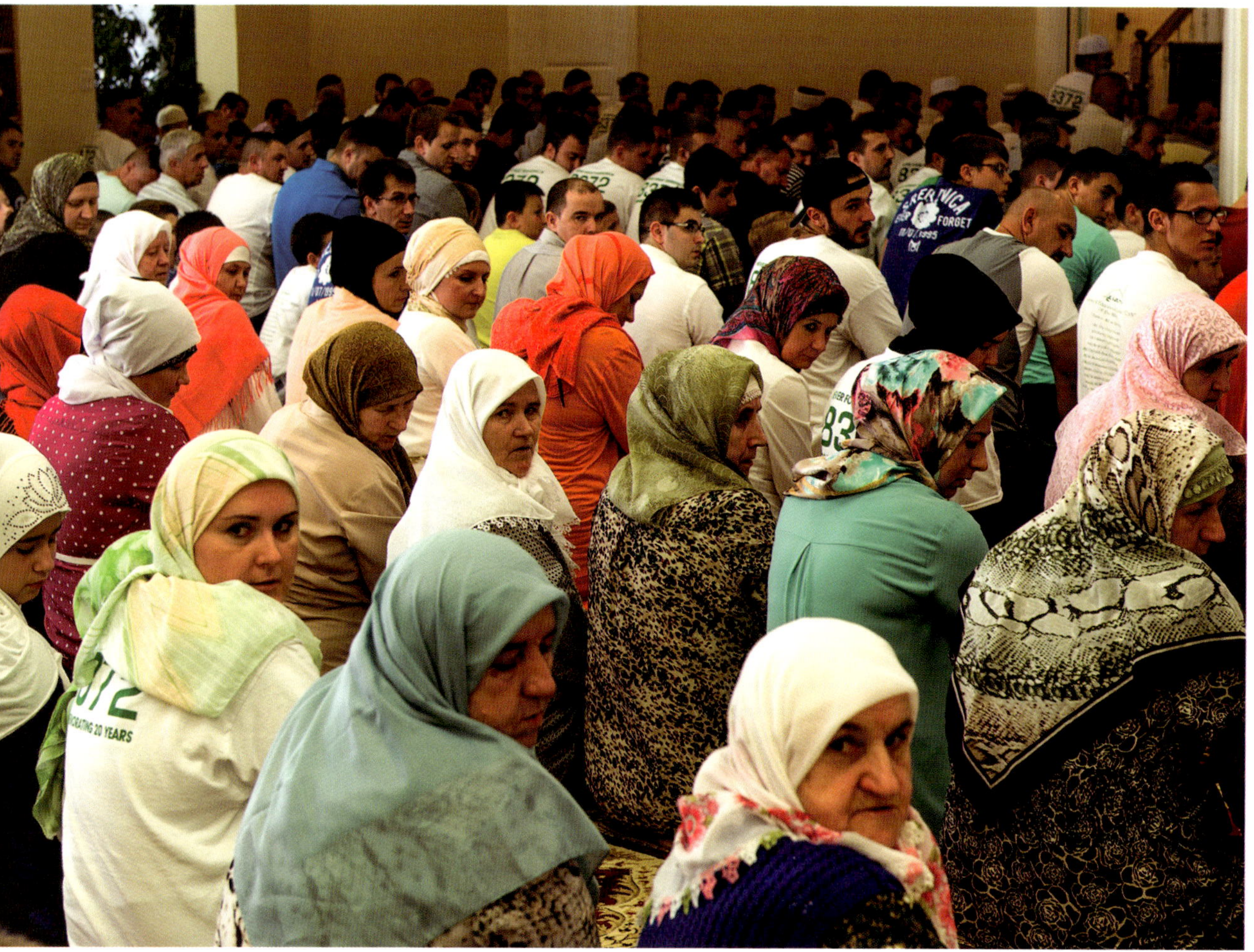

The members of Ezan conclude one unit of prayer (*rakat*) by addressing the angels over their right and left shoulders

Their professional degrees were useless in the United States. But here, now, they have hope for the future again, and social mobility.

Ezan has found a moment of peace.

SPACE A former commercial building on a busy street in Central Des Moines provides an inconspicuous façade for the mosque of Ezan: a spiritual sanctuary lies within.

One of the hardest things to replace after war is a sense of belonging. Establishing a home in a foreign land is integral for refugees to begin the process of regaining what they have lost. At first, finding work and learning American customs take precedent. Eventually, with these initial goals achieved, a community begins to yearn for a space to call their own.

As the refugee community of Ezan grew, members decided to look for a building suitable for a mosque. Money was tight. They didn't always agree about what they were looking for. But in order to fit both property and a building into their budget, they did agree they needed a fixer-upper. Location mattered greatly, as the mosque would host at least five prayer times each day. Eventually they found an old former car dealership and mechanic shop close to where many of the community lived. Auspiciously, they purchased the building on the first day of Ramadan in 2008.

A fixer-upper, indeed—there was no ceiling, an empty interior, nothing but bare concrete walls. New plumbing, electricity, heating, and air-conditioning would come first. Drywall had to be installed throughout the building, and the room's focal point had to be altered to face northeast, the direction of Mecca. For *wudu*, the ritual cleansing prior to prayer, the bathroom would need remodeling. Undeterred, this small group of dedicated people took what little money they had and transformed the old building into a beautiful mosque and community center.

The community did all the work. By day 27, the mosque was ready to host prayer services. Gladly, the community moved from rented space in a local school to a space they could call their own. People who came to this country with nothing but a determination to rebuild their lives—these are the people who built Ezan. They did more than remodel an abandoned building; they transformed themselves from displaced survivors of war to established Americans.

How best to utilize their new building? Everyone knew it would host regular prayer services. But the congregation of Ezan wanted to offer more. First, they established a weekly Islamic education program for youth—a big step toward that important goal of religious and cultural preservation of their roots. But why limit educational opportunities to children when so many Americans knew little about the Islamic faith? Today, Ezan's doors are open to any person interested in learning more about Islam. Through education, understanding becomes possible. It was this spirit of education and understanding that persuaded me to join the community of Ezan during the month-long observance of Ramadan.

PRACTICE Leaning against a metal porch rail behind the mosque, I take in the sound of the Bosnian language being spoken by the twenty men who surround me. They will switch to English as soon as I attempt to engage, but for now I sit back and enjoy watching the men interact with one another on one of the last nights of Ramadan. The prayer service just prior to the breaking of our daily fast was full of anticipation for the upcoming meal. We have refrained from eating and drinking the entire day, so the aroma of the savory dishes being brought in is profoundly enticing. Sweet dates are passed out as we wait for the prayer to begin. Then, men, women, and children alike focus their attention towards Mecca. The *ezan*—call to prayer—is recited, and the followers of Allah commence the physical and mental portions of their worship.

You know the prayer has finished when the children race one another to the several tables laden with food, the grown-ups poised but chuckling softly in understanding at their haste. Classic Bosnian dishes of meat, rice, vegetables, and potatoes seem both foreign to me and yet

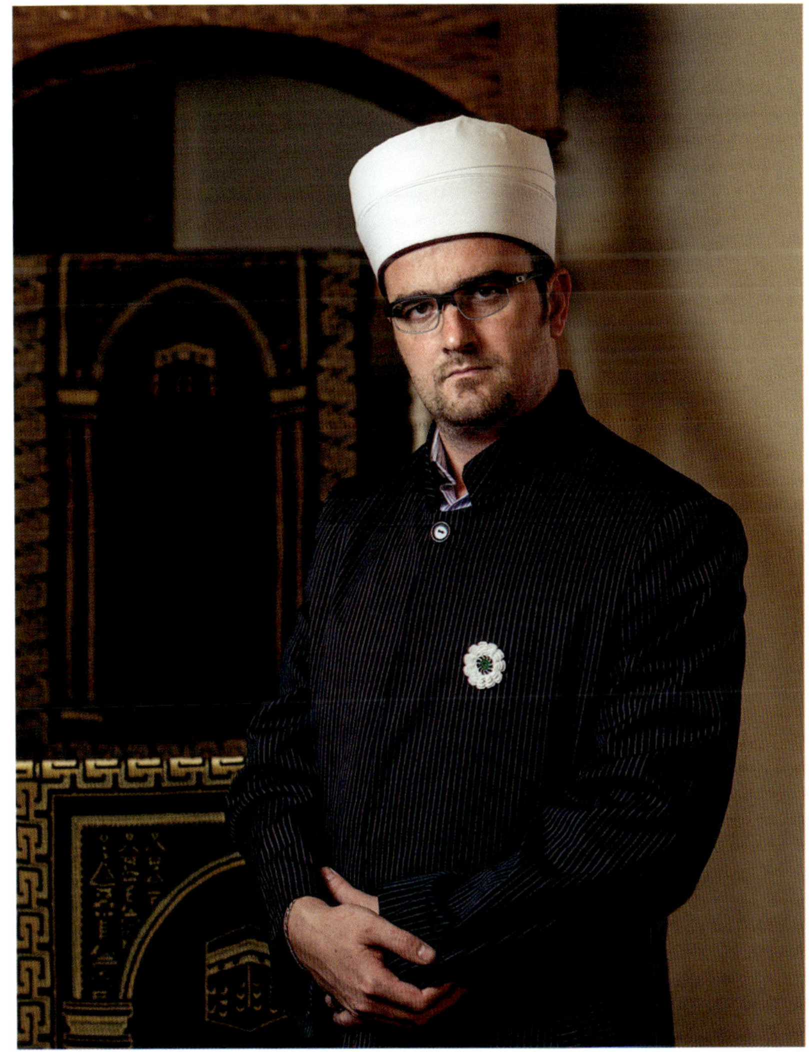

Imam Nijaz ef. Valjevcic

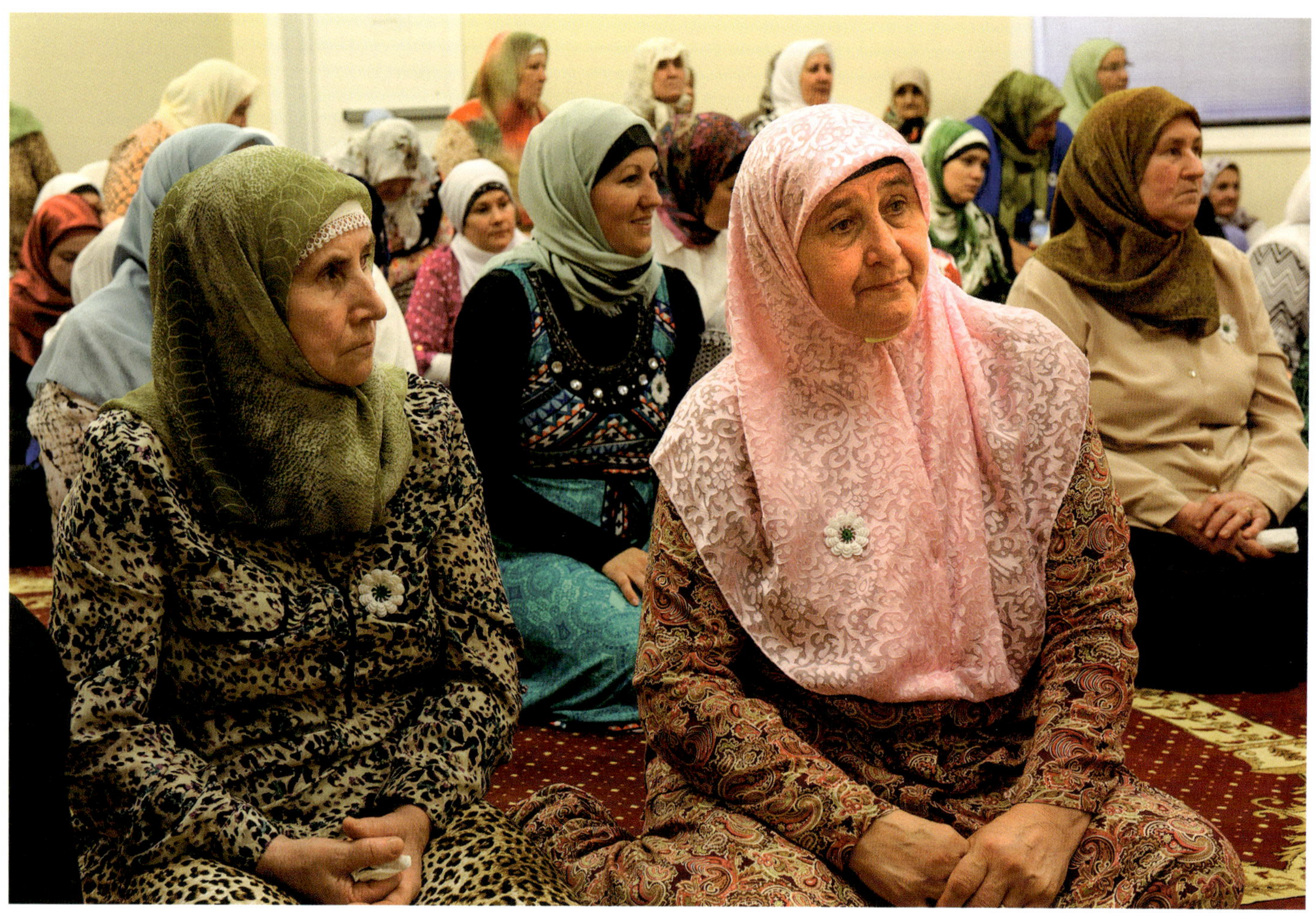

Female members of Ezan listening to a program about the Srebrenica genocide

strangely familiar. There is pizza for the children, along with soups, salads, and desserts as sides. This community meal, called *iftar*, is potluck style and welcomes all, regardless of race, religion, or nationality. As we eat, sitting cross-legged on the ground, I converse with a few of the men who attend regularly but have been sharing *iftar* at different locations each night—there are three Bosnian mosques and eight mosques altogether in Des Moines—to show solidarity within the larger Islamic community. After the meal, the men step outside to gather around a few picnic tables and drink the Bosnian coffee that will help sustain them through the final prayer of the day, *isha*. The summer evening is warm. They try to ignore the cracks and pops of nearby firecrackers. For Americans, this signals the coming of the Independence Day holiday. But for Bosnians the sound is all too familiar: it's the sound of a city under siege.

Occurring during the ninth month of the Islamic lunar calendar, Ramadan is also one of the Five Pillars of the Islamic faith and a central practice for all Muslims. All healthy followers past the age of puberty fast from the moment dawn's light is discernible in the morning sky until the sun has dropped below the horizon in the evening. Muslims use this time of sacrifice to settle into awareness of the divine while also reminding themselves to stay thankful of life's basic necessities.

Although the practice is physically, emotionally, and mentally demanding, it is not meant to punish the body. Rather, Muslims view this practice as a catalyst for the spirit—it's self-purifying. Fasting builds willpower. It also gives the digestive system a break. Combatting human desires creates an excellent opportunity to focus on what is truly important in life. When you're subsisting without food and water, material possessions quickly lose their luster. Life is simplified. *Iftar* becomes a chance to connect with others and affirm the good things that arise from sacrifice.

The first week is the hardest, as the body attempts to adjust to the new schedule. I found myself unusually irritable, so, embarrassed and seeking guidance, I asked the imam for clues on how to control my negative emotions. The same willpower you exercise in abstaining from food and drink can also be directed towards controlling your thoughts, he told me. With life thus simplified, you can begin to weed out negative thinking and behaviors. Yet, transmuting these internal struggles into moments of growth is a humbling and difficult process. Eventually, I found that by altering my outlook so that anger became not a negative emotion but a positive opportunity, I not only successfully completed the fast but have since found greater control over my thoughts and actions.

Although Muslims have *iftar* to look forward to each evening, practitioners are asked to be mindful that millions will remain thirsty and hungry long after the setting of the sun. At Ezan, members are mindful that they were the ones in need of help not long ago; thus, they embrace any opportunity to give back to the community that helped them. Giving a portion of one's salary to the needy, or *zakat*, is expected of all Muslims and is often completed during Ramadan. Ezan is just one of thousands of Muslim communities in America that regularly collects and distributes money to the poor. While it is true that money makes our world go round, I am also told that simple acts of kindness are a form of *zakat* and highly favored by Allah.

Inclusiveness and acceptance are some of the most important values stemming from my experience with the faith community of Ezan.

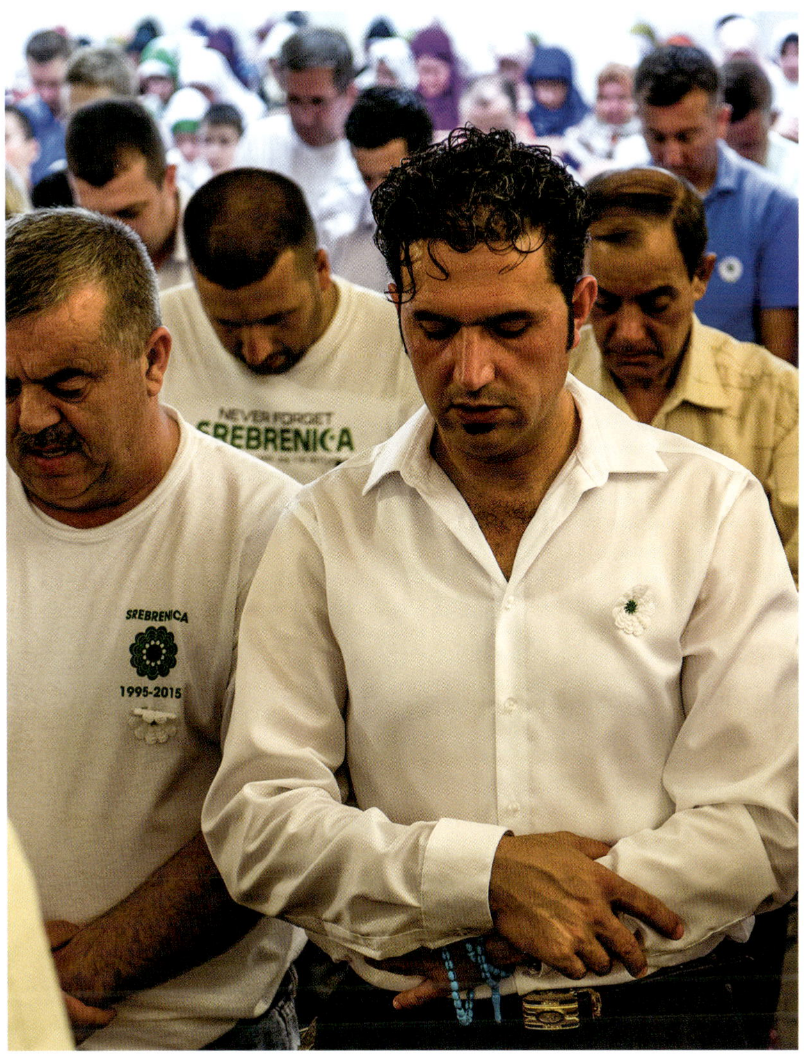

Salih Kocher and other members of Ezan perform one of the daily prayers (*salat*)

Unlike most mosques, women stand behind the men for the daily prayers—not behind a screen or in a separate room. For Dzana Memic this custom "makes you feel more a part of the community." Women can not only hear but also see Imam Nijaz when he speaks, and this gives a better emotional connection to his words.

For me, the kindness and hospitality of Ezan have reminded me how fortunate I am never to have experienced the hardships these Muslims, Bosnians—and, now, Americans—have faced. We stand to learn from their courage and fortitude. All Americans stand to learn from those different from ourselves. Therein manifests our greatness.

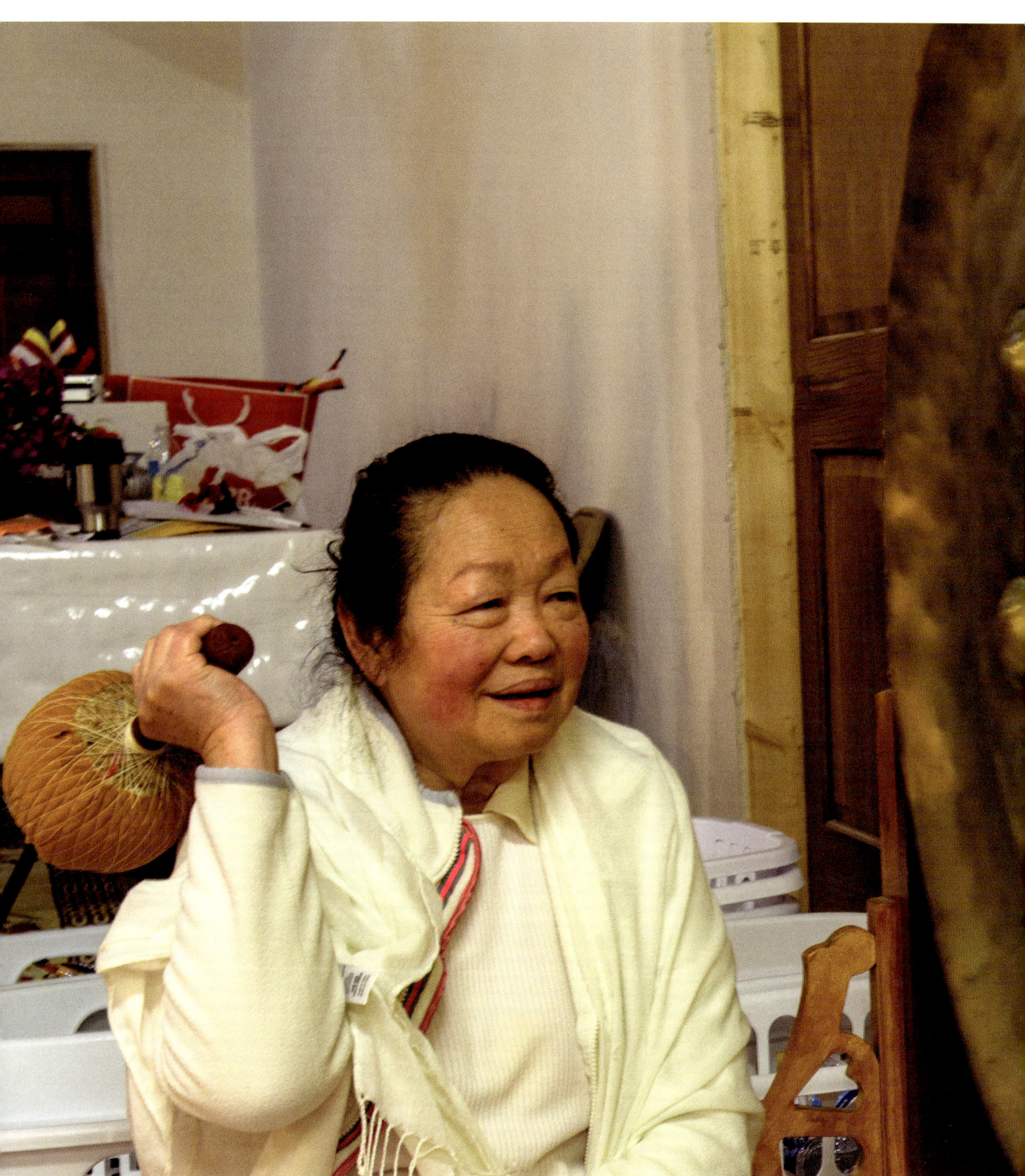

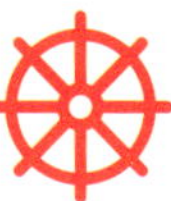

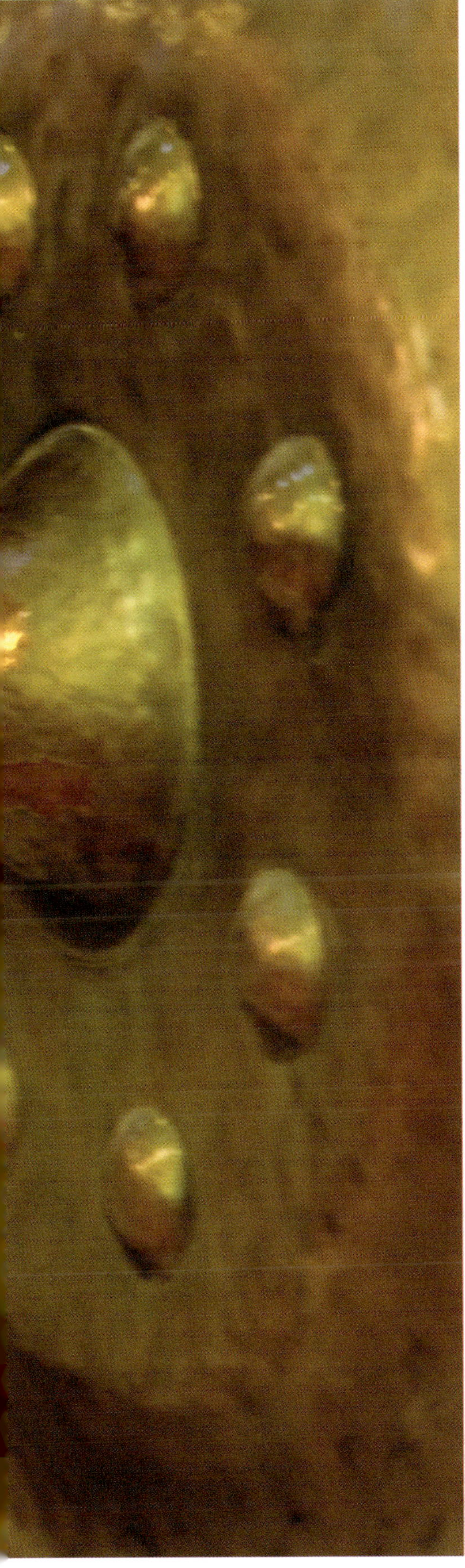

Wat Phothisomphan

W. A. Chamindi Wijesinghe

IDENTITY "I am the disciple, follower, replacement, and teacher."

Phra Ajahn Somphan's powerful words embody the heart of Wat Phothisomphan, or the Meditation Monastery, allowing Buddha's legacy to speak to people's lives. One of many monks from Laos, Phra Ajahn Somphan came to America to create a safe haven for other Laotian Americans in the name of Buddha. His vision is not unique: *Dharma*, the teaching or truth of Buddhism, intertwines every action, thought, prayer, and chant emphasized by all visiting and permanent monks, who are known as *ajahns*. These ancient Buddhist teachings meld with everyday practices so that people always feel connected to the Enlightened One: Lord Buddha.

When Lord Buddha taught the *Dharma* 2,500 years ago, he fostered a new religious philosophy that would attract thousands of followers. As his teachings travelled from India, they took different cultural forms, which led to the creation of different schools of Buddhist practice and thought. However, Theravada Buddhism—the form of Buddhism practiced in Laos and many other Southeast Asian countries—prides itself on remaining true to Lord Buddha's original *Dharma*. Today, Wat Phothisomphan is

Tu See banging the temple gong during a ceremony

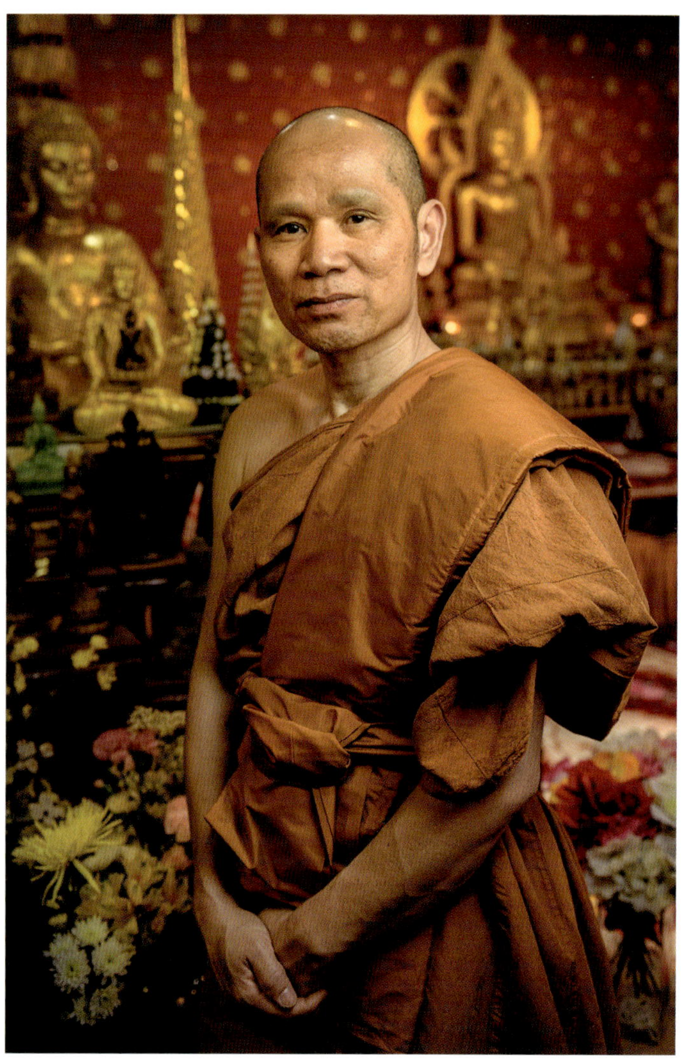

Ajahn Somphan, Wat Phothisomphan's head monk

one of two Lao Buddhist temples in Iowa that embraces this "Way of the Elders."

"I can't think of a dharma-talk without the word *dukkha*, meaning suffering," explains Ajahn Jackson, an American monk from Sioux City who was ordained in the U.S. by a *bhikkhu* from Sri Lanka and serves as a prominent teacher at Wat Phothisomphan. Indeed, *dukkha* is present in all of Buddhism's Four Noble Truths:

- ordinary life brings suffering, especially since everything always changes;
- suffering is caused by attachment to permanence;
- cessation of suffering is attainable;
- cessation of suffering happens by following the Noble Eightfold Path, also known as the *Ariya Atthangika Magga.*

In turn, the Eightfold Path provides guidance for Buddhists in how to live—through right view, right resolve, right speech, right action, right livelihood, right mindfulness, right effort, and right concentration. But on an even more basic level, the Buddhists of Wat Phothisomphan look to one simple line from the *Dhammapada*, a central teaching of the Buddha: "Cease from doing evil. Practice doing good. Purify your mind."

For many lay Buddhists who cannot devote as much time to meditation and study as monks can, this central teaching finds everyday expression in the Five Precepts, which ask that Buddhists refrain from harming living things, taking what is not given, sexual misconduct, false speech, and intoxicants. A strong belief in these teachings knits together the community of Wat Phothisomphan, giving them a sense of belonging and hope in a place so far from their homeland.

Laotian refugees first came to Iowa not long after the end of the Vietnam War, which roughly coincided with the end of the Laotian Civil War, known to the CIA simply as the "Secret War." In 1975, Governor Robert D. Ray began resettling the Tai Dam people who had been displaced by the wars in Laos and Vietnam. Later, ethnic Lao loyalists, who had fought on behalf of the American-backed Royal Lao Government, came too. The first Lao temple in Des Moines, Wat Lao Buddhavas, dates back to the purchase of land in 1983. Not until much later, in 2010, was Wat Phothisomphan established. Both temples now serve as homes for Lao immigrants, and, as Ajahn Somphan attests, as means of enlightenment: "I want to help people—teach them and help them find the way to end suffering."

As Laotians continue to immigrate to central Iowa, new friends help those newly arrived to hold on to their identity. Buddha's *Dharma* envelops the hearts of all members. In turn, they

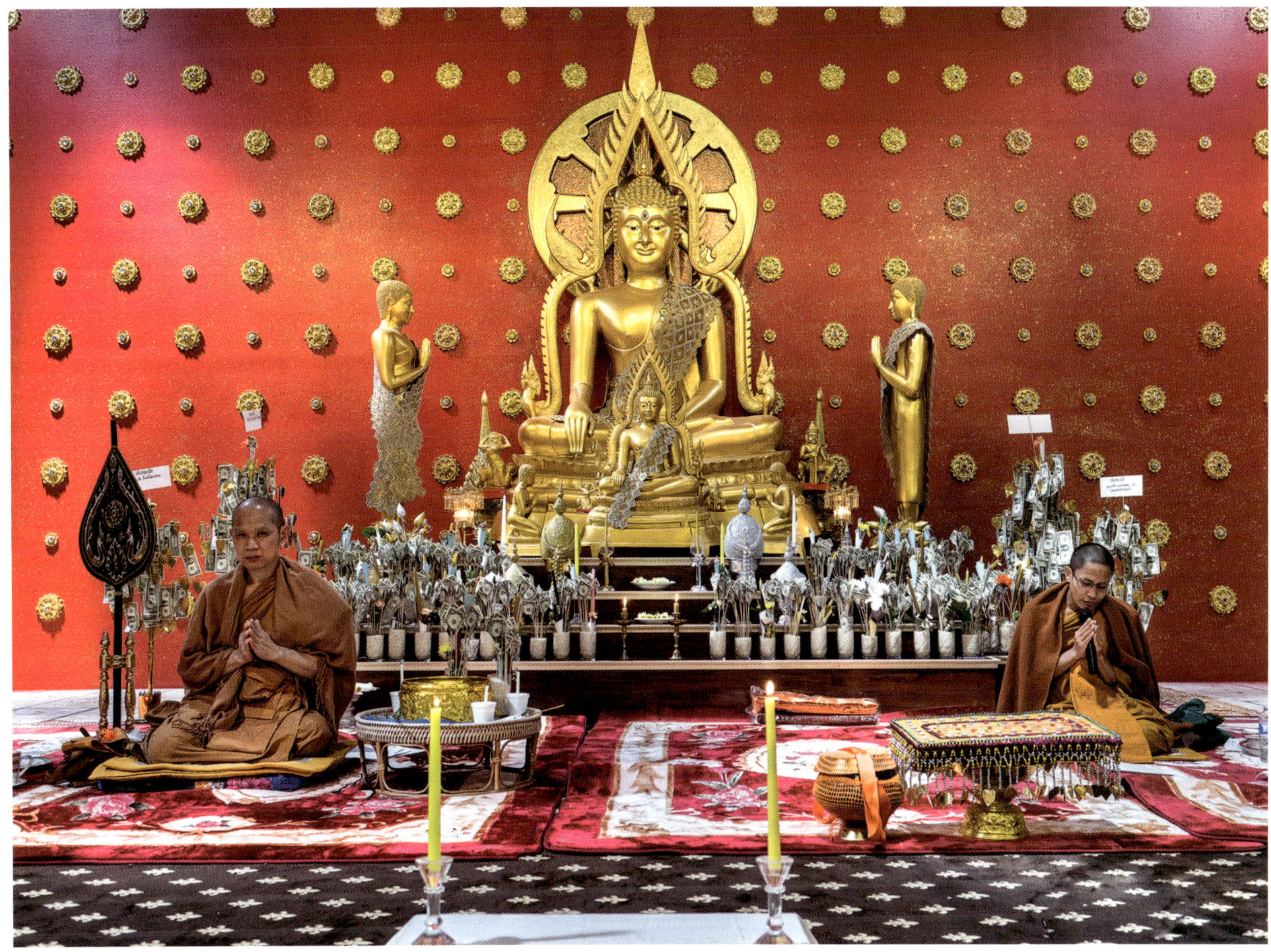

offer their support to each other. Despite any difficulty a member might face, they never have to fear. As Tu See, an elderly grandmother, told me one Sunday, grabbing my hand and leading me to the gigantic Buddha statue, "Remember: Buddha is good, Buddha is love, Buddha is happiness, Buddha is compassion."

HISTORY The Laotian community is united because of something that was once as powerful as the Buddha but much darker: war.

"My parents left due to the communist takeover. My dad was a judge and would have been taken to a concentration camp had we not escaped," shares Kate, a member of the temple. Many Laotians suffered the same insecurity after the communist Pathet Lao seized power in 1975.

Golden statue of Lord Buddha on the temple's main altar

They were forced to leave their homeland, often under perilous conditions, and travel west seeking a more secure future. According to the Center for American Progress, the demographics of the Laotian population in the U.S. grew to 150,000 by 1990 as conditions worsened in Laos. Today, 4% of the Laotian population in the United States resides in Iowa, the first state in the nation to offer resettlement to refugees.

The community continues to welcome new members. Moving to an unfamiliar place is never easy, but having people they can count on lessens the ache of homesickness. Recently, a family of four came to seek Ajahn Samboun's blessing; as they left, they bowed with gratitude. "There is an organization within the community that sponsors new families, and everyone helps out because we know how hard it is to come to an unfamiliar place," Law Saysinuan says. Law and her husband, Samboun Saysinuan, are devoted community members. Samboun is a fount of information about Buddhist practices.

The generation of Laotians born in the United States had a different experience than their parents did. For most of them, Laos is a dim memory. Their path is influenced by their parents' Buddhism, but they are also Americans. Samboun's son took a trip to Laos recently to learn more about his religion and the place where his family is from. "He grew up here, so he finds it quite hard there," Samboun explains one Sunday morning, showing me a hand-woven basket that his son brought back from his recent trip. "From the food to sleeping… it's different, you know? Laos's cuisine is spicy! But, my son loves it, being with his grandparents, and I have friends who took good care of him…following and learning the Buddha's teachings. He might go again sometime, with me. But the plane tickets are so expensive!"

The people of this temple have integrated American culture into their homes, but Laos is still in their hearts. Sunday gatherings for the children help to assure parents that the next generation will remember their origins. The Laotians' daily activities are steeped in the language and culture of their homeland.

An enormous golden-hued statue of the Buddha presides over the religious life of worshippers in a huge hall on Southeast 14th Street. Behind each layer of paint in this building lies a story. "I was not here at the beginning, but the people who were did a great job rehabilitating and transforming the place," Kate says, beaming with pride.

A Baptist Gospel Assembly Church was the building's first occupant, established in the 1950s. It flourished for dozens of years until its dynamic and charismatic leader, Pastor Miller, passed away due to cancer at the turn of the century. Unable to continue upkeep of the church, the community had to abandon it. Years later, Ajahn Jackson discovered its untapped potential beyond the drug dealers and prostitutes that it sheltered at the time. The pivotal moment in Wat Phothisomphan began in 2010.

One day, a group of Thais, Vietnamese, European-Americans, and Laotians came to him with their desire to start a temple. Ajahn Jackson had been trying to persuade others that the dilapidated church had potential. "Finally, I got one of the [group] to come with me," he reports. "It was springtime." The dirt, grass, weeds, rusty cans, and general mess of the place wasn't easy to look at. "Every single window was broken out," said Ajahn Jackson, "and there was graffiti…all over the place." But his companion also saw the potential. So Ajahn Jackson called up Pastor Miller's daughter and negotiated a price. Soon, the old building, nearly five acres of land, and a dilapidated old house became the property of a non-profit established to manage it—all for only $135,000.

Through many ups and downs over the years, Ajahn Jackson and the founding members of the temple embraced the challenge of transforming the church into a suitable place for Buddhist worship. "We put in a lot of money," he said, "and I think we came out OK."

Members of the temple now look toward a bright future. The Land of the Million Elephants, which is one of Laos' nicknames, and the Land of the Free each hold a special place in the hearts of this congregation.

SPACE Wat Phothisomphan has an underlying peacefulness in a humble-looking, secluded haven. The monk's residence, a quiet house called the *kooti*, sits to the side of the driveway amidst the trees. All Sunday gatherings were once held here, though the small space made things cramped. To the south lies the new temple, where practitioners gather for special occasions. The Buddhist flag hangs alongside the American flag at the entrance to the new worship area, symbolizing peace. Together, the

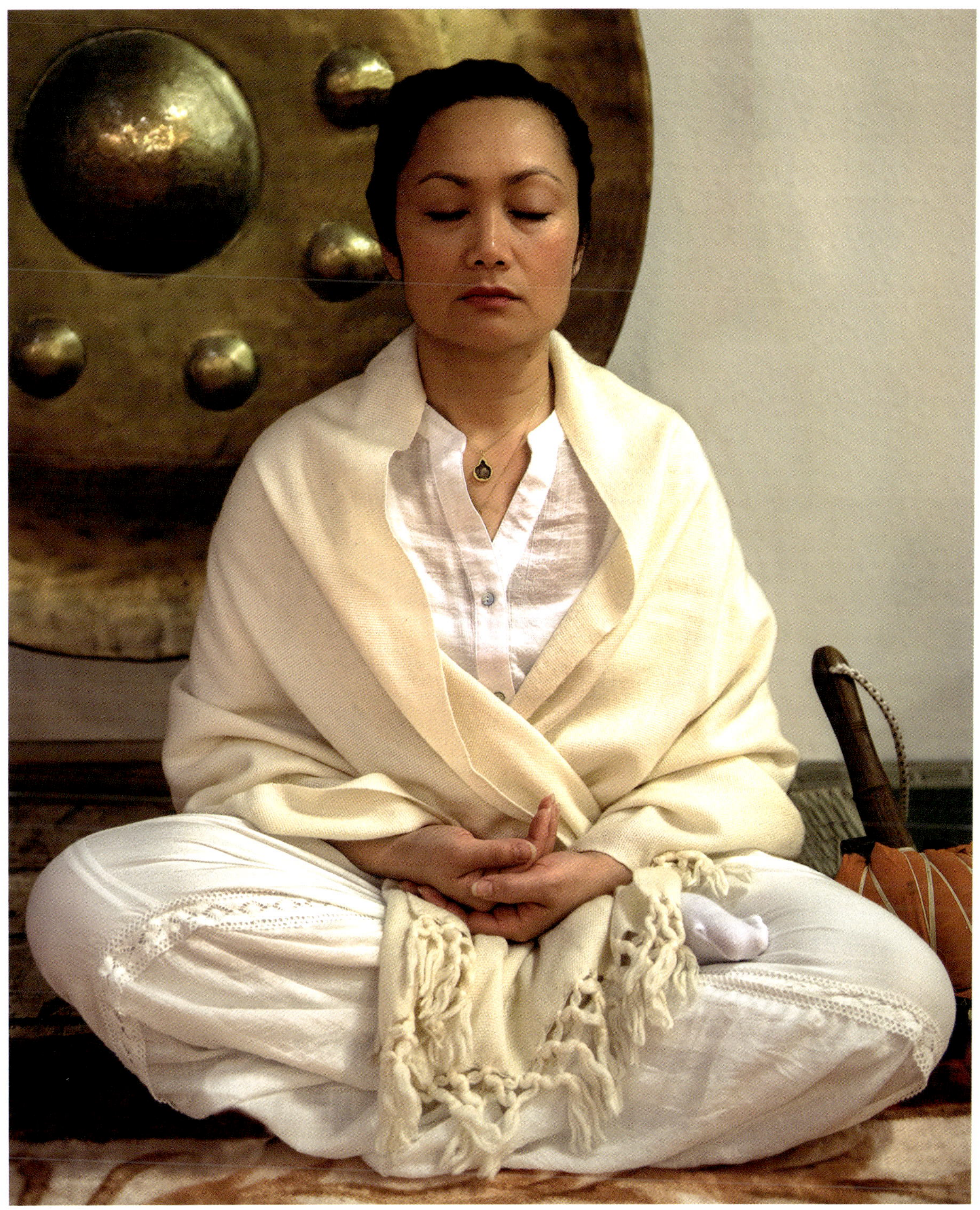

Kate Phanmaha sitting in lotus position

flags represent the timeless faith of the East mixed with the culture of the West.

As I enter the temple for the first time that chilly Sunday morning, I remove my shoes and walk across the colorful mats and tapestries covering the floor. I enter the prayer hall where, elevated on a podium, the majestic golden statue of Lord Buddha sits. This statue was originally bought by a Laotian temple in a different state and later sold to the community. Amongst the warm colors of the temple, it stands glorious against a white wall. Along the left wall lies a bed clad in orange and gold. This symbol, reserved for the departed, shows the devotion of community members to the dead. They place clothing, blankets, and other items on the coverlet, hoping these items will be useful for their departed loved ones.

A long cream-colored drape adorned with bodhi tree leaves and the wheel of the Eightfold Path hangs on each of the bedposts. Buddha reached enlightenment underneath the bodhi tree, so it has great significance for this temple. Three tree-like structures are placed around the room, onto which members clip their donations. A large gong hangs on the same side of the room. The opposite wall, clad in prayer flags, exudes a more subdued atmosphere.

Changes at the temple continued throughout the weeks I attended. A plain white wall one week became a bright red wall adorned with gold decorations by the next.

Samboun greeted me, saying, *"Sabai dee baw,"* meaning, "How are you," in Laotian. "Beautiful, isn't it? Ajahn Somphan himself painted the wall, and I helped with the decorations," Samboun explains. To outsiders, it is just a wall, but to the temple family it is part of the transformation process. Some weeks a new statue appears at the temple. Other times, a white thread appears, spreading from one end of the room to the other, keeping evil away. The temple is constantly embracing change. The Laotian community writes its history under the guidance of the Ajahns. They imprint their journey and culture into the trees and walls of the temple on SE 14th street.

PRACTICE Sunday mornings come to life at Wat Phothisomphan. "We come here at 6 in the morning on the weekends to prepare breakfast for the monks and lunch for everyone," says Euy Cha, an active member. People begin arriving around 9:30 almost every Sunday to participate in the *Tak Bat* and Sunday chanting.

In Theravada Buddhism, *Tak Bat* is a tradition of giving offerings of food to the monks. To the left of the entrance is a table heaped with baskets of food: snacks, sticky rice, and Capri Sun are among the offerings. Each basket costs about $5, with the money collected going toward temple funds. The baskets are for devotees that do not already have a homemade offering basket for *Tak Bat.* Food is placed in these baskets, beginning the *Tak Bat* ceremony.

Brown and orange bowls decorate the surface of the *Tak Bat* table in the middle of the *sala*, or gathering hall. These bowls collect the food offerings from members' baskets to be given to the monks. A small statue of Buddha stands on the table, facing its larger counterpart at the front of the temple in the *sala.* A golden donation basket sits on the table to hold the numerous blessings that will be given to the monks. But before members leave their offerings for the monks, they seek blessings for themselves and others.

Members bring blessings to themselves in many different ways. Some touch the whole basket to their forehead and then recite various requests. "There are many forms of blessings that you can ask for... for your friends, family, and even enemies. I practice loving kindness meditation, so I always say these four: May I be healthy, may I be free from danger, may I be happy, may I be able to love with ease!" says Kate.

After receiving blessings of our own, Kate guides me through the rest of the process, offering baskets in hand. We drop money into the golden basket and move down the table, placing food in the remaining five bowls as more people follow behind us. By the end of this procession, the participants' baskets are empty of food. Members then seek blessings a final time.

Powerful words resound throughout the hall: *Namo Tassa Bhagavato Arahato Samma Sambuddhassa,* meaning "Honor to the Blessed One, the Exalted One, the fully Enlightened One."

The Ajahns are seated in a row on the podium, while the devotees sit on their knees or with legs to the side, their heads always lower than the monks and the statue of the Buddha. They join hands and bow their heads in prayer. Despite the reverent atmosphere, children run about, and the room is filled with activity. A comfortable vibe settles over the congregants, and prayers lift from the hall.

When the chanting ends, the monks sit down to lunch prepared by the community members. Monks abstain from solid food after noon every day, so this is their only true meal. After the monks have been served, the first round of chanting ends with the water blessing ceremony. "*Sadhu! Sadhu! Sadhu!*" the Ahjans chant—"Well done!"—pouring water from a golden container into a bigger one as the voices of the faithful blend into a powerful echo. Then there is silence.

In the calm, people move outside to pour the water on soil. This is one of many ways that members of Wat Phothisomphan "make merit," earning themselves a better rebirth. "Merits are an important concept," Kate explains. "This way we share more of our merits with Earth and also seek its blessings." The temple also supports projects in Laos that aid development.

After the ceremonial watering, an elderly woman chirps "*Ma gin khao!*"—come eat. Now that the monks have been served, the rest of the community assembles to enjoy a Laotian feast. Laughter fills the hall as members gather to share chicken, sticky rice, *pandan* cake—a type of sponge cake—and much more, as one family.

Members here are eager to showcase their culture. During events like CelebrAsian, held each spring in downtown Des Moines, Iowans are treated to a small piece of Laos through their food and culture.

* * *

A gong's sounding soaks up the silence of the temple one Friday evening. I look around. Deep concentration envelops the faces of others. This level of devotion among believers has become synonymous with Wat Phothisomphan.

The practice of meditation requires diligence and discipline, and to reach this level of discipline, one must not give in to distractions. "Don't be afraid," Samboun told me. "If you hear something [distracting], don't get up. Keep practicing." He

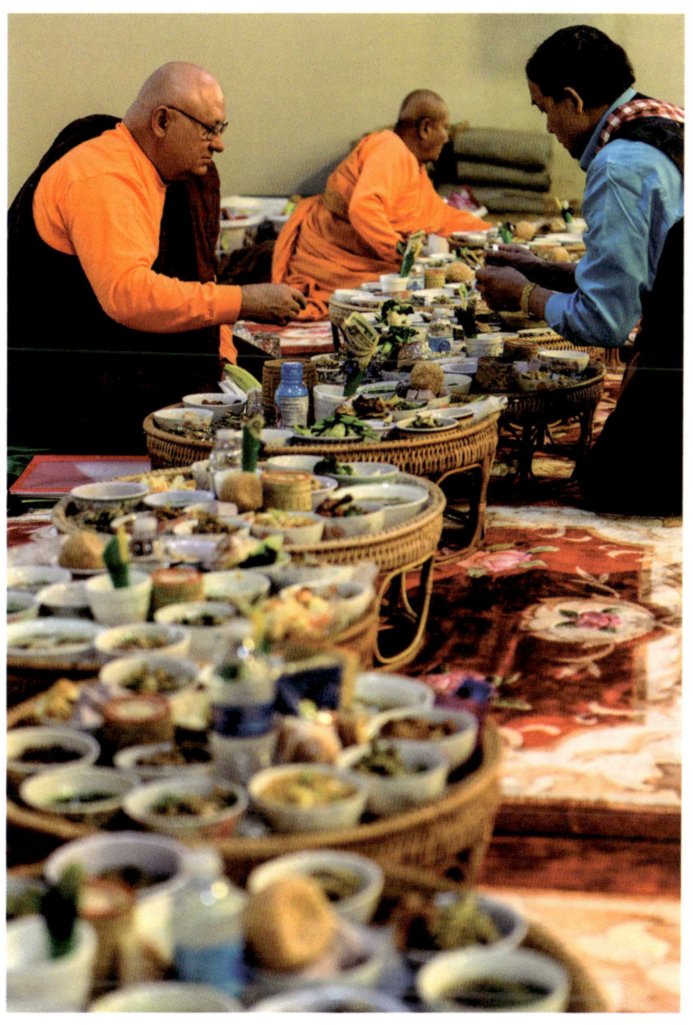

Monks are offered a meal through the practice of *Tak Bat*

continues, "I recommend meditation to people for a reason. When you practice deep meditation, you see a change happening." It brings calm and clarity to the practitioner.

Meditation can benefit anyone who diligently practices, leading them to a purposeful life. Following Buddha's path requires more than meditation, however. According to Buddha's teaching, chanting cultivates the mind; that's why the Laotian Ajahns emphasize it, as well. Services begin and end with *Namo Tassa Bhagavato Arahato Samma Sambuddhassa* and *Sadhu! Sadhu! Sadhu!* Members embrace these sayings of Buddha.

As Kate put it, "Our community is to help and support each other to be good and do good by the teaching of the Buddha."

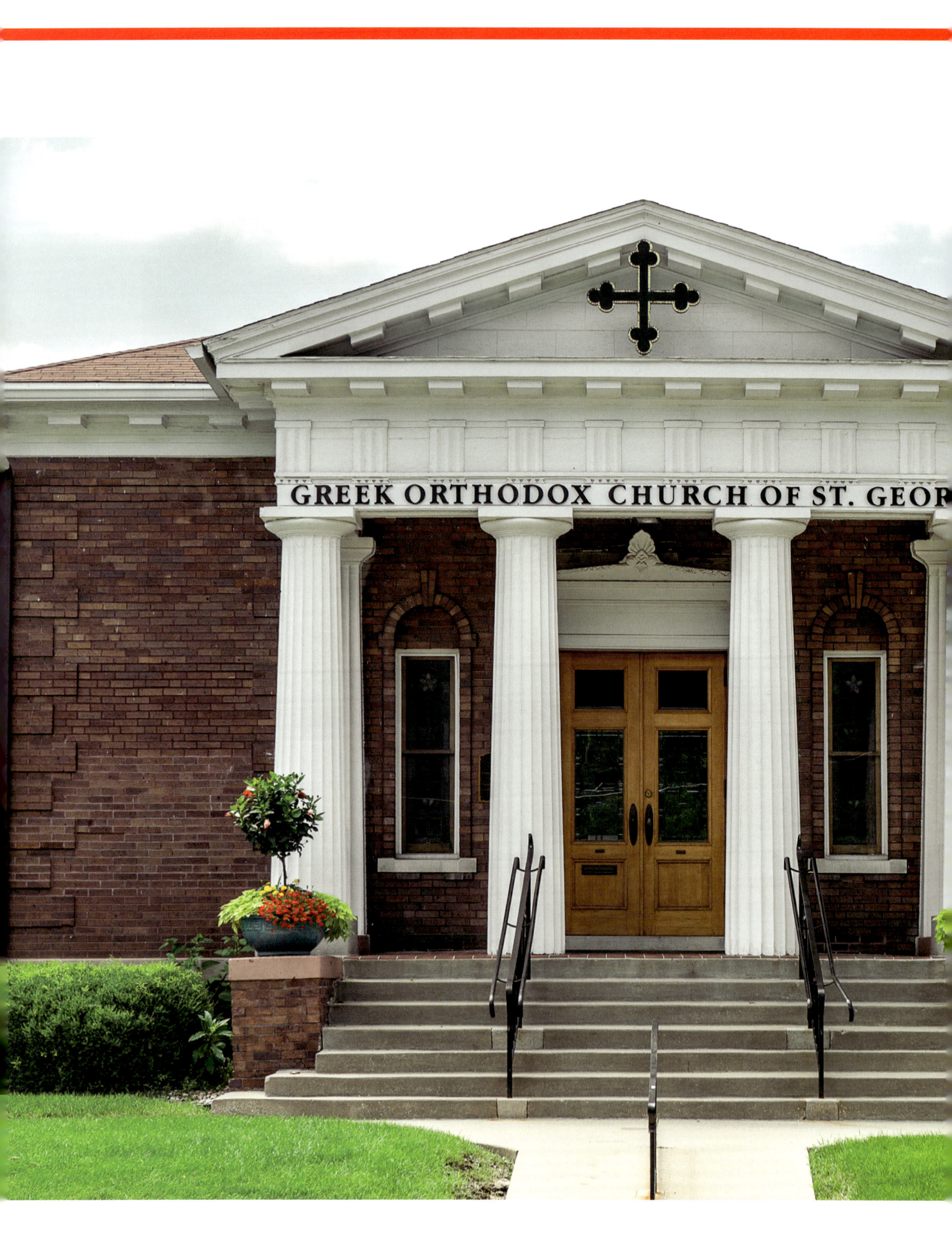
GREEK ORTHODOX CHURCH OF ST. GEOR

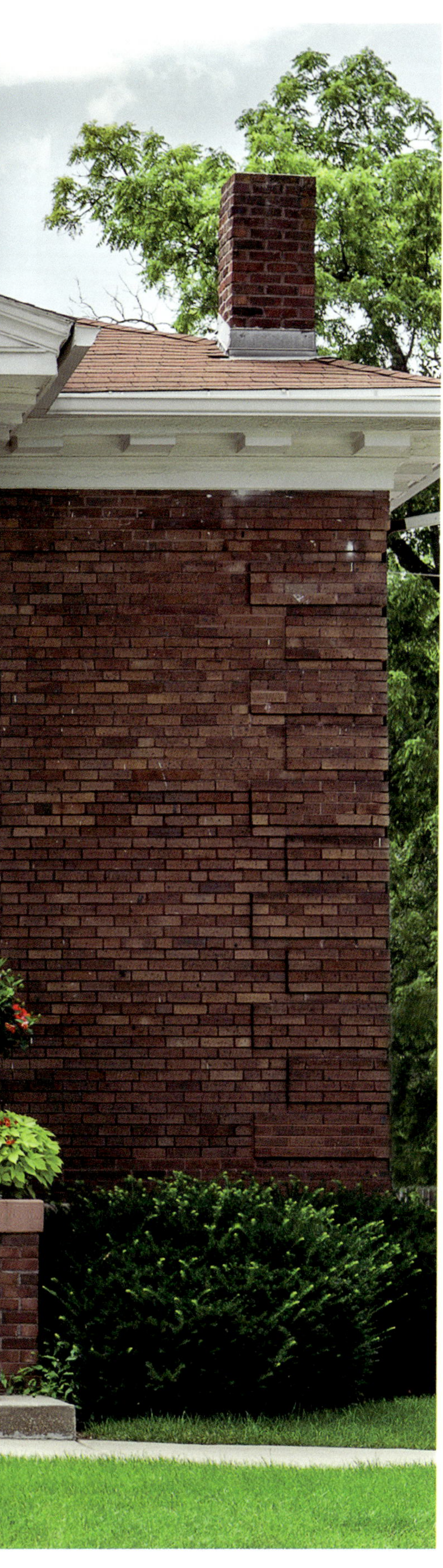

Greek Orthodox Church of Saint George

Alliyah Greaver

IDENTITY The first thing to know about the Greek Orthodox Church of St. George is that members aren't just Greek: they come from many cultures. Some have converted or have backgrounds from Russia, Syria, Lebanon, Ethiopia, and other cultures belonging to the Orthodox tradition. It is this tradition that binds these diverse backgrounds together within one faith community. The familiar icons, liturgical order of service, and shared beliefs based on the strong regard for tradition in the Orthodox Church ensure continuity for members at St. George's.

On a typical day of worship, the soft sound of chanting in both Greek and English greets the faithful as they enter. Although some congregants arrive well after the service begins (a phenomenon known as "Greek time") the chanting sets the tone for each service. In different seasons throughout the church year the chanting takes on the quality of the worship: somber during the lamentations of a Good Friday service, triumphant during the *Pascha*, or Easter, service.

Father Basil cues the congregation to sit or stand as they sing, "Lord, have mercy," or the Greek equivalent, "*Kyrie, eleison* / Κύριε, ἐλέησον." Attenders join in these chanted phrases so that

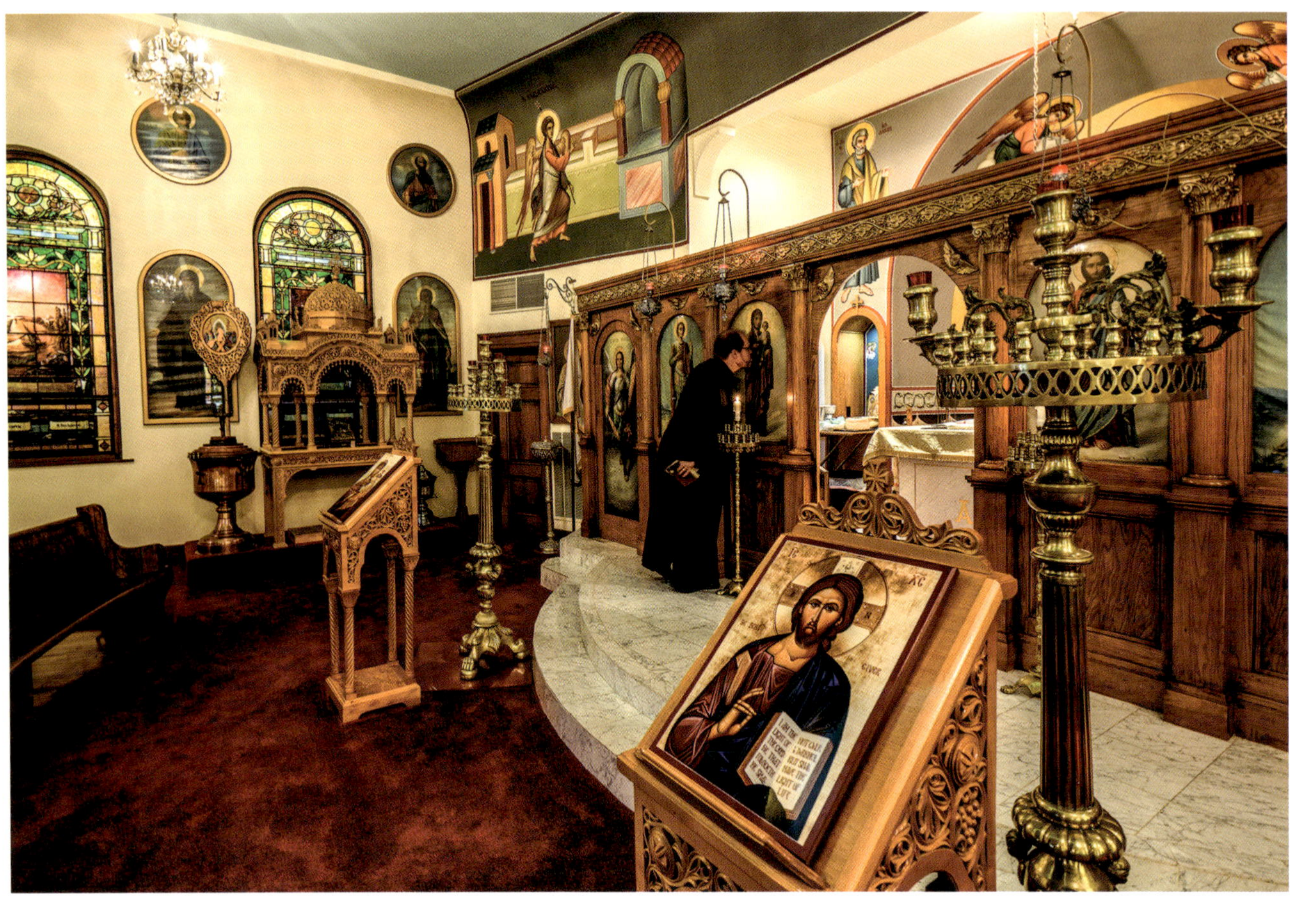

Father Hickman venerates an icon of the Virgin Mary and Christ Child on the icon-screen (*iconostasis*)

by the end of the service even visitors can follow along. During the Forgiveness Vespers, "Lord, have mercy" is petitioned forty times in a row, and in the Easter service, members sing "Christ has risen," "*Christos Anesti* / Χριστός ἀνέστη" joyously throughout, crossing themselves with the lit candles each time the verse is sung.

The Forgiveness Vespers marks the beginning of the Lenten season, a more somber time in the church. Father Basil changes from his usual red or gold vestments into dark purple to embody this transition. His strong, clear voice reverberates throughout the special liturgy, even without a sound system. At the conclusion of the service each member comes forward to venerate the icon of Christ. Then they ask forgiveness of one another with a kiss on each cheek, in the Greek way. The words "Lord, have mercy" are the theme, meaning, and emotion of the entire service.

"Christ has risen!" members call out triumphantly during the Pascha Vigil service at Easter. Just before midnight, the faithful gather in the nave carrying unlit candles in the darkened sanctuary. Meanwhile, in the closed altar area, Father Basil removes his black robes and dons his white-and-gold-trimmed vestments. He bursts through the Royal Doors in the *iconostasis*, or icon screen, saying, "Come receive the light from the unwaning light, and glorify Christ, who is risen from the dead." Carrying the *Paschal* Candle, he lights the dark as, one by one, congregants tip unlit candles to the flame. "Christ has risen!" Father Basil calls out in the various languages of his congregation. In celebration of the risen Christ who has conquered death, each calls back in English, or, perhaps, Russian or Arabic, "Truly, He is risen!"

Visitors and members may follow along with a book of the Divine Liturgy—written in both Greek and English—which are provided during services. At one recent memorial service, a young altar boy in an elaborate golden robe whispered the congregation's and the priest's part from memory. Altar boys carry the candles around the nave following the tradition they've been taught. The chanters demonstrate their knowledge of the service as well: standing by stacks of books propped open on the *analogion*, or book stand, they alternate swiftly between English and Greek, calling out the ancient melodies and prayers.

Use of the Greek language during the bulk of the regular service preserves the traditions and heritage of the Greeks and of ancient Christianity. "Ten years ago, maybe 75% of the service would have been Greek," says Angela, one of the regular chanters. "But today it's closer to half and half." Nowadays, Father Basil does a large portion of the service in English. "It's a natural and slow transition that adapts to the needs of the congregation," Angela explains. The Greek language helps preserve the history of the congregation and the ancient faith traditions, while incorporating English makes the service accessible to all.

At the conclusion of the service, Peter, a member and frequent worshiper at St. George's, notes, "The after-liturgy coffee hour really shows community because it'll often last for the whole hour." It covers everything from planning for the yearly Greek Food Fair to teasing the children darting around the room. The more informal setting is just as vital to what it means to be a part of St. George.

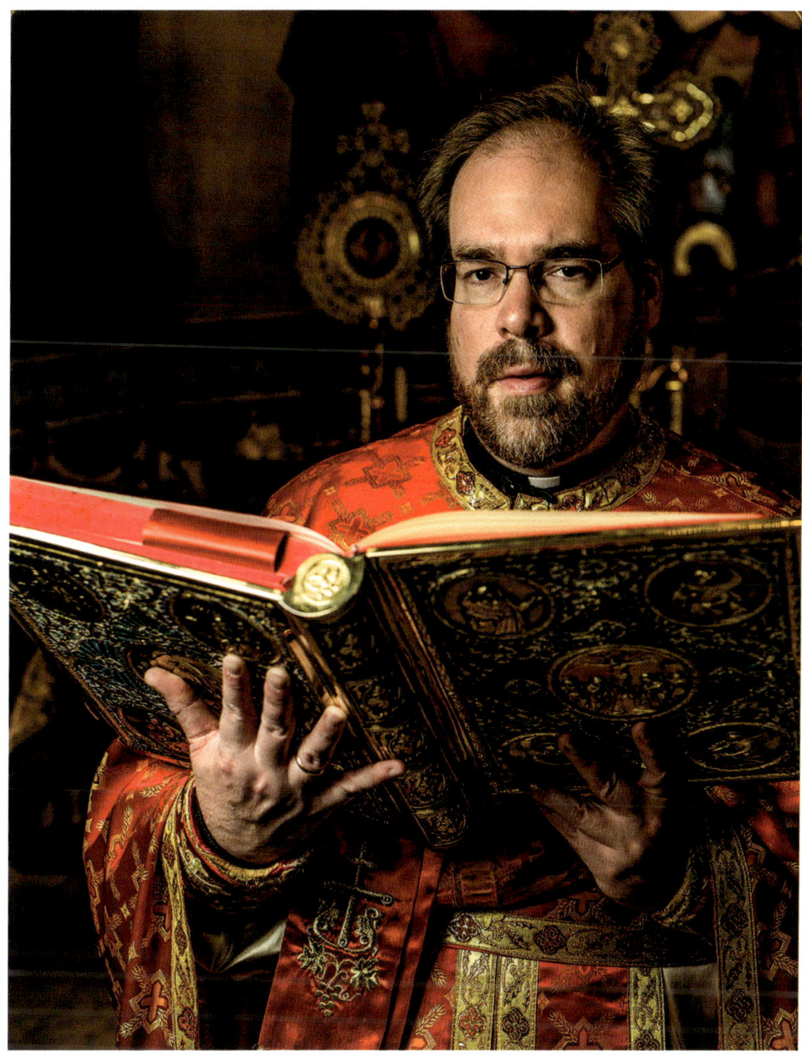

Father Basil Hickman

HISTORY When the Greeks first immigrated to Des Moines, many opened shops and businesses, but a Greek Neighborhood never truly developed. In 1928, a Greek parish was founded and named after St. George. In 1930, the parish finally purchased its own building, a former Presbyterian church. To suit the needs of the congregation, members quickly modified the building, which is now equipped with an *iconostasis* and an elaborate separated altar space. The *iconostasis* holds the beautiful painted icons of Jesus, Mary, saints, and angels.

The church provided a gathering place throughout the years and in 1997 earned a listing on the National Register of Historic Places for its role in contributing to the Greek community.

Binders of newspaper clippings about the Greek community in Des Moines line the shelves in the fellowship hall. Photo books document changes to the building and the individuals who have worshipped here through the decades, even as the services remain the same. Members from all backgrounds can proudly tell the story of how St. George's acquired its building or how the liturgical service has been passed down through generations. While St. George's has accommodated somewhat for the changing times, a high respect for tradition remains. The same can be said of Orthodox Christianity.

"We're obviously not Greek," explain Fred and Carolyn, two regular worshippers at St. George's. They didn't grow up going to Orthodox services, but like many, they have connected to the heritage of the Orthodox faith by participating in chants, learning the history of St. George's and Orthodoxy in general, and immersing themselves in the life of the church.

Memorial services are another tradition keeping St. George's history alive. Father Basil reads the names of those both recently- and long-departed. Relatives and friends prepare the *koliva*, a dish of boiled wheat with dried fruit, nuts, sugar, and honey. They mound the dish to look like a grave with a cross drawn in powdered sugar on the top and a candle in the middle. The service ends as Father Basil recites, "May your memory be eternal, for you are worthy of blessedness and everlasting memory." Afterwards, members relay stories about departed loved ones and then share the *koliva*.

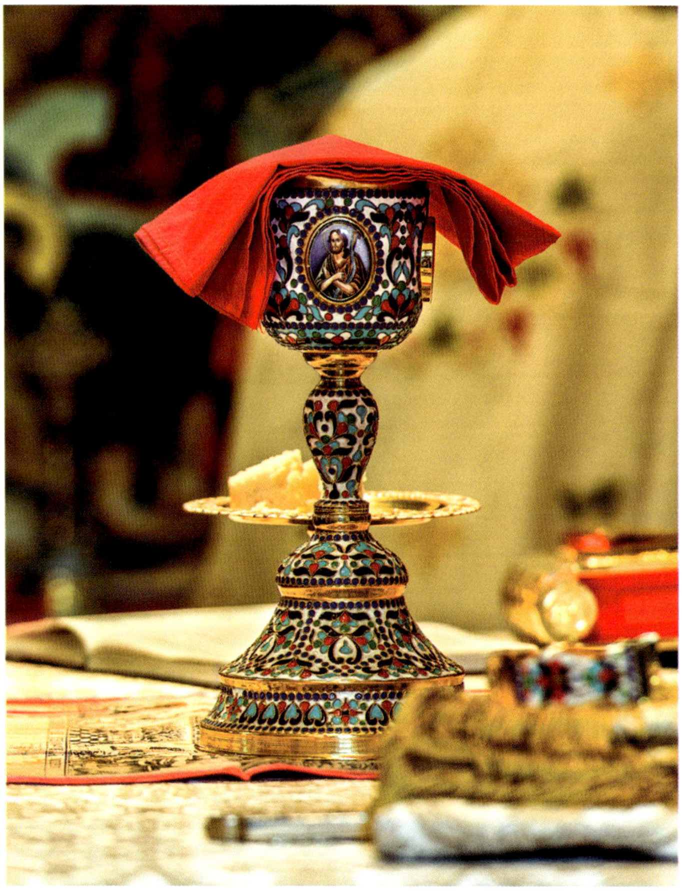

Like many elements of worship at St. George's, the *koliva* is layered with meaning and symbolism but also offers a tangible way of engaging in the service. The bitterness of the almonds, according to Father Basil, reminds us of the sadness of death, but the sweetness of the honey and sugar reminds us of the resurrection. The wheat and fruit come from the Bible verse, John 12:24: "Truly, truly, I say to you, unless a grain of wheat falls into the earth and dies, it remains alone; but if it dies, it bears much fruit" (Revised Standard Version).

Memorial services may be added to the end of a service. In the weeks approaching the first week of Lent, the church offers three Saturday morning services during what is called the Saturday of the Souls. After the Saturday of the Souls service, some members take cups of the *koliva* and fondly recount names they recognize. "Nitsa was such a dear woman. Even when she was ailing in health she'd make it to church. She had a sharp mind and warm heart." A few weeks later, a Holy Week book with Nitsa's name scrawled in cursive inside the cover finds its way to me. The stories others shared of Nitsa came to mind, sustaining her memory.

SPACE "It was sort of on the edge of Des Moines civilization," Jim Zeller, the tour guide at St. George's, recounts, referring to the building the Greeks moved into in the 1930s. At St. George's, history is brought to life through art and prayer, and for that transformation over the decades to take place, changes had to be made.

The building did have some architectural elements that lent themselves to a Greek Orthodox space. A small, intimate nave and

Eucharistic chalice and paten, containing the blood and the body of Christ

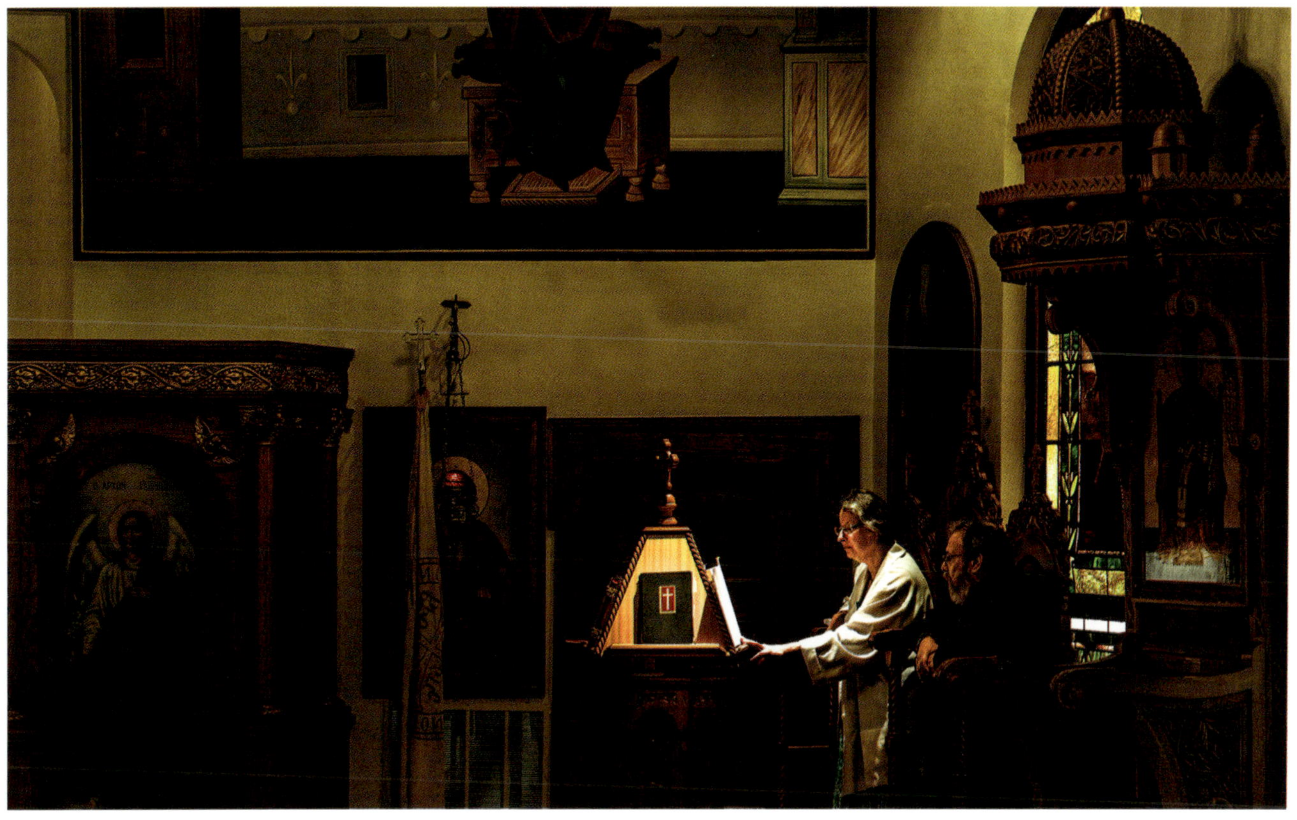

Chanters Angela Sweet (left) and Dr. William Bitsas (right) chanting hymns from liturgy books resting on the *analogion*

domed ceiling provided familiar features for those coming from different Greek Orthodox communities. Eventually, the massive depiction of Christ the *Pantocrator*, or All-Powerful, was painted on the domed ceiling. They retained the stained glass windows—a nod to the building's history. Between the windows they added tall icons of saints as well as the iconostasis separating the altar space from the central part of the church, called the nave.

The altar space posed a bit of a challenge. In a typical Orthodox church, the altar faces east. At St. George's, the façade of the building faces the opposite direction, and the floor inclines to the west, making an east-facing altar difficult to achieve. The solution for this dilemma? Compromise.

Meanwhile, St. George's deepened its transformation into a place of worship in the Orthodox faith. Topped with intricate woodwork and the icon of Christ as King and High Priest, the Bishop's Throne sits near the front of the nave to the right of the *iconostasis*. The Throne represents Christ's leading role in the church and sits empty unless a bishop is present. Members proudly recount a very special occasion in 1997, when the seat was used by the Ecumenical Patriarch of Constantinople, Bartholomew I, who stopped at the church on his tour of the United States. It was a significant honor for St. George's.

A large wooden bier topped with an elaborate canopy rests on the opposite side of the *iconostasis*. This is the *kouvouklion*, which symbolizes Christ's tomb. Not just an item to be admired for its beauty, the *kouvouklion* serves a vital function in the Orthodox Good Friday services.

The icons are another way of keeping history alive. One of the largest of these, filling an entire wall behind the altar, is the *Theotokos*, or God-Bearer, depicting the Virgin Mary and Holy Child. On the domed ceiling, the massive Christ the *Pantocrator* holds the Gospel book in one hand and with his other raised in blessing reminds the

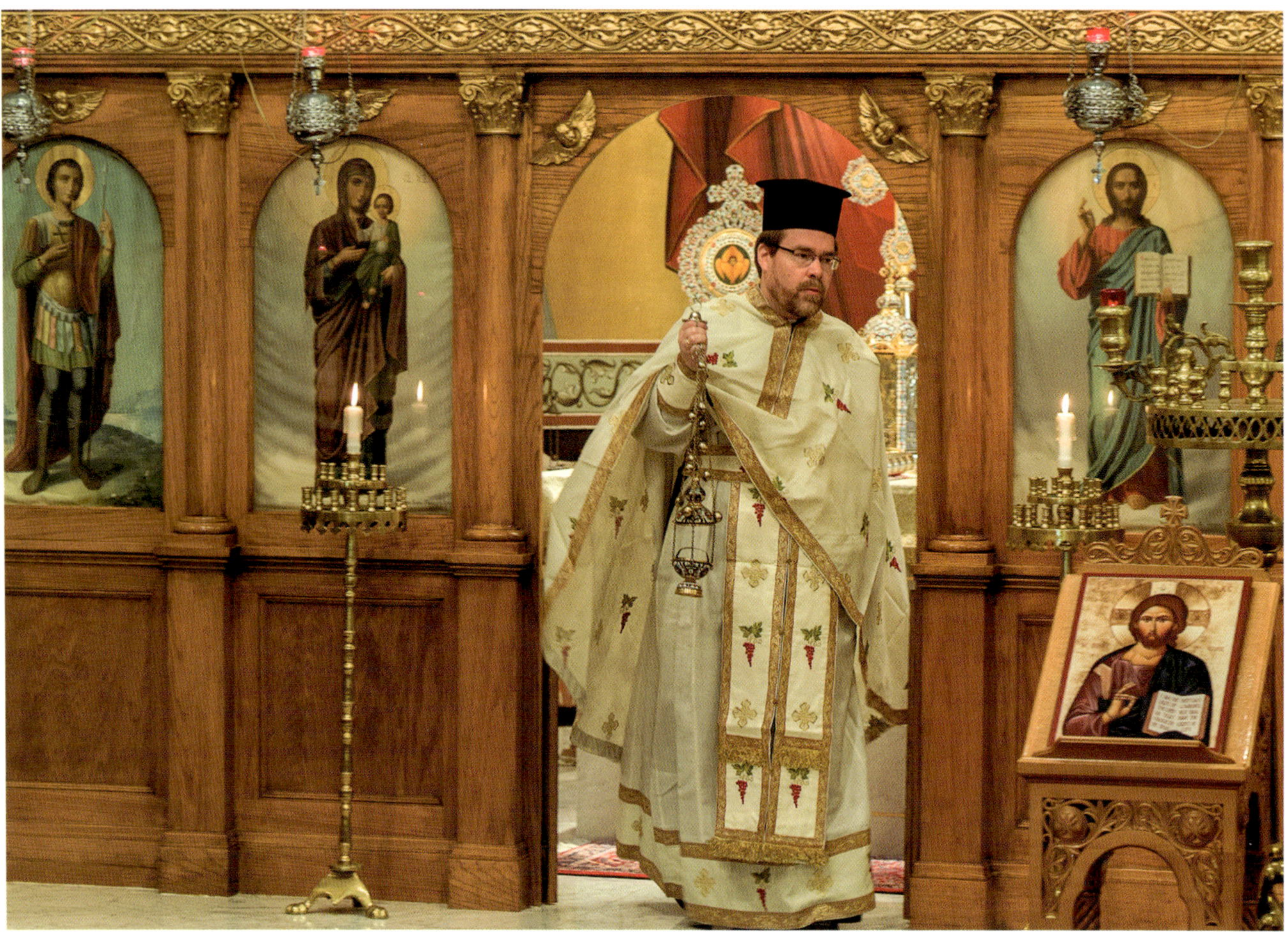

Father Hickman emerging from the *iconostasis* with a censer

faithful that Christ, who upholds the law and bestows forgiveness, is always in their midst.

Inside the nave, icons depict the visage of the spiritually transfigured by featuring larger eyes, ears, and noses and smaller mouths. Their halos illuminate the light of God that surrounds them. Far more than simply decorations, these icons act as "windows to the heavens." When a member kisses or venerates an icon, Father Basil explains, "It's like kissing a picture of a loved one. You know the picture isn't the person, but you are honoring who they are." When icons are venerated, "Christ and the Saints know that we are honoring them."

Although the meaning behind the icons in the church often requires an explanation from Father Basil and other parishioners, the beauty of the transformed space is clear. We bring our best to God in the church because "Christ is especially in our midst when we gather to worship," says Father Basil. The artistry reflects the beauty of the heavenly kingdom. This beauty, in turn, should be "revealed in our actions and words."

PRACTICE Not a crumb shall be left on the altar. Father Basil makes sure of this as he finishes his taking of Communion. The congregation waits.

A large portion of Sunday services revolves around the anticipation, preparation, and reception of the Eucharist, or Holy Communion, and one aspect of that preparation is that the priest himself asks for mercy and forgiveness of his sins. Jim Zeller explains that although priests are highly respected in the Orthodox Church, even they are not free of sin. When he is finished, Father Basil brings the bread and wine, believed to have become the body and blood of Christ, to the front of the nave. The faithful then turn toward the Holy Communion, crossing themselves.

"With the fear of God, faith, and love, Orthodox Christians draw near," he exclaims, holding up the ornate chalice and spoon. Communion is offered to all Orthodox members, young or old. As each takes communion, two members hold a red cloth under the receiver's chin, ensuring that not a drop falls from the spoon onto the floor.

One woman prostrates herself when approaching the chalice. Another member brushes the floor with her hand to finish crossing herself; others don't bow at all. Small differences like these come from different cultural expressions of Orthodoxy. Some might stand, while others prefer to kneel during certain parts of the service. During the coffee hour a church member points out that despite some differences in exterior rules and customs—such as how you might find women in Ethiopia wearing head-coverings—"the beliefs are largely the same between Orthodox communities." Diversity of culture and practice is common, but the main beliefs are shared.

"When we offer the bread and wine to God," explains Father Basil, "it is like a child offering a dandelion to their parent: the parent doesn't need the dandelion, and God doesn't need the bread and wine, but the parent accepts the gift in love." According to Orthodoxy, sin obscures our authentic self. By living according to God's will and growing in relationship with Him, we can become closer to our authentic self, which was created in the image and likeness of God. Through baptism, prayer, Communion, and obedience to God's will, we become unified with Him. This is only possible through the Grace of the Holy Spirit and the Incarnation of Christ.

This belief clarifies why such care is taken in the preparation and reception of Holy Communion. The role of the congregation during the service and the importance of the Eucharist arise from the process of *theosis*, or deification, which is the Orthodox model of salvation. Each Divine Liturgy service is an opportunity to encounter Christ and participate in the Eucharist.

Aside from the practice of Holy Communion, the conclusion of every service involves bodily participation. Members come forward to kiss Father Basil's hand and accept the *antidoron*, or blessed-bread, which comes from the same loaf as the Communion bread but has not been consecrated for Holy Communion. Visitors, too, are invited to receive this blessing.

Jamie, a student who began attending St. George's in college, sums up living a life of Orthodoxy: "Let us commend ourselves and each other and our whole life unto Christ our God" is her favorite line of the service. "I make a sign of the cross whenever I hear it," Jamie says, "because Orthodoxy isn't just, 'let's go to church on Sunday.' To me, if you're living a life of Orthodoxy, you are making decisions based on your faith and based on God. It's commending my *life* to Him."

At the end of Lent, before the faithful celebrate the resurrection of Christ, several services are devoted to remembrance of Christ's crucifixion. Women transform the *kouvouklion* with red and white carnations and roses into a beautiful and poignant reminder of what it symbolizes. During the Good Friday evening service, the *kouvouklion* sits in the front of the nave while members sing verses from the Lamentations.

Afterwards, the structure is brought around the outside of the church in a funeral procession. Despite the sorrow of the evening service, excitement builds in the night air as members follow solemnly, holding lit candles. Whispers fill the darkness. Behind the priest, choristers' voices fill the air with Byzantine chanting. "This is more than a funeral procession," Father Basil reminds the congregation. "As we enter into the darkness of the night, singing hymns and carrying an icon of Christ lying in the tomb, we commemorate Christ entering into the darkness of death and conquering it from within, filling even death with his light and life."

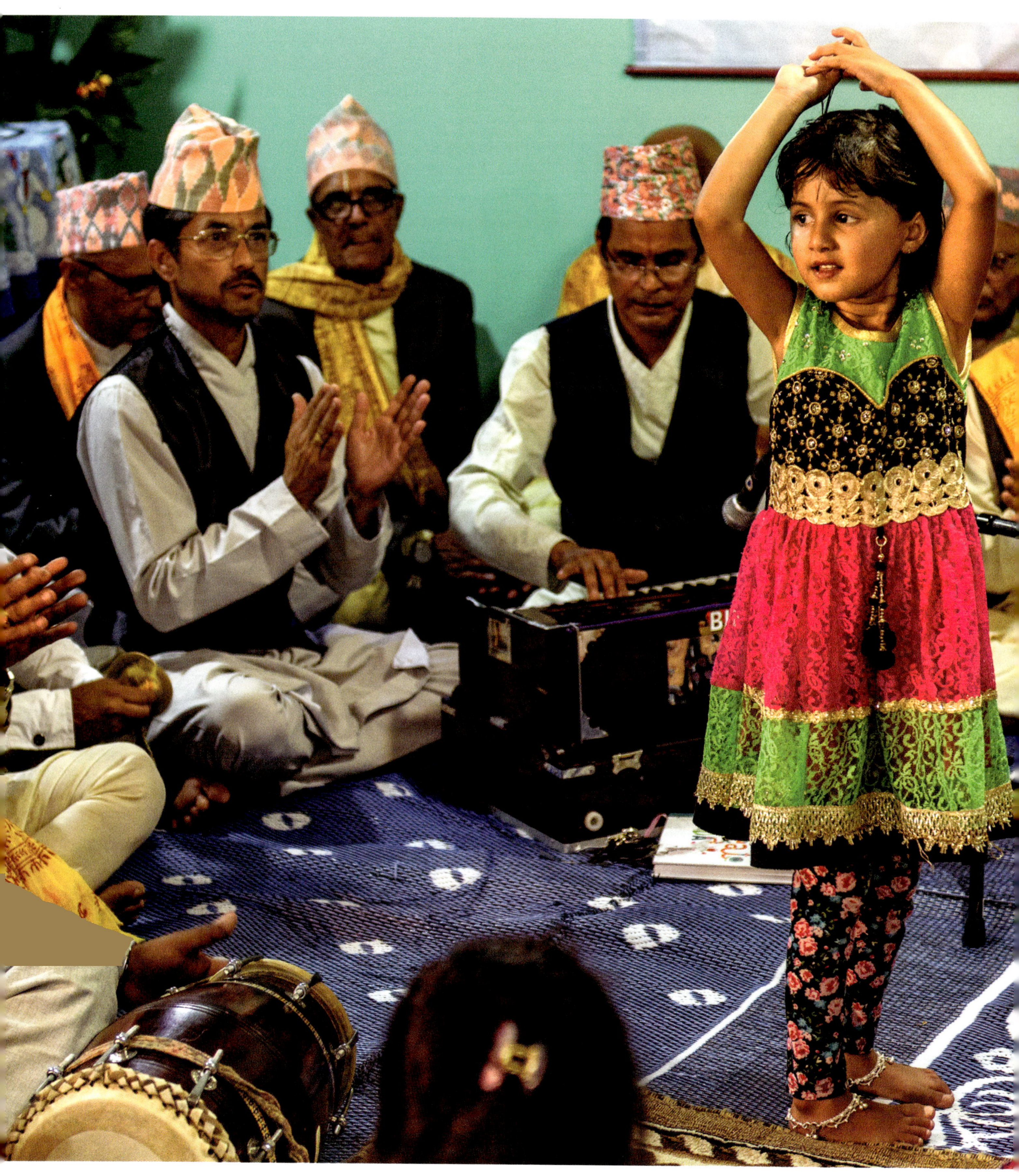

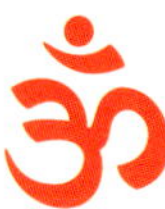

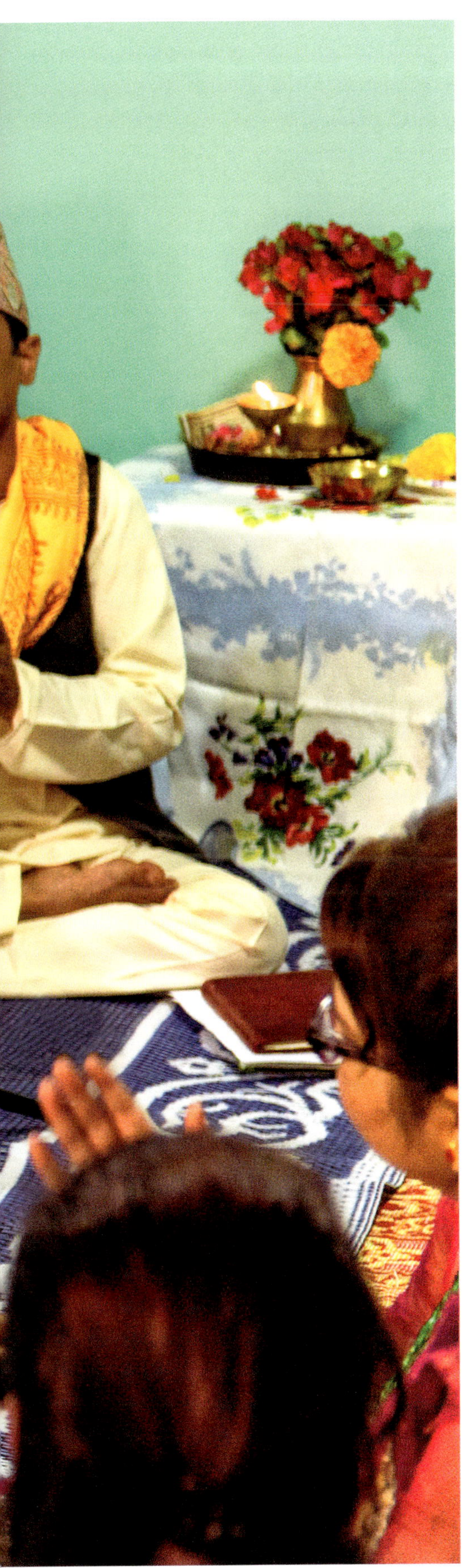

Hindu Cultural and Educational Center

Taylor Donaldson

SPACE In the basement of a home in the neighborhood of Easter Lake, a little girl smiled at me and placed a rainbow-colored lei of flowers around my neck, a symbol, she said shyly, reserved for welcomed guests. Live music with a steady drumbeat accompanied by chanting and bells animated the space with color, movement, and sound. It was not my first experience at *bhajan*—worship through song and dance. But it was the first time one of the young women of the group succeeded in pulling me up from the floor where I sat and into the circle of dancers.

I had no idea how to dance like that, I protested. But everyone cheered when I joined in. Out came a slew of phones pointed in my direction with much laughter and merriment. Dozens of dancing bodies can generate a lot of heat, especially in a basement filled with live music and drumming, along with bells and gourds, chanting and clapping. But I decided that being "on-stage" wasn't so bad, after all. In fact, at that moment, even with my face red from both heat and self-consciousness that I was doing it all wrong, I realized I felt something new: finally, I'd become more of an insider than an outsider among the Bhutanese Hindus of Des Moines.

* * *

Shradha Humagai dances during a *bhajan* service

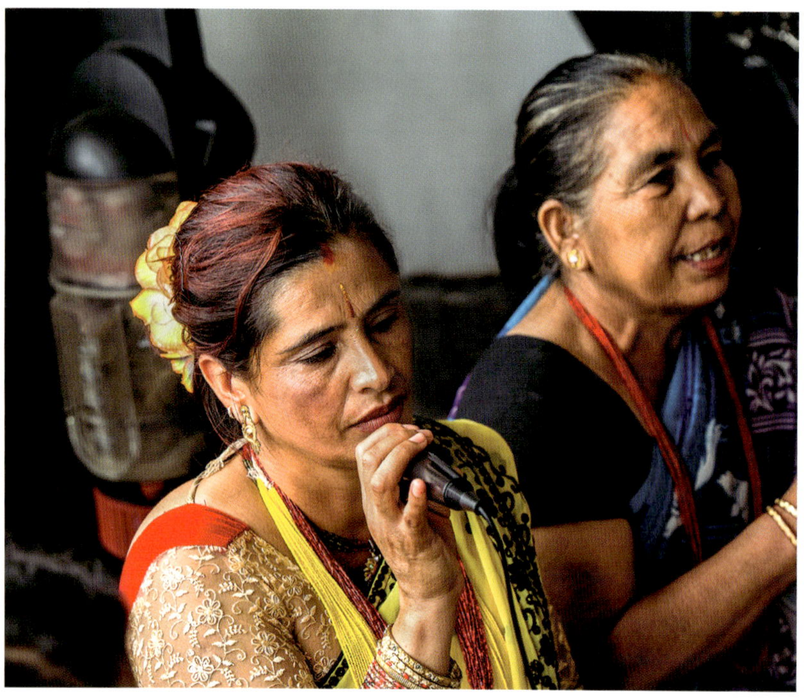

Lila Bhattarai leads singing at one of the *bhajan* services

A shrine adorned with posters of deities and religious leaders sits at the front of the basement room when members arrive for *bhajan*. They lay offerings of fruit and flowers. Incense is lit. Some of the faithful kneel at the altar before the Hindu gods and goddesses whose presence they anticipate when worship begins. The Bhutanese Hindus don't yet have a permanent place of worship, so the faithful take turns hosting the service in their own homes. Each week the basements change, but the service is always the same.

"*Namaste*," they say—hello—greeting one another with affectionate warmth. Some stop to chit-chat or laugh together as they seat themselves on the floor, creating a vibrant visual mix of colors and sequins among the bright saris and tunics, blouses and T-shirts, sweatpants and skinny jeans. Many women wear the traditional *bindi*, a small red dot on their forehead, while married women wear an additional forehead marking called a *sindooram*. Men occasionally wear a *topi*, a Nepali hat adorned in a traditional pattern, for worship or special events.

After announcements and greetings, the priest and musicians gather at the altar. Soon, singing, dancing, and clapping keep time with the music's driving rhythm. Bells jingle and tock, welcoming forth the gods. Joy and movement fill the room, but still an air of serious devotion reigns. This is not a party, my friend, Tanka, explains. Yes, it is jubilant celebration, but it is also the practice of religion free from persecution.

Now that this community has begun to settle into their new country, they seek a more permanent worship and education space. The Hindu temple in Madrid, Iowa, is one option, but many of them can't make the forty-minute drive each week. That's why the group recently founded an organization in Des Moines to promote outreach and educate the community about Hinduism. Now they are looking to the future with two grand projects: first a Multicultural Center, then a Hindu Temple, both on a newly acquired plot of land in southeast Des Moines.

HISTORY "The refugee camps were crowded," shares 21-year-old Pratima. She remembers how she and the other children made the most of their time there despite camp conditions—"going to school, playing outdoors, and helping our parents when needed." Pratima was born in the camp in 1995 and lived there until the age of 14 when her family moved to the United States. Because her parents had lost their state and nationality, they were motivated by the prospect of moving to a country full of opportunity. Only after many tumultuous moves across the globe did they secure the chance to build a life for themselves in Des Moines. The transition from life in the small, cramped houses of a Nepali refugee camp to life here hasn't been easy. But through hope and through their connection to one another, this community perseveres.

What made them refugees in the first place? According to Tanka, the government of Bhutan aligns itself with the concept of "One Nation, One People." As such, it is under Buddhist control. In hopes of unifying its people, this mantra made mandatory the practice of Buddhism, and the Bhutanese language spoken by only a small group of people became the official language. These requirements left the Nepali-speaking Hindus of Bhutan marginalized. Things turned ugly when Hindus were physically punished for failure to comply with the unification. Hundreds of thousands of Hindus fled for their lives from the south of Bhutan, making their way through India and into Nepal. There they faced equally harsh, albeit different, judgment being that they were from Bhutan and therefore not accepted as Nepalese. It was a choice between persecution or statelessness. That was when they achieved refugee status, and the United Nations High Commission for Refugees relocated them into the camps in the eastern part of Nepal.

"I think it was hard for my parents because they had to work and take care of us," Pratima continues. "We lived in a hut that was too small for our family, and we would always share a bed." But children will be children. Pratima remembers running, laughing, and playing games like any little girl. She also recalls early mornings at the Temple where *murtis*—statues of Hindu deities—lined the walls. In the camps, they learned about their religion and the Sanskrit language. They also learned the ritual of bathing, robing, and offering food to the *murtis*—theirs depicted on posters rather than statues, given their temporary surroundings. The priest recited passages, Pratima recalls, which the children would repeat and commit to memory. Pratima, along with her family, now holds tightly to her traditions and attends weekly services despite—or perhaps because—life is so different here.

While many of the Nepali Hindu community re-settled in Seattle, the state of Iowa's job opportunities, lower living costs, and the chance to live close together attracted many of the refugees. Imagine adjusting to life permanently in a country whose official language is foreign to you. No matter their high education levels or abilities, relying on others for assistance became the only way to adapt. Children and teenagers were placed in school shortly after arrival. When possible, adults obtained jobs through local refugee services and took advantage of English as a Second Language (ESL) courses offered through refugee assistance programs such as the Lutheran Services of Iowa (LSI). The group has been fortunate in this way, but that hasn't made it easy.

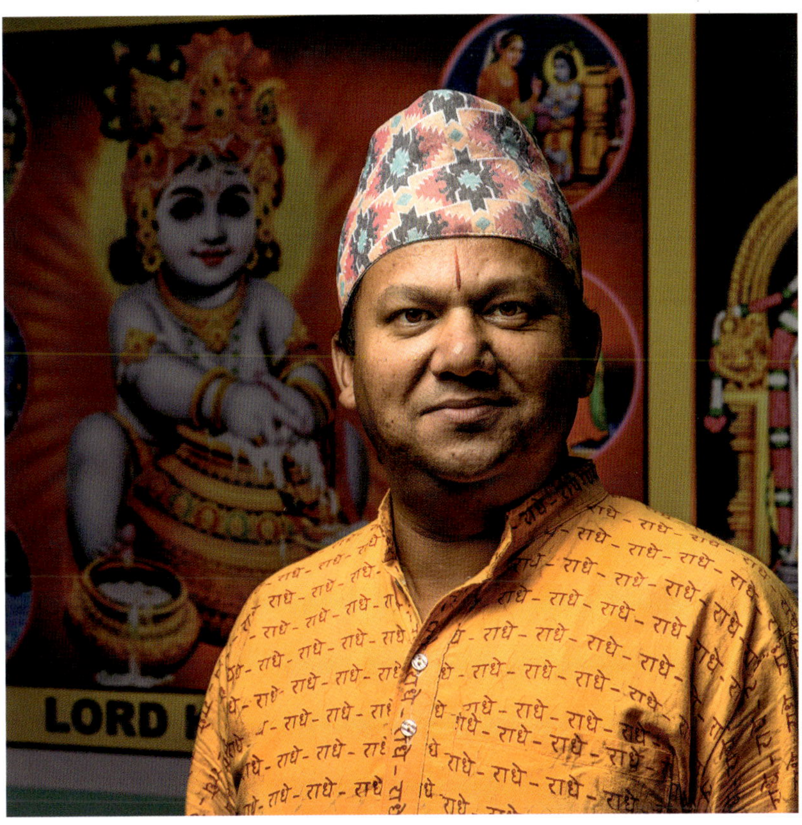

President Tanka Dhital

PRACTICE Everyone scoots closer to the head of the room to be near the musicians and altar as the *bhajan* service begins. The first song is always about Ganesh, the Hindu god of auspicious beginnings, but after that any member of the typical crowd of 30 to 70 people can choose to sing a piece about any deity. To accompany the religious songs, musicians play several instruments including the harmonium, *tabla* drum, and hand-held cymbals. And, of course, there is dancing. As the music begins, the lead priest starts to sing a set of call-and-response phrases, to which the audience eagerly responds in rhythm.

A handful of priests and regulars sing most of the songs—the languages vary from Nepali to Hindi to Sanskrit—but other singers are always welcome to lead. Few in the group understand every language being sung or spoken, of course. Music is what connects them. And as the beat settles into a steady rhythm, women, girls, and sometimes men get up and form a loose circle as their dance area. In lithe, free-form movements, they twist and turn to the beating of the drums and the jingling of the bells, calling forth the presence of the gods. The particular gods they're dancing for during any given song matter less than the time they are taking for praise and devotion. Anyone can join in. Worship that takes the form of chanting, music, and movement makes plain why many of the songs are devoted to Krishna: He is the God of love, movement, and song.

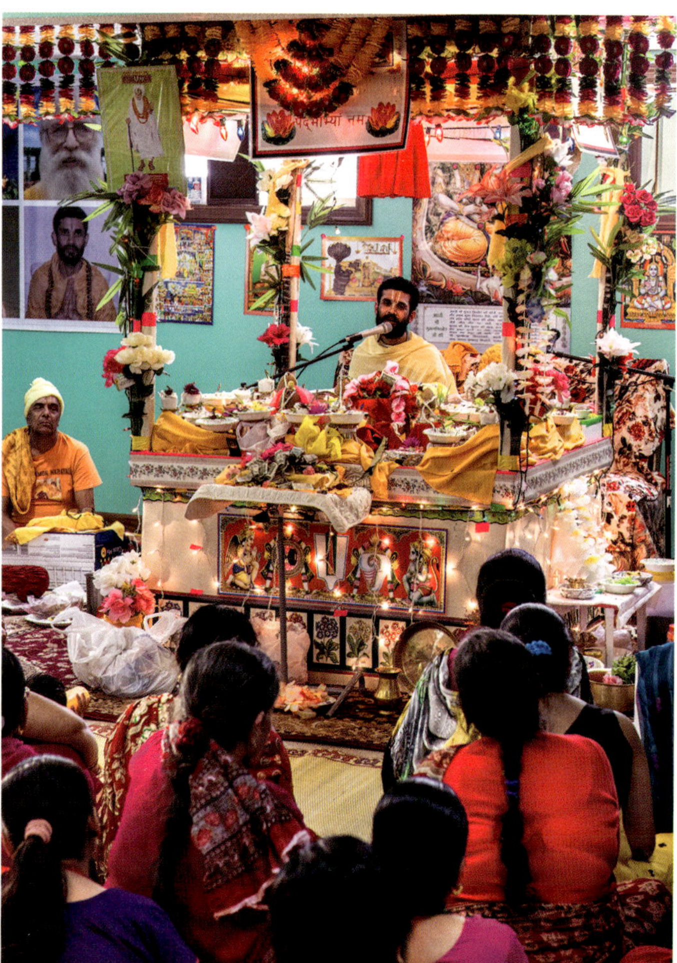

More and more dancers get up, while others sit down to rest and watch for a while. Some songs are especially popular, and dancers crowd the floor. At the close of each piece, the priest says a short prayer into the microphone, his voice blasting throughout the room. *Jaiye*, he calls out in praise, followed by the group's echoes of response.

After two hours of singing, dancing, and music-making, people are ready to eat. The priests close with a group prayer. Members of the hosting household then serve *prashad*—offerings of food made to the gods who have been invited into the space—which is subsequently enjoyed by the congregation. The musicians pack up their instruments, friends and families visit and share laughs, and the feasting begins.

Delighted to learn I am vegetarian, Tanka and his wife, Purna, served a traditional Nepali meal of white rice, cooked green beans, and greens, with a clear broth poured over the top. Did I like spicy food? They smiled when I nodded yes and brought me some hot and flavorful sauce mix for my rice and veggies—delicious! But even better was the sense of belonging that I felt as a welcome addition to their entourage.

* * *

A time of year when members gather for a more solemn focus happens during *Puran*. For this memorial ceremony, held over several days in the spring, members gather to pray for those who have passed away. This year's hosts, Tanka and Purna, have transformed their basement into a worship space with a large altar laden with fruit, spices, candles, flowers, and money. Ringing bells and cymbals accompany the chanting of Sanskrit texts, and the priests offer their gifts to the gods, praying for peace for the assembled and for the world.

Swami Damodar Nepal, a Vaishavite priest, leads the seven-day celebration of *Srimad Bhagavad Maha Puran*

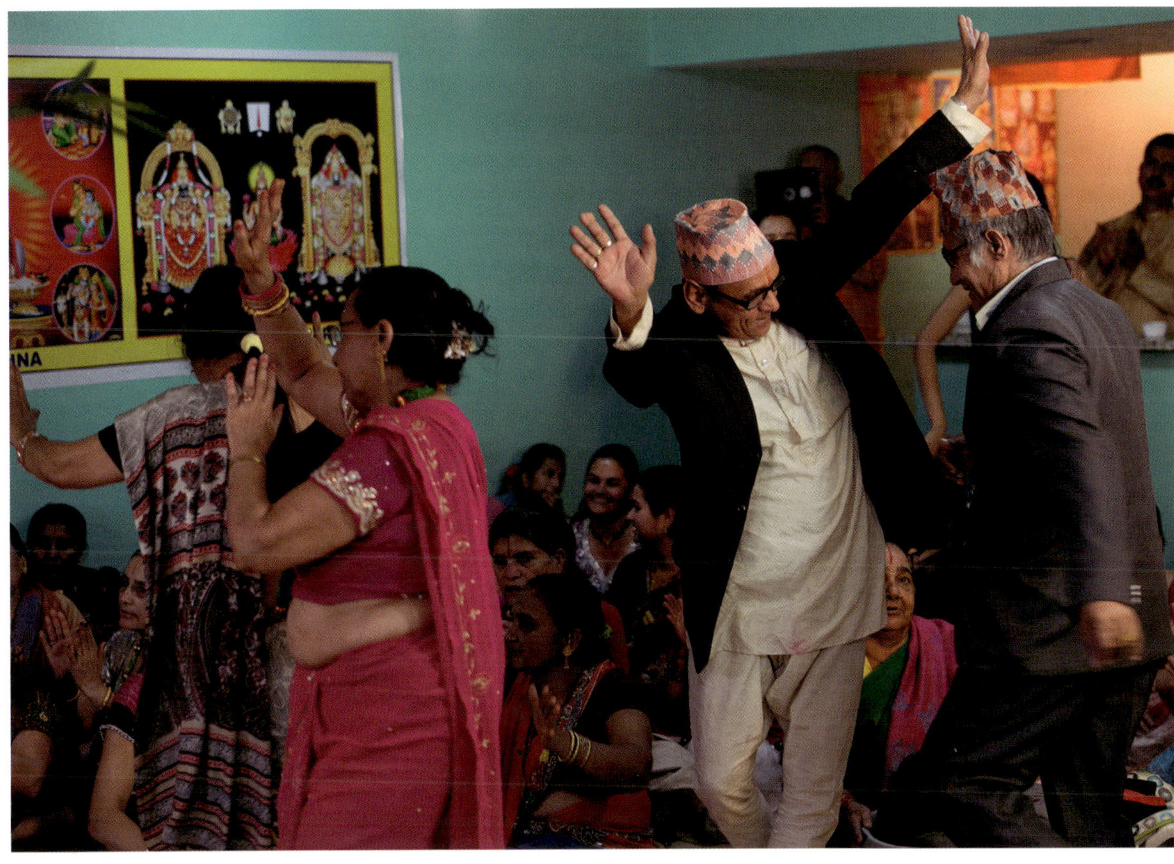

Members of the Hindu Cultural and Educational Center dance and sing during one their *bhajan* services

Over the next several days, people take time to enjoy traditional Nepali food and socialize with friends and neighbors. Come afternoon, festivities continue while workers prepare a bonfire for the evening *homadi* fire ceremony. Smoke from the fire contains healing energy that cleanses the atmosphere of negative karma, purifying and replacing it with positive karma that will guide practitioners to their highest spiritual devotion. All are blessed with holy water and also receive a *tika* marking on the forehead, showing that they are *Vashnaivite* Hindus, devotees of the God Vishnu and his ten incarnations, or *avatars*, especially Krishna.

Because the priests recognize that Bhutanese Hindus have families, work, and school just like the rest of us, they can alter the timing and length of *Puran* to fit the hectic schedules that accompany American life. But the worshippers wouldn't miss it: taking time out from regular life to deepen their devotion rejuvenates the spirit as well as their connection to one another. For Pratima, religion is "love and hope and faith. It's something that combines us all for who we are today and what we can be in the coming days. It's definitely family as well; it unites us all."

IDENTITY Each week as I sit and enjoy the service, a little girl about two or three years old dances freely among us, bestowing smiles and kisses on her favorites, like Pratima. Although Pratima didn't know her before she started attending services, the two became fast friends, and now they sit together every week. With me, the child is still a bit wary. We don't speak the same language, after all. But recently, she began a game of peek-a-boo with me. When I finally got up to dance, she wrapped her arms around my neck and kissed my cheeks.

When I think about this girl's future in the United States, I can't help but contrast it with

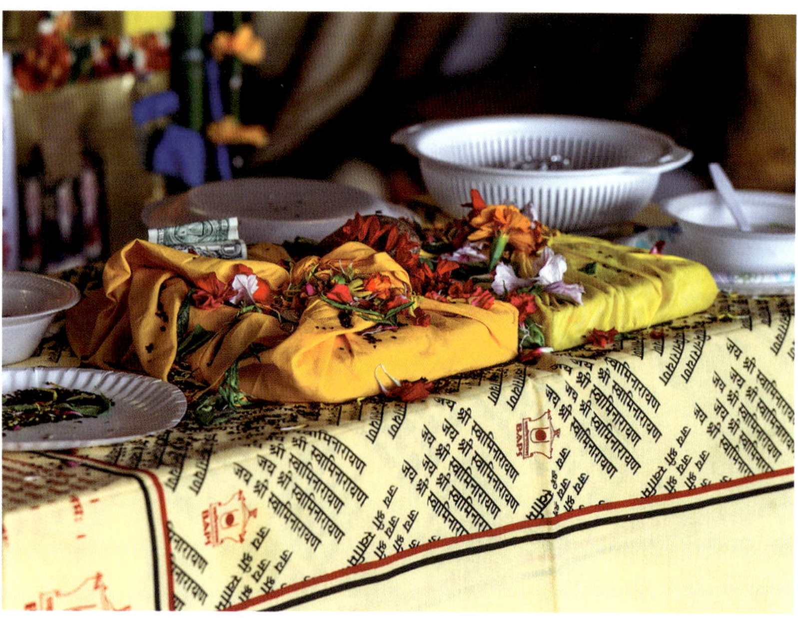

The *Bhagavad Gita* rests on a table amidst offerings for Lord Krishna

some of the community's older members, the ones who often have the toughest time adjusting to life here. Tanka is familiar with everyone; he knows the issues. And he put it frankly: the suicide rate among Bhutanese refugees is extremely high. Pratima explains that while local agencies provide resources and assistance when families arrive, those families don't automatically know how to use these programs and services. Like many, her own family preferred to seek the help of others in their own community. "Our neighbors offered to help us," adds Pratima. "If they wouldn't have been so willing to teach us, we would be starving." That's why attending weekly religious services is not just a spiritual practice for the Bhutanese. It's also the opportunity to have fellowship with those who understand their customs and speak their language. After having been uprooted many times in their lives as refugees, that time together helps them adjust to life in the United States. As Tanka puts it, "People sacrifice for their religion, so we must preserve our practices for ourselves and our community."

Will the young people grow up not knowing their religion, customs, or language? Worse—will they not be interested to know? Parents have expressed that fear to me. In the United States, busyness is part of the culture. With work and school, so much goes on in the lives of families that some get pulled away or don't take the time to attend services. To counter this, parents want to establish not just a temple, but a community center, so that children can be educated in both the religion and the language—and have fun.

A small space provided by the Lutheran Services of Iowa (LSI) headquarters in Des Moines currently acts as the Hindu Cultural and Educational Center's location for Nepali, Sanskrit, and culture classes, which are split by age for children of refugee families. Each week between 15 and 40 students gather in a crowded classroom working to improve their language skills and sustain cultural practices for the next generation. The teachers know that learning Nepali is difficult for the children since they are being raised in the United States; still, they hope the cultural tie of language will help these children remain close to their family, their community, and their religion.

Plans are underway to construct this center and a temple in the Des Moines area on land purchased off of East Army Post road. The community hopes to attract more Bhutanese refugees but also to provide outreach for anyone interested in learning more about Hinduism and their culture. Already, they offer cultural and religious education as well as services such as citizenship preparation and case management, greenhouse and farmers-market opportunities, and ESL classes. As Tanka puts it, Hinduism, like any religion, inspires people to do good with the limited time they have in their life by guiding them on the proper path. It's the path he hopes to lead his own children down throughout their lives, wherever they may go.

Upashna Dhital (right) and Archana Dhital (left), the daughters of Tanka and Purna

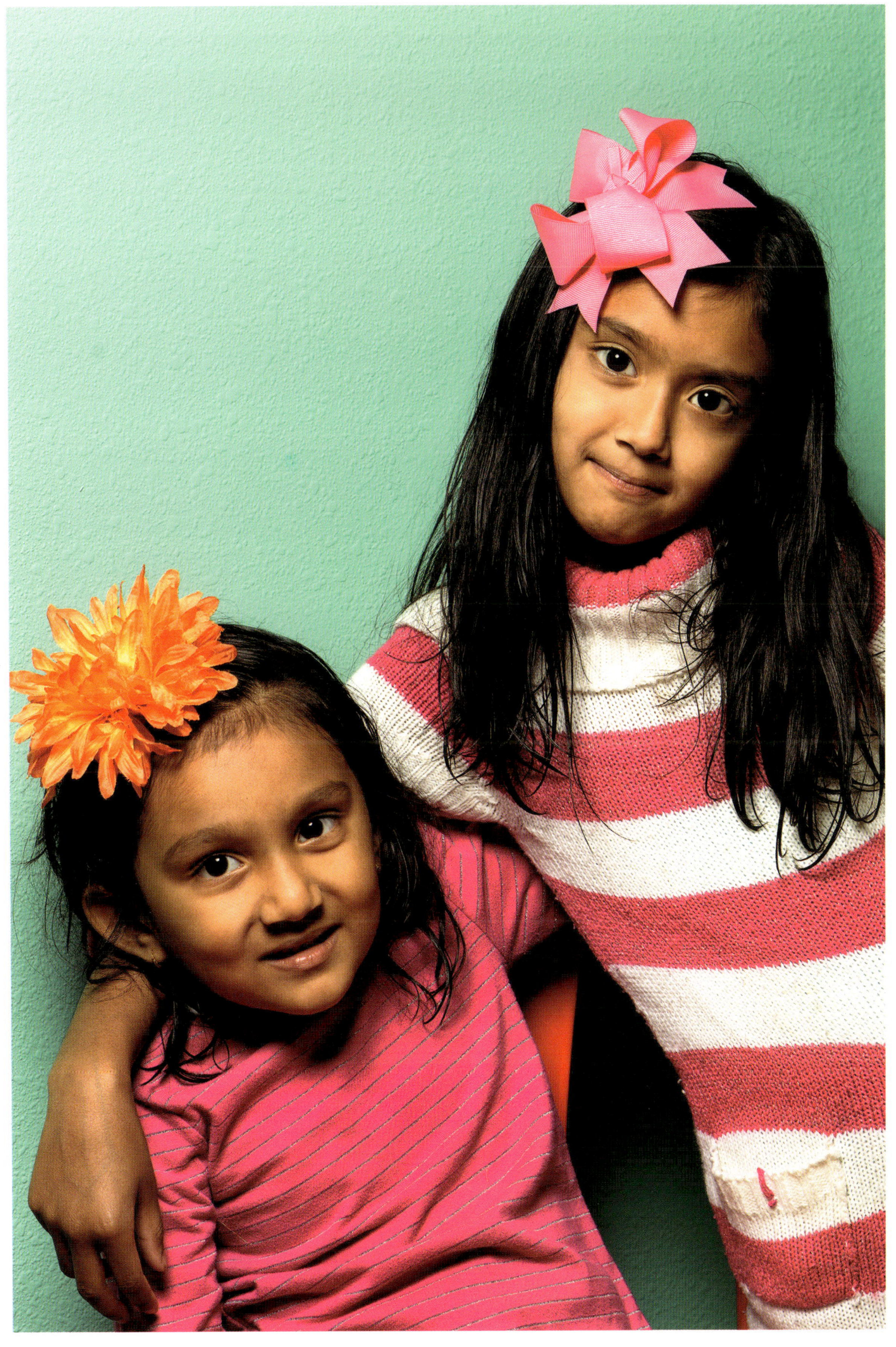

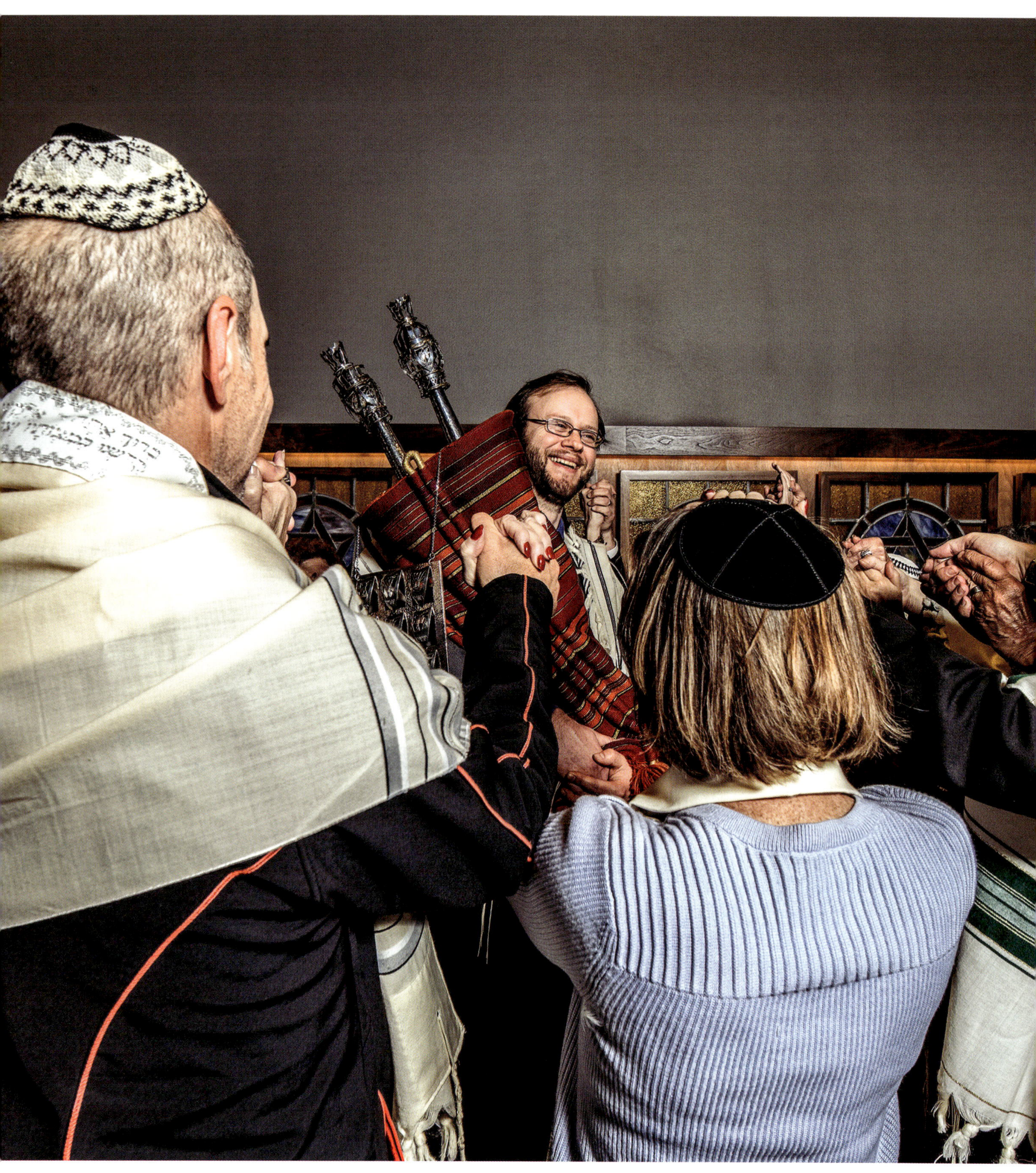

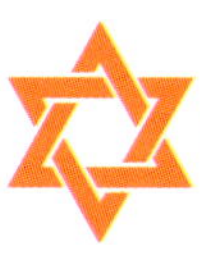

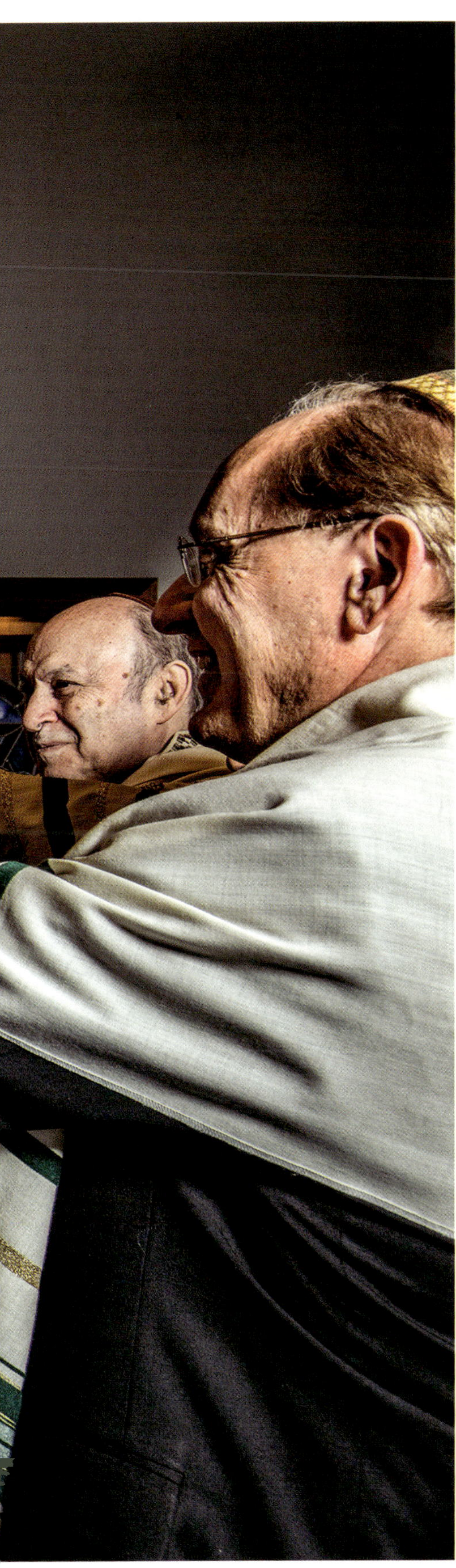

Tifereth Israel Synagogue

Anoushe Seiff

HISTORY *We are a sacred community. We are unique Jewish souls. We are a caring and engaging family. We are a transformational force. We are the foundation for your search.* Although Tifereth Israel Synagogue's five core ideals were formalized only recently, they have guided the congregation ever since its first meeting at the home of Mr. and Mrs. Marks on April 16, 1901. Thirty-five years prior to that first meeting, Des Moines' Jewish population totaled no more than two-dozen people. But toward the turn of the 20th century, that number began to climb, and the Marks family sought to cultivate the religious roots of a new generation of young people from which Tifereth, the "Glory of Israel," would eventually grow.

In 1906, the congregation built its first dedicated synagogue, a building at 3rd and Crocker. Before long, the congregation outgrew this facility, moving to its present location on Polk Boulevard soon after the cornerstone was laid in 1929.

"Tifereth has been around a lot longer than the physical property," says Army veteran and Drake University graduate Will Rogers, who began attending services in the late 1990s with his wife. Indeed, Will and his fellow congregants would come to witness Tifereth's most remarkable act of resilience through transformation.

Celebration of the festival of *Simchat Torah*

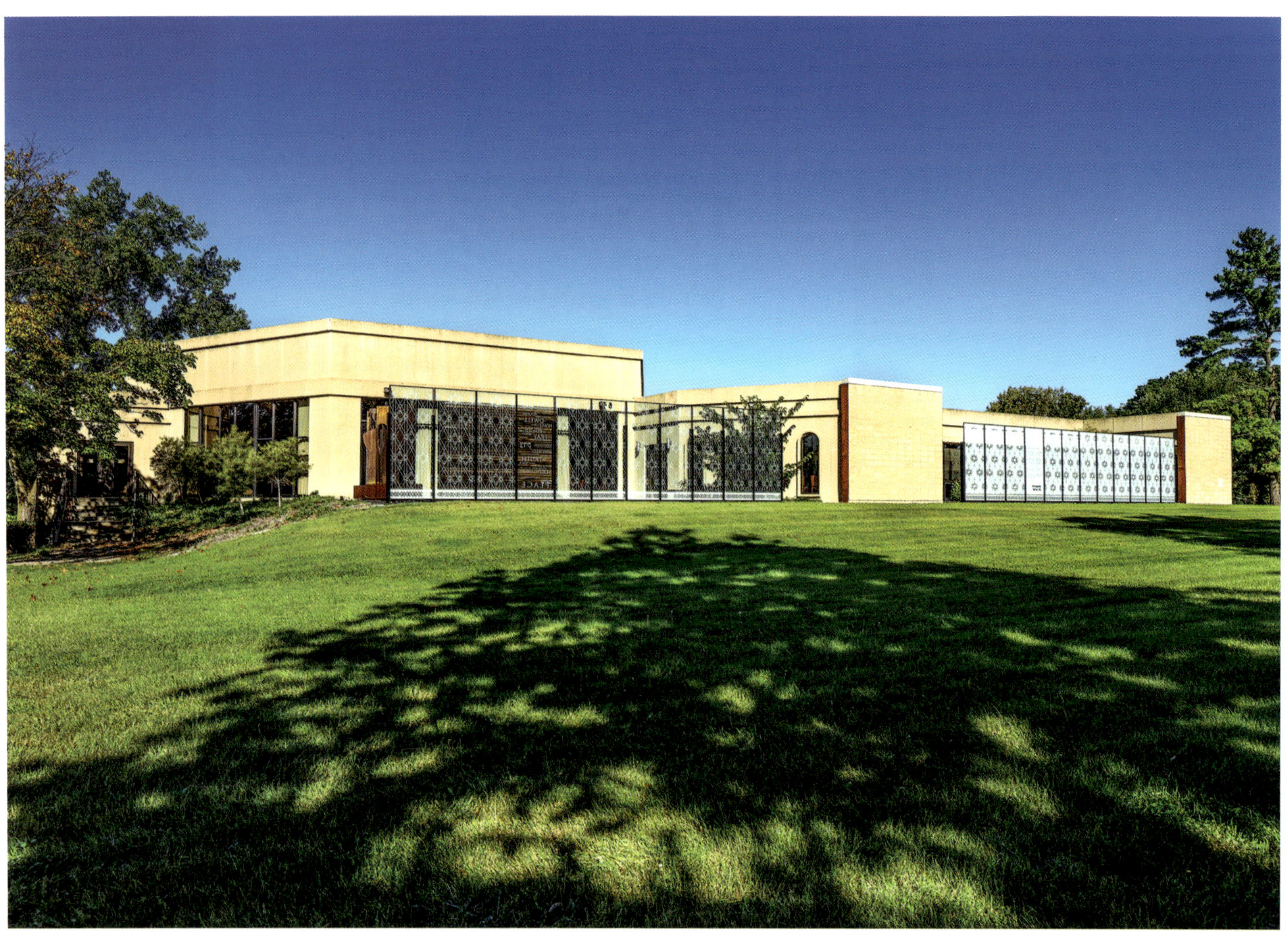

Tifereth Israel Synagogue

By the early 21st century Tifereth's sanctuary had fallen into disrepair. Restoring the building seemed too costly, so they considered building a new synagogue in the suburbs where land had been offered to them. Ultimately, though, members chose to remain in the building where worshippers had gathered for decades. That meant raising the money to construct a new sanctuary and renovate the other facilities. By 2012, they achieved their result—a structure at once strikingly modern but at the same time dedicated to preserving tradition. It is here, as Tifereth's mission statement reads, that the community *strives to enrich our cultural and spiritual lives as Jews by connecting with our community, the traditions of our People, Israel, and with God.*

Fittingly, then, Tifereth's synagogue symbolizes the branch of Judaism practiced there—Conservative Judaism. Standing midway between the more traditional branch of Orthodox Judaism and the more liberal branch of Reform Judaism, Conservative Judaism preserves the old while welcoming the new. As its name indicates, Conservative Judaism takes a "conservative" approach to modernizing the *halakhah*, or Jewish law.

In the early 20th century, modernization included removing the screen that separates men from women in synagogues and allowing congregants to drive automobiles on the Sabbath. Later in the century, modernization took increasingly social forms: Conservative Judaism came to permit female rabbis, same-sex marriages, and LGBT rabbis. For Conservative

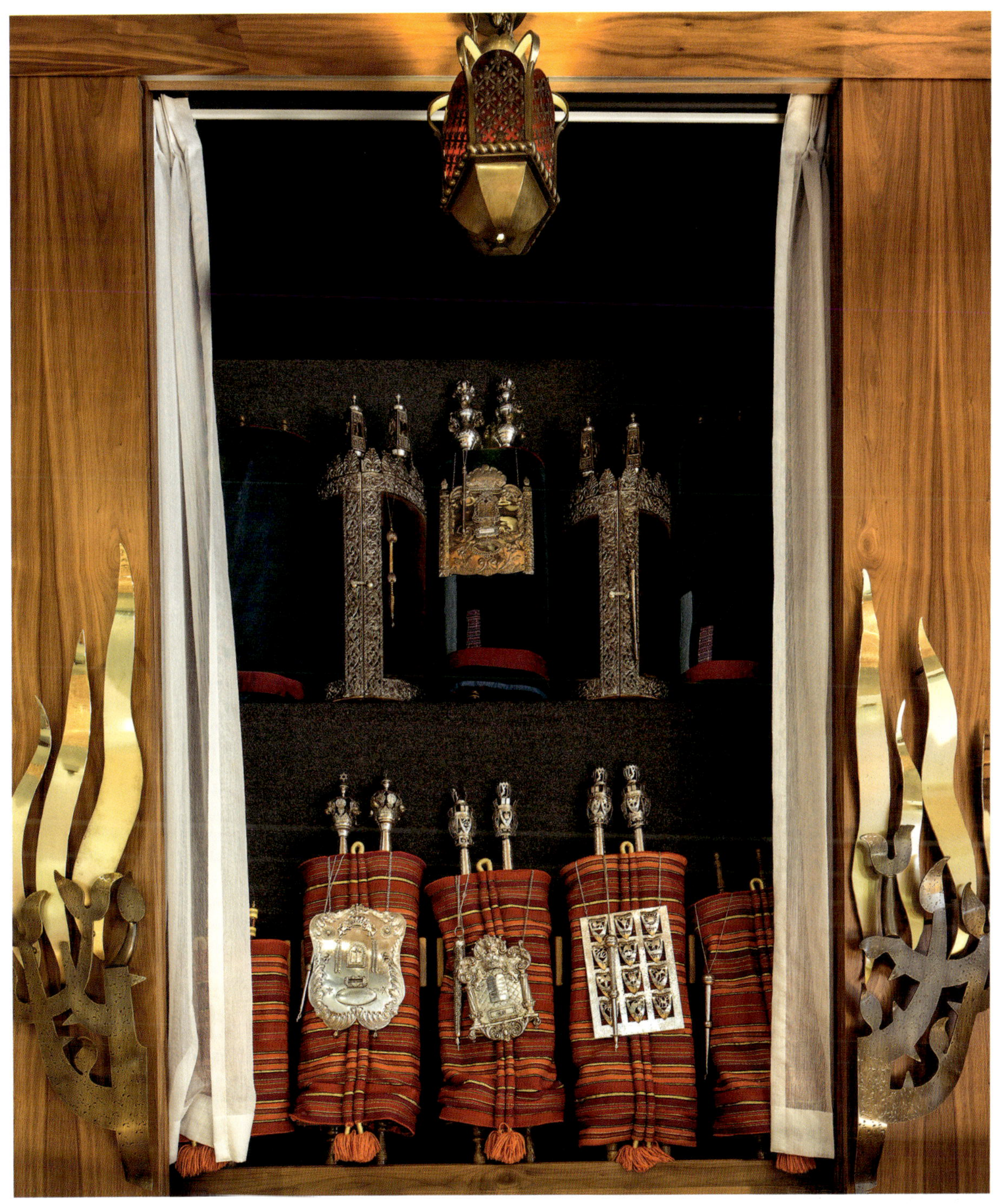

Torah scrolls in Tifereth Israel's Torah Ark (*Aron Kodesh*)

Jews, these changes are not violations of *halakhah*; in fact, they are fulfillments of them in the name of divine justice and equality. They welcome the new while preserving the old—just like Tifereth Israel's redesigned synagogue.

SPACE At the center of Tifereth's redesigned synagogue is a spacious sanctuary where up front sits a giant wooden cabinet with sliding doors. Inside these doors lies the *Aron Kodesh*, or Holy Ark, the holiest place of any synagogue and the location of the Torah scrolls. Facing in the direction of Jerusalem, the Ark serves as a reverent representation of the Holy of Holies in the Jerusalem Temple where the Ark of the Covenant, which itself housed the Torah, was once located. A *parochet,* or thin white curtain, veils the entrance to the cabinet, much like a *parochet* once veiled the entrance to the Holy of Holies. And just as a menorah once illuminated the Jerusalem Temple, the Eternal Light (*Ner Tamid*) continually illuminates the Holy Ark from above.

Most synagogues have one or two Torah scrolls; Tifereth is blessed with ten. Because Torah scrolls contain the very words of God as spoken to Moses on Mount Sinai, they must be cared for in precise ways and can never be destroyed. Over the last few decades, many small-town Iowa synagogues have been forced to shutter their doors. Fortunately, Tifereth Israel volunteered to take in and care for their Torah scrolls, which are handwritten sheets of parchment sewn together and bound on each end with a wooden roller. A breastplate and a crown adorn the scrolls, each of which also includes a pointer, or *yad,* used in reading, so that bare skin does not touch the parchment. However, none of these physical features encompasses what is most important about these marvelous documents. They constitute the covenantal relationship between Jews and God, binding the faithful into a relationship with the divine.

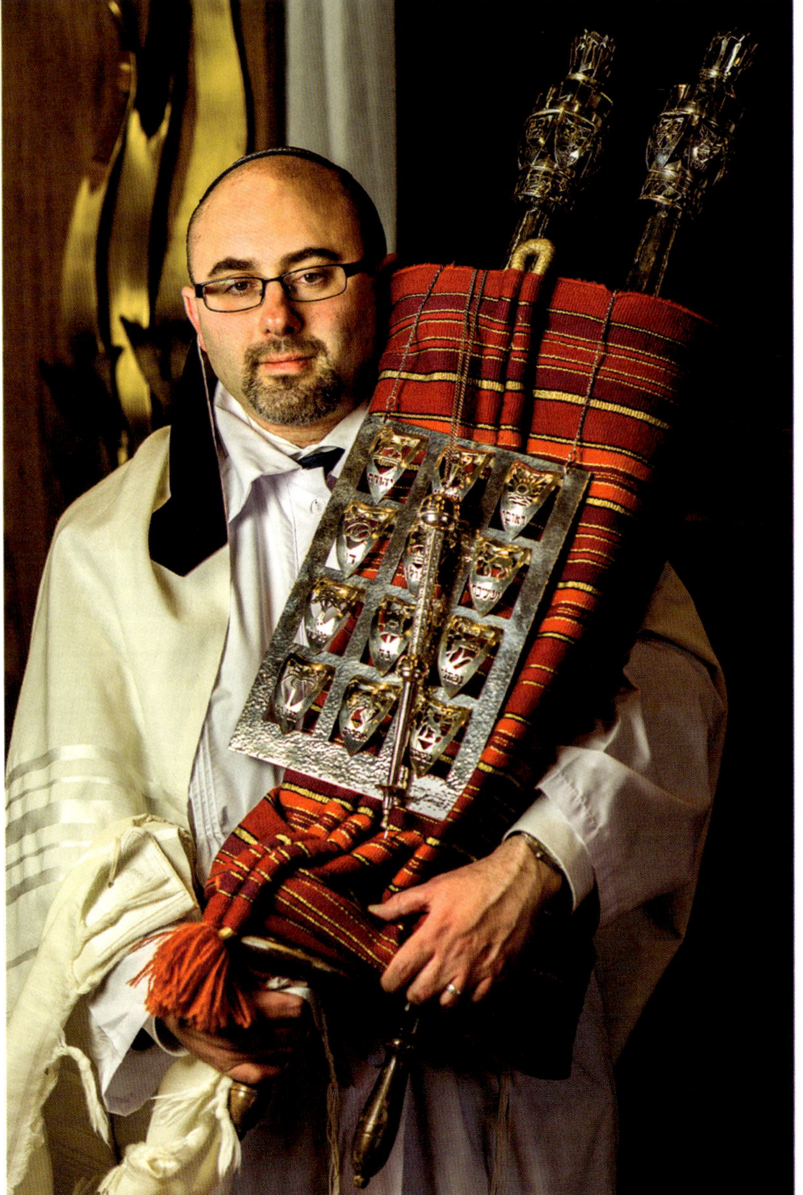

This relationship extends well beyond Tifereth's sanctuary and into all areas of life. On the other side of the sanctuary's retractable wall—which gets pulled back for the High Holidays of *Rosh Hashanah* and *Yom Kippur,* as well as for Passover (*Pesach*) and many *bat* and *bar mitvahs*—lies the social hall, where the congregation enjoys fellowship and food prepared in the nearby kosher kitchen at least once every week and during festive gatherings. Outside the social hall/sanctuary, an atrium is used for receptions as well as *kiddush,* a blessing to sanctify the Sabbath. Original artwork by Andy Warhol and Mauricio Lasansky adorns the atrium walls. Warhol's "Ten Portraits of Jews of the Twentieth Century" features notable Jewish luminaries such as Einstein, Freud, and Kafka, while Lasansky's "Kaddish Series" depicts haunting imagery of the Holocaust (*Shoah*). Tifereth's other facilities include classrooms, offices, a gift shop, and the library. As Will Rogers puts it, these are all sacred spaces that bring Tifereth together as a community apart from the rest of the world.

IDENTITY The aroma of coffee and pastries fills one of Tifereth's classrooms early one Sunday morning as a woman settles into a seat holding

Rabbi Steven Edelman-Blank

her bagel piled high with egg salad. The Sunday Torah Education Program—STEP for short—will soon be in session.

STEP has become an essential part of Torah education at Tifereth. Educator Mike Kuperman has led STEP for the last ten years at Tifereth as well as at other synagogues in the Des Moines area. He describes Tifereth as "active in education and doing," focusing not only on teaching Torah and Judaism to its own congregants, but also on opening dialogue with the members of other religious communities in Des Moines.

This particular STEP class features a discussion of Aviya Kushner's book *The Grammar of God*, which takes a look at various translations of the Torah into English. "Translations are different versions of what people thought," Mike explains. Each translation influences the interpretations that follow. The translator must decide on a meaning, which can cause problems with later understandings of scripture. Since meanings change over time, a word used thousands of years ago may mean something completely different today. His message is not lost on the class, one member of which is fluent in Hebrew, another of which already knows the meanings of many key Hebrew terms in the Torah.

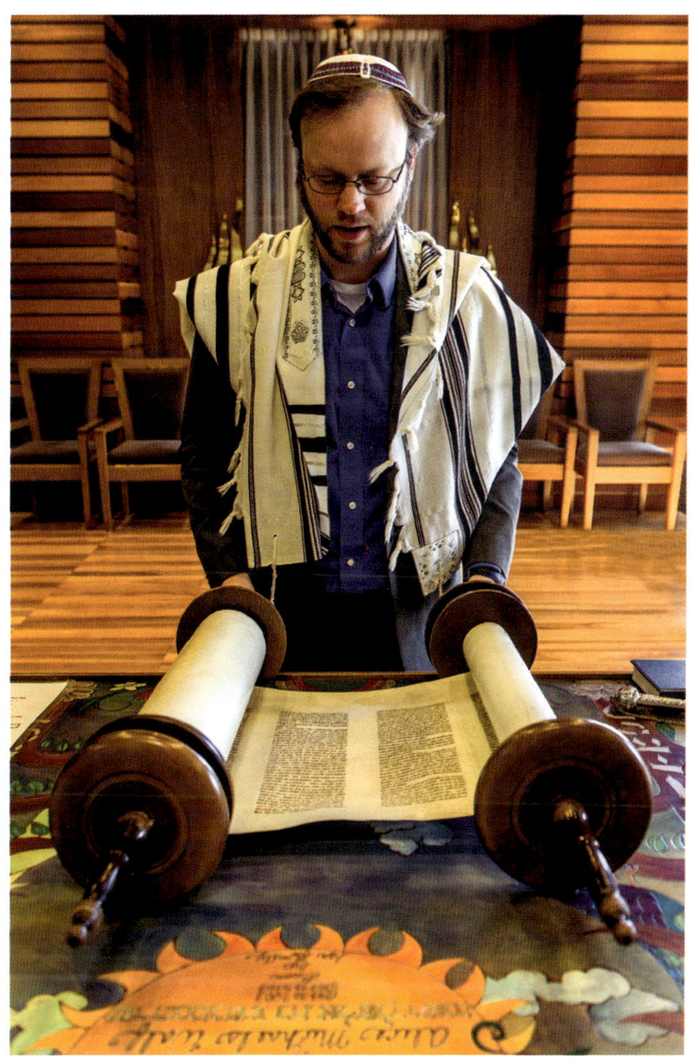

Cantor Patrick Courtney reads from a Torah scroll

According to Patrick Courtney, individuals "come to Judaism on their own terms." This means that "those belonging to the faith can certainly decide how much they follow it." As a lay cantor at Tifereth, Patrick was not ordained and does not have any formal training as a rabbi, though he is musically trained and helps lead the congregation in prayer. Raised by a Christian father and a Jewish mother, Patrick comes from a diverse religious background. In his own family, those identifications are reversed—it is his wife who is a Christian minister. Patrick says that he doesn't neatly fit into a specific category of Judaism. But since Conservative Judaism lies between Orthodox and Reform, he feels it's the best fit for him, as is Tifereth's particular expression of it. For Patrick, Tifereth is everything he's looking for in a synagogue—"small, active, unique, close knit, and open."

In this spirit of openness, Tifereth has changed over the years, seeking to extend justice and equality while also preserving fidelity to Judaism's laws and traditions. *Bat mitzvahs* are one example. Tifereth celebrated its first, the *bat mitzvah* of Miriam Levine, in February of 1940, just 18 years after the first ever *bat mitzvah* was held. In those days, young women were not permitted to become "daughters of the commandments" in the same way that young men became "sons of the commandments"—that is, young people who pledge to observe the commandments, or *mitzvot,* of the Torah.

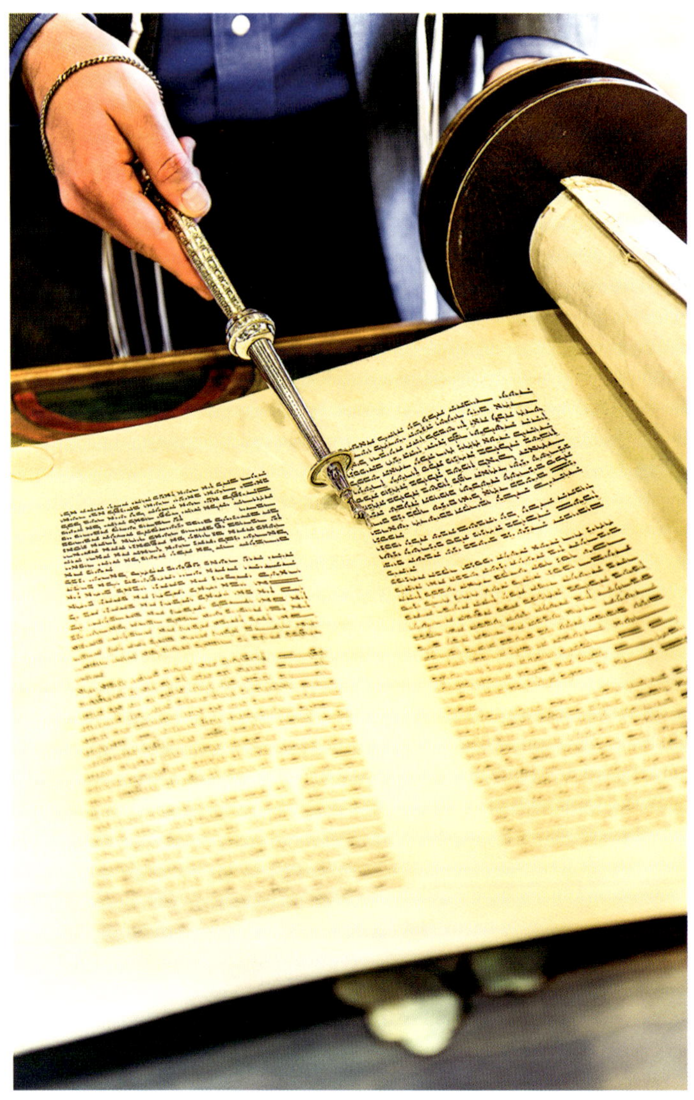

Torah scroll with Torah pointer (*yad*)

Nowadays, both *bar* and *bat mitzvahs* are the norm in Conservative Judaism, welcoming through the practice of the *mitzvot* both young men and women into covenantal relationship with God.

Sheila Bloom-Roehmer, who grew up in Tifereth, still fondly remembers her own *bat mitzvah* and notes, "The community has really changed." Families now benefit from *mishpacha* (family) services as well as "Tot Shabbat" services for children. Once a month, a musical Shabbat puts portions of the Torah to music. And for those wishing to embrace the Jewish faith, there are now confirmation and Torah classes. For Sheila, though, the traditional Saturday morning Shabbat service at Tifereth is where she feels most at home.

PRACTICE Brightly colored sweets are about to fly in all directions, as teens and children armed with candy wait for Patrick to give the word. Then, blue, pink, and yellow wrapped sweets will rain down on the *bat mitzvah*, a 12-year-old girl who has just completed the rite of passage entering into her faith community as a "daughter of the commandments." She has been called up to the Torah where she led the *aliyah* blessing and recited her selected Torah portions. Having successfully performed this duty, the *bat mitzvah* will attempt to dodge the pieces as other children race to the stage to collect the candy.

The throwing of candy comes from traditions pertaining to *aufruf* in which a soon-to-be married couple is called up to the Torah for an *aliyah* blessing, after which the congregation showers them with candy to symbolize the start of a sweet life.

According to Tifereth's rabbi, Steven Edelman-Blank, life cycle events like the *bat* and *bar mitzvah* "are a really big deal" since they are "times when people have a special space to celebrate."

Another such occasion is *Purim*, a holiday celebrating the beautiful and righteous Jewish queen, Esther, and her defeat of the evil minister to the Persian court, Haman. As the book of Esther is read, every mention of Haman's name produces stomping, booing, and the rattling of *graggers*, or noisemakers. But when Ester's name, or the name of her uncle, Mordecai, is read, congregants instead cheer wildly.

This carnival-like springtime celebration begins with games and crafts for the children, although some just run about madly rattling their *graggers*. Never is Tifereth louder! After these preliminary activities, the children's celebration commences with a reading of a censored version of the scroll of *Esther* (which has been scrubbed of all the sex and most of the violence). Patrick,

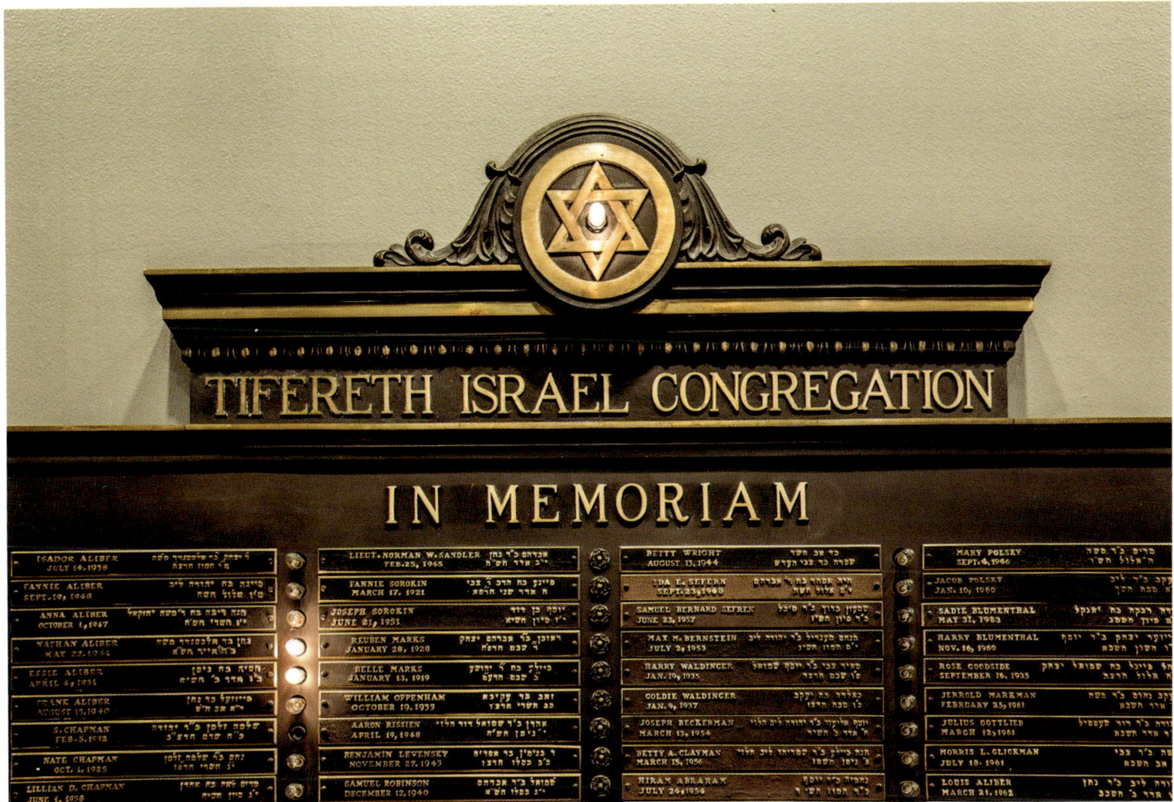

Yahrzeit memorial plaque at Tifereth Israel Synagogue

Tifereth's cantor, reads the story dressed in a bathrobe to mimic Haman's robes.

After the children's reading, the entire community gathers for a meal. *Hamantashen* is the featured delicacy: triangular-shaped, fruit-filled cookies that resemble Haman's three-cornered hat. Once most of the families with young children leave, the un-censored story can begin. Adult members of Tifereth engage in the *Purim* tradition of drinking until they cannot tell the difference between the phrases "cursed be Haman" and "blessed be Mordecai." Wine and liquor flow freely in this particular Jewish revelry.

Purim and *bat* and *bar mitzvahs* aside, the real life of the community revolves around weekly Shabbat services held every Friday evening and Saturday morning. According to Jewish custom, Shabbat begins at sunset, since this is how God created the first day: "And there was evening, and there was morning—the first day" (Genesis 1:5). The setting of the sun, particularly on the Shabbat—the day when God rested after creation—marks a holy time to give thanks and reaffirm God's covenant.

Equal participation is the goal for all Tifereth services, so women are fully involved. As for Jewish law and tradition, individual members decide on their own level of observance. As Rabbi Edelman-Blank explains, "People in this community don't really connect with commands to do things...they do see it as a choice." Many, though, choose to follow the commandments, including keeping kosher dietary guidelines, attending services, and wearing both a *kippah*, a small head covering, and a *tallit*, a prayer shawl. On the four corners of the *tallit* are fringes called *tzitzit*, which remind the faithful of God and His commandments. As the Torah scrolls are paraded around the sanctuary during services, members of Tifereth press their *tzitzit* to the Torah then to their lips, bringing God closer.

For the men and women of Tifereth, daily life, congregational fellowship, and a belief in justice and equality are grounded in the commandments and traditions of Judaism.

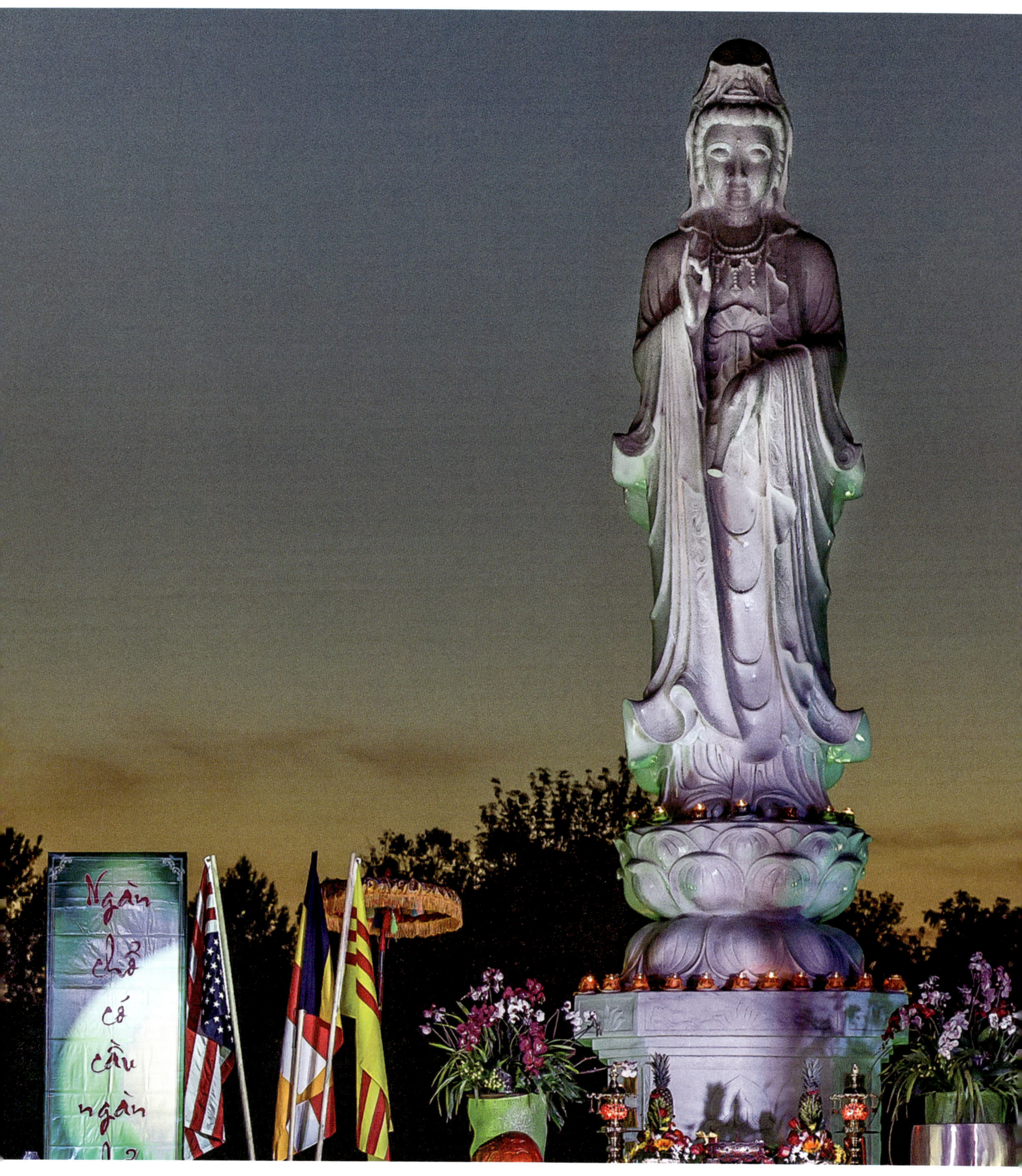
Ngàn
chỗ
có
cầu
ngàn

Tu Viện Hồng Đức

Logan Potter, with Tim Knepper

HISTORY I can't understand a word of Vietnamese, but Thầy tells me that I will understand the meaning of his dharma-talk if I study his face. As he stands at the front of the room on a raised platform in front of three Buddha statues, I remember what he has told me—that all human beings bear resemblances to plants and animals. He himself, due to his Buddhist name—Thich Nguyen Thong—resembles a white pine, since *thong* is the Vietnamese word for that tree. Like the white pine, Thầy is unmoved by the wind and unchanging through the seasons. His faith is strong in the principles and practices of Buddhism and in the community of Tu Viện Hồng Đức.

Although "Thầy" means master or teacher, Thầy's birth name, Minh Huu Nguyen, means "bright," "sunny," or even "smiling." This master is young in spirit and body. In fact, when I first met him, one of his legs was in a cast because he had broken it playing volleyball with the kids. Thầy has been my teacher on my quest to get to know the community of Tu Viện Hồng Đức and the mixed form of Pure Land and Zen Buddhism that they practice.

Tu Viện Hồng Đức would not exist without Thầy's guidance, but this community's story goes back much farther than he does. It begins

Quan Âm dedication ceremony

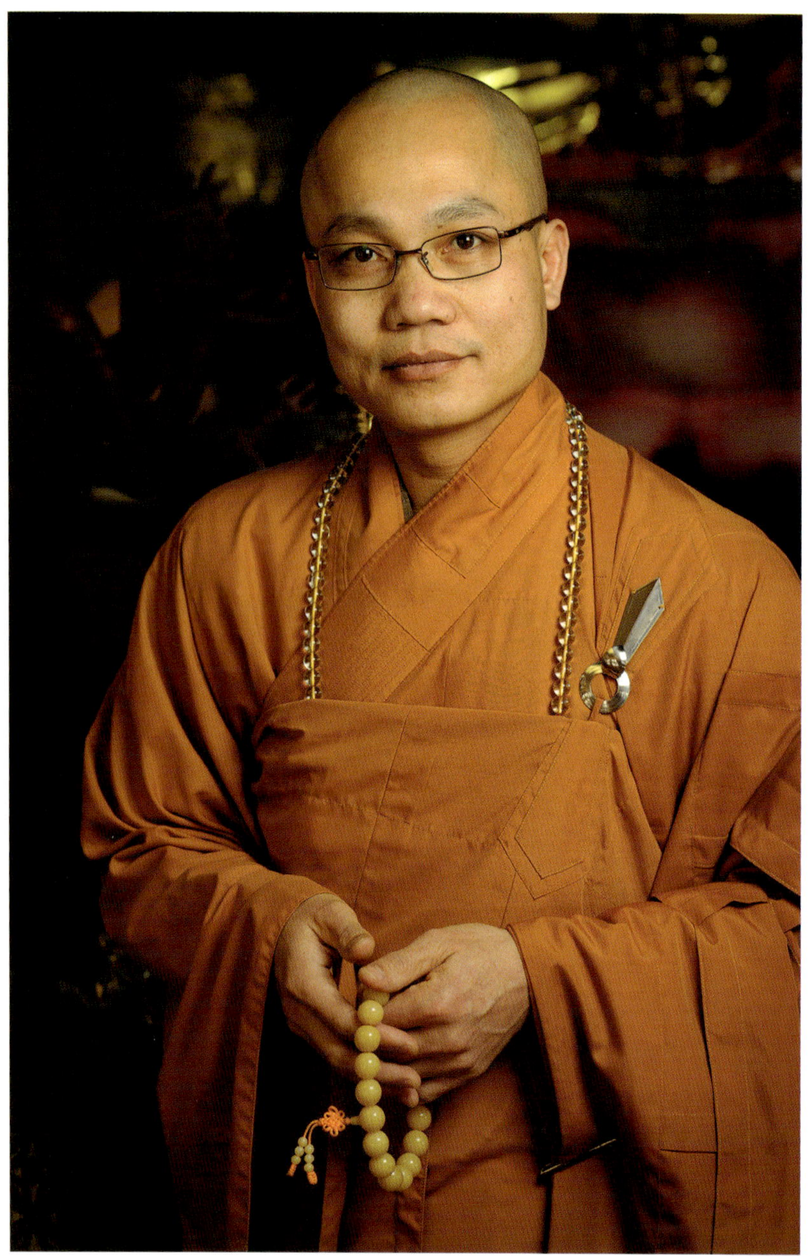

Thich Nguyen Thong, who is simply known as Thầy, meaning master or teacher

with an Iowan, Governor Robert Ray. In July 1975, Governor Ray responded to a letter from President Ford urging states to help resettle refugees after the Vietnam War. Over 2000 ethnic Tai Dam people came to the state of Iowa from Laos. Four years later, Governor Ray again opened Iowa's doors to victims of the Vietnam War, this time to the South Vietnamese "boat people."

A house on 17th Street became the first meeting place of the Vietnamese Buddhist community. Then, in 1998, they established their first temple—Chùa Hồng Ân—on Martin Luther King Junior Boulevard. When Thầy first attended this temple in 2005, he saw potential. The Vietnamese Buddhist community had outgrown Hồng Ân, and Thầy dreamed of a new facility that could better serve them. It would have room in which to grow, space for a monastery, and grounds for a sculpture park. In 2007, the community's dream became reality in the form of an office park on Southwest 9th Street.

Here, the community can preserve and celebrate Vietnamese culture. Just as Thầy had once envisioned, a monastery—the "Tu Viện" portion of the community's title—houses a few Buddhist monks and a nun. A sculpture park features a forty-foot statue of the Vietnamese Buddhist *bodhisattva* of compassion, Quan Âm, along with over forty other Buddhist statues.

Nowadays, Des Moines is a city blessed with two Vietnamese Buddhist temples. The smaller, original Vietnamese Buddhist temple, Chùa Hồng Ân, remains.

SPACE When entering Tu Viện Hồng Đức for the first time, you're asked to take off your shoes, and people are quite eager to give you a tour of their "home." Evidence of the former office park lingers in certain portions of the building, but for the most part the place has been totally transformed. People of all religions are welcome here, a member, Xuân-an, tells me.

After dharma-talk and chanting meditation on Sunday afternoons, I sit amidst the Vietnamese members of the temple, young and old alike, in the community room at Tu Viện Hồng Đức. Aromas of pho and sticky rice, spring rolls, and vegetarian "lobster" fill the air—much of it prepared milder than normal on my behalf and despite my protests. Up on stage, the temple band alternates between Vietnamese pop and traditional music, a festive backdrop to the laughter and fellowship in the

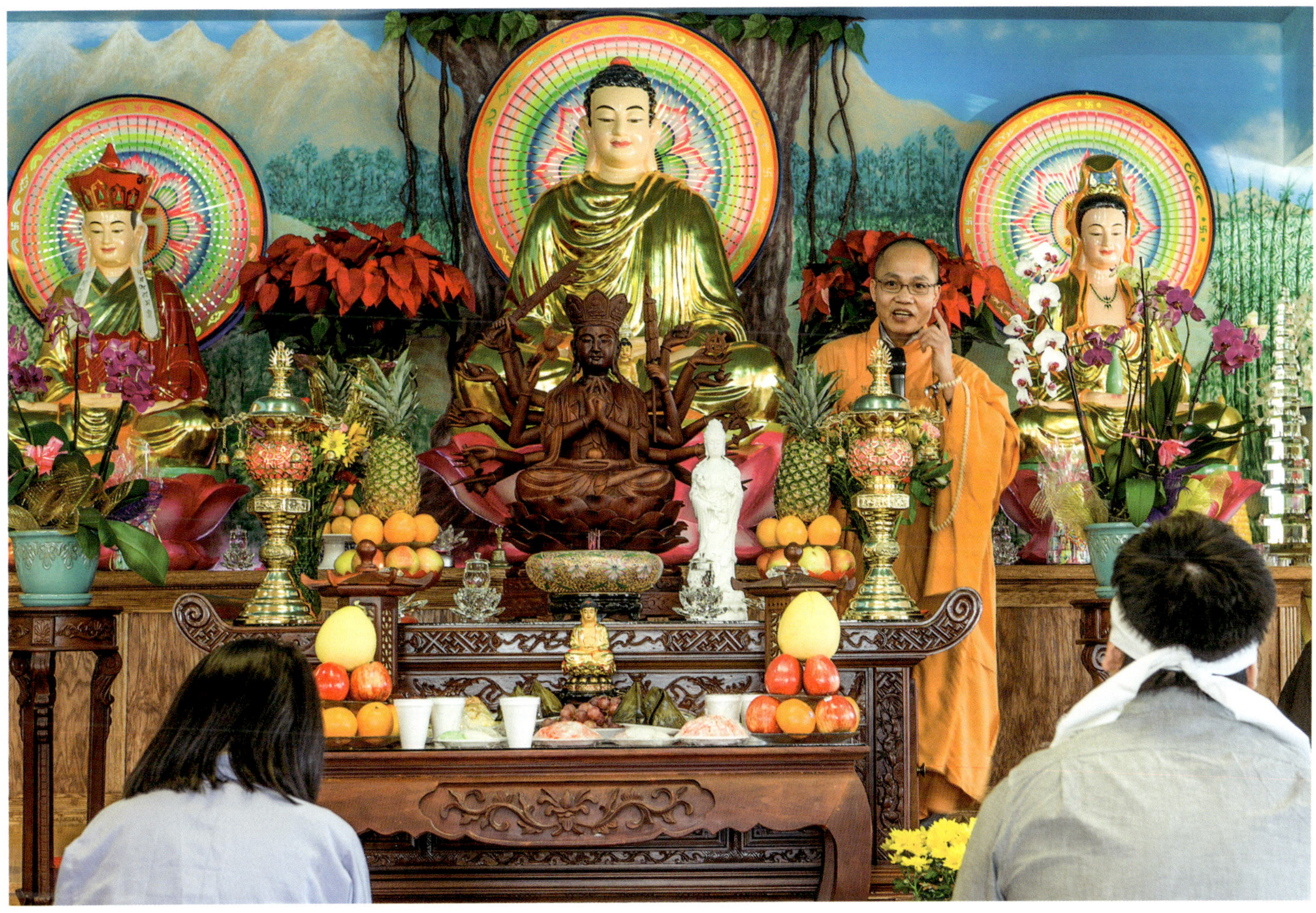

Thầy delivering a dharma-talk on the main altar

community room, and all of it a contrast to the solemnity of the earlier service. Then comes dessert: squares of lime cake, rosy diamonds of gelatin, tapioca pearls in sweet cream, and doughy, sesame-seed covered globes.

Two young girls, Ngọc and Hương, show me around a bit. There's a classroom where young people learn Vietnamese Buddhism, language, and culture. The girls say these lessons are important to them, especially the ones that teach principles through the life of the Buddha. In another room, kids can "chillax" together or play video games.

Thầy's suite lies on the other side of the community room. It includes a tea room for visitors where Thầy has spent hours with me, sharing both his tea and his wisdom. For larger events, the community eats on the back patio under a canopy. There is even a stage for the band.

Inside, a statue of Siddhartha Gautama, the historical Buddha, occupies the center of the main worship space flanked on either side by *bodhisattvas*. These are enlightened beings who take a vow not to enter into the state of final Nirvana until all sentient beings are saved. On the right is the *bodhisattva* of compassion, Quan Âm; on the left, the earth *bodhisattva*, Địa Tạng.

Thầy gives his dharma-talks and leads his chanting meditations from this platform, accompanied by a large bell and gourd-like woodblock that keep time during the chanting. Members seat themselves with cushions on the plain hardwood floor or along the bench at the back wall to hear the talks and participate in meditations. Here, where serenity and silence prevail, a temple community member named

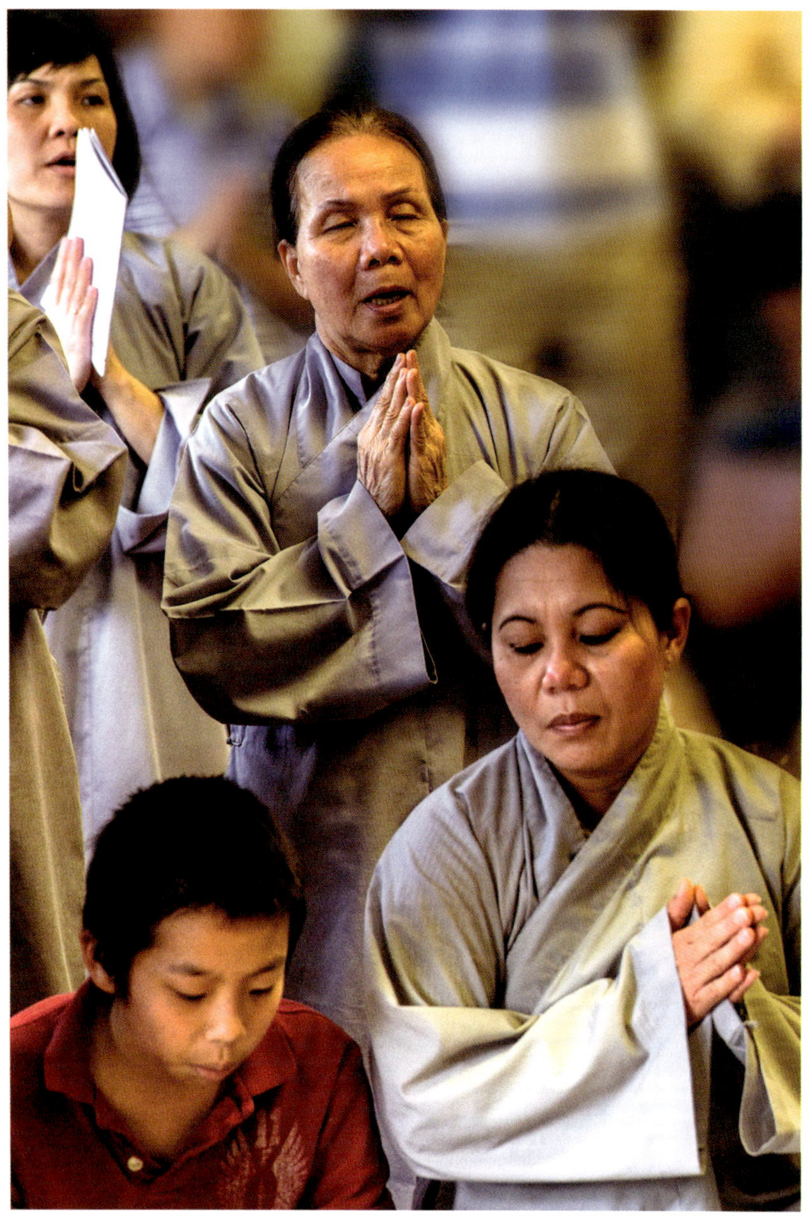

Members of Tu Viện Hồng Đức chant during the Quan Âm dedication ceremony

Xuân-an encounters the sacred. She feels hopeful here. A recent graduate from Drake University and Des Moines University, Xuân-an shares that this space helps her understand where she came from and where she is going in her own life.

For Vietnamese Buddhists, the deceased are still considered a part of the community; they are not purely inaccessible. Therefore, these faithful attend their dead. Through open doorways leading back from either side of the temple stage, one room contains shrines for the recently departed and cabinets in which their cremated remains are kept for a period of time. Three times a day, Thầy or the Temple's nun, Nun Đức Thiện, bring to the deceased a bowl of uncooked rice and water, chanting and ringing a bell in a brief ritual.

Outside in the open air, the statue of Quan Âm towers over Tu Viện Hồng Đức and pours from her bottle infinite compassion upon those who pray for her help. Around her, twelve smaller statues of her personage correspond to the twelve signs of the Vietnamese Zodiac. Elsewhere in this "peace park," as Thầy calls it, sculptures depict scenes from the life of the historical Buddha. People come, seeking peace and petitioning the *boddisattva* for help. One member, Phúc, comes often to pray to Quan Âm, especially when he has a problem or challenge. During such times, he comes to realize that "everything has a solution."

IDENTITY As a Vietnamese temple, Tu Viện Hồng Đức practices *Mahayana*—the "great path" form of Buddhism practiced in East Asian countries like China, Japan, and Korea. More specifically, Tu Viện Hồng Đức practices a mixture of Pure Land and Zen Buddhism, both of which are sects of Mahayana Buddhism. The former emphasizes devotion to Amitā Buddha, the Buddha of Immeasurable Light and Life, who created a heavenly "Pure Land" into which devotees will be borne upon death and from which it is easy to attain final Nirvana. Remembering and repeating the name of Amitābha—*A-di-đà Phật*, in Vietnamese—is vital to these ends. Indeed, "A-di-đà Phật" is never far from the lips and hearts of the members of Tu Viện Hồng Đức. It also functions as "hello," "goodbye," and "thank you."

Quan Âm's grace and compassion center this community. In both a physical and spiritual sense, she is a savior. She is also a *bodhisattva* and, daily, performs miraculous deeds. One member, Hiếu, tells of how Quan Âm protected him during a recent car crash. His airbag had failed to deploy, and instead of suffering a tragic accident during a high speed collision to his side of the car, a "white light" enveloped him, shielding him from the flying glass. It was Quan Âm who brought the faithful to safety after the war, guiding them from Vietnam to Iowa. And it is Quan Âm who will guide the community to Amitābha's Pure Land upon death.

Despite the centrality of Pure Land Buddhism, however, it is the practice of Vietnamese culture that makes Tu Viện Hồng Đức the temple it is. The largest gatherings take place on Vietnamese holidays, festive with traditional songs and dances. Lately, however, Thầy observes a growing divide that separates the older, first generation immigrants who usually speak only Vietnamese from the younger, second and third generation immigrants who usually speak only English. Thus, leaders like Thầy agree: Buddhism alone is not enough. Their youth must learn the Vietnamese language and culture. Unfortunately, it's not always clear if these efforts are paying off.

Wonderful moments do happen, however, in which their hard work comes to fruition. At the dedication of the Quan Âm statue in 2014, for example, Paula and Grace were among the fourteen young women and girls who performed the "Thousand Hand and Thousand Eyes" Quan Âm dance. During one moment, the dancers line up one behind the other, creating what appears to be one being with a single face but the swaying arms of thirteen other dancers, recreating the "thousand helping hands" of Quan Âm. When the girls saw so much of the audience moved to tears that day, their nearly endless repetition of rehearsals suddenly seemed worth it. Monks and nuns who had come from around the country called it the most beautiful rendition of the dance they had ever witnessed. They even invited the performers to come dance at their own temples.

Thầy remembers smiling from ear to ear that day, and fittingly so, given his "sunny" name. He wants to be known for his smile, he tells me, not just his intellect, and then bursts into laughter. The congregation also enjoys a good laugh often, since humor punctuates the wisdom and compassion in Thầy's dharma-talks.

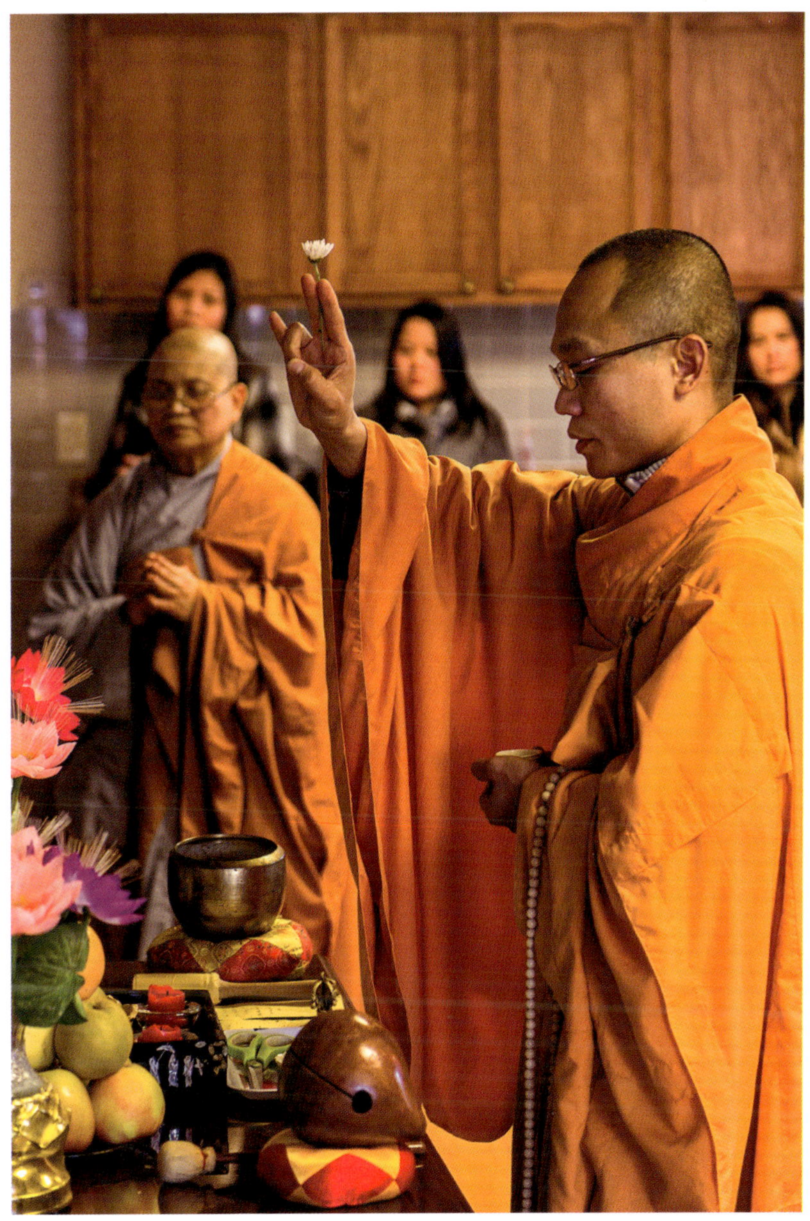

Thầy performs a ritual for a recently departed member of Tu Viện Hồng Đức

PRACTICE We walk three paces, drop to our knees, and lower our foreheads to the asphalt, then rise and begin the pattern again. After nearly 45 minutes, our procession reaches its destination—the 40-foot high white marble statue

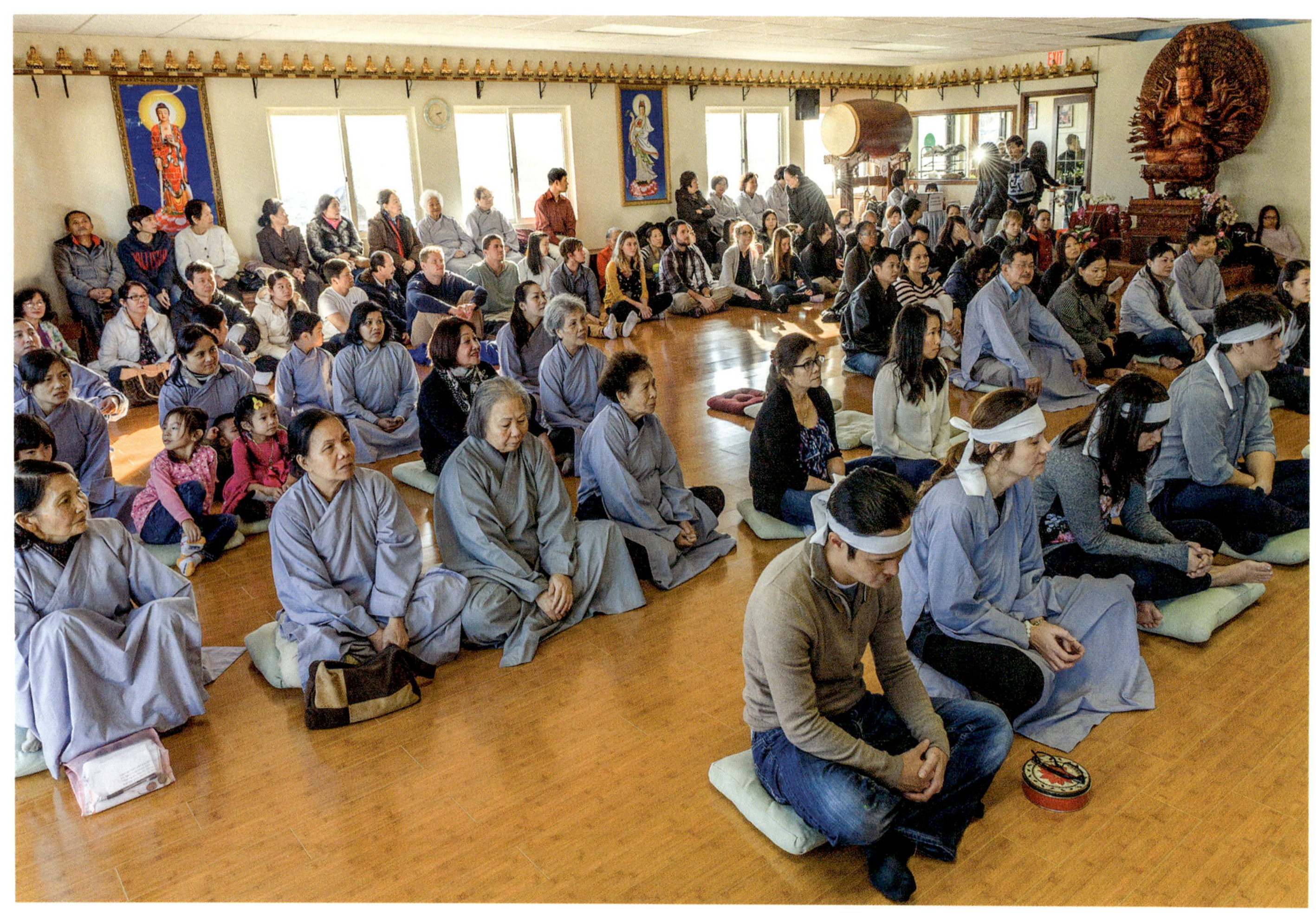

Members of Tu Viện Hồng Đức listen to Thầy's dharma-talk

of Quan Âm. We have arrived to commemorate the occasion of one year ago, when the statue was installed. Then, the installation was part of an entire weekend of events that included a delegation of Vietnamese monks and nuns from all over the United States and a bevy of famous Vietnamese performers. But the highlight of the installation ceremony was, of course, the Quan Âm dance with its stunning visual representation of the "one thousand" helping hands of Quan Âm.

One Sunday, Hiếu translated a service at which Thầy gave a dharma-talk about Quan Âm. As a *bodhisattva* of compassion, Quan Âm resides in every one of us, Thầy explained and Hiếu translated. We can—indeed, we must—become "Quan Âms" for those in need. The temple's Sakya Care Foundation program is an example. Teams of doctors, nurses, and other volunteers travel to India and Vietnam to provide free health care for the poor and sick. For Xuân-an, currently in residency as a family practitioner, this is what makes her most proud of Tu Viện Hồng Đức.

It is unsurprising, then, that the meditation following Thầy's dharma-talks always features Quan Âm, as well as the Buddha of the Pure Land, Amitābha. For these practitioners of Pure Land Buddhism, saying the name of Amitābha is vitally important, especially in helping to reach Nirvana. But Thầy reminds the congregation of Tu Viện Hồng Đức that the Pure Land is right here, right now—and that the faithful must work to manifest its reality.

A smaller crowd attends weekly Sunday services, but the temple swells over capacity

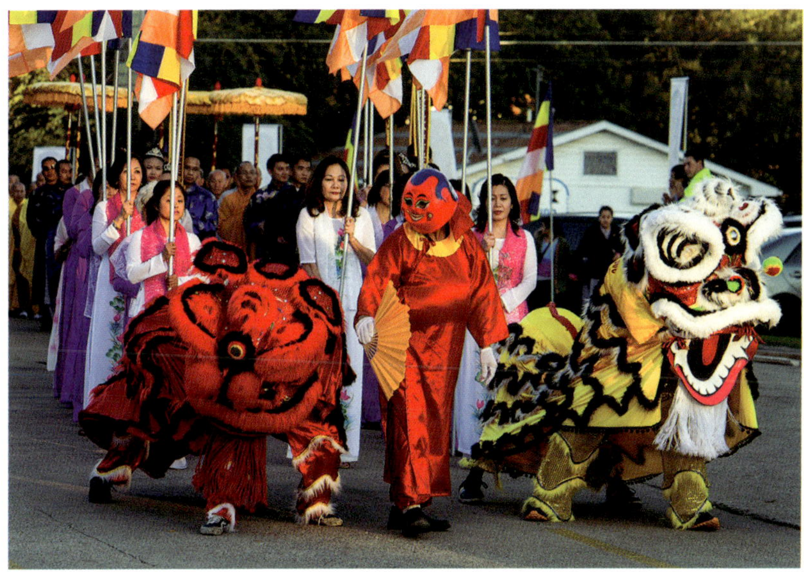

Members of Tu Viện Hồng Đức, some wearing "dragon dance" costumes, commemorate the one-year anniversary of the Quan Âm dedication ceremony

for special yearly events, whether they are religious ones connected with the life of the historical Buddha or cultural ones that celebrate Vietnamese heritage. *Vesak* is one example of a Buddhist holiday—Buddha's birthday, in fact. The faithful form long lines waiting to bathe the figure of the Baby Buddha with ladles of water. As for Vietnamese holidays, members perform traditional songs and dances, a favorite being the Dragon Dance, during events such as New Year's, *Tết*, and their version of Mother's Day—more accurately, Parent's Day, called *Ullambana*. As with most celebrations, it's both a religious holiday and a cultural holiday rolled into one, complete with songs, dances, and, of course, food. Prayers are offered to deceased ancestors as well as to living parents and elders.

One Sunday afternoon, as I went to throw away the uneaten food on my plate, Thầy instructed me to "take it outside to the garden." (For Thầy, every occasion, no matter how mundane or unusual, is an opportunity to live and teach the principles of Buddhism.) Puzzled, I handed my bowl to a man who, I discovered, regularly takes the leftovers outside. "We feed the animals of the temple," the man told me, in halting English. He was referring to the squirrels, birds, opossums, raccoons, and various other critters that live in the trees and grounds of the temple. The karma inherent within animals who are properly fed and cared for might be reincarnated into higher life forms, possibly even humans.

* * *

Once, Thầy and a few other members of Tu Viện Hồng Đức invited me on a "road trip" to West Liberty, Iowa, a full two-hour drive. When we emerged from the vehicle, however, it wasn't a temple that greeted us; it was a saltwater fish store. In we went to the so-called "Sea of Marvels," where numerous colorful glittering tanks of plants and animals endeavored to live up to the store's name. Among the massive tanks of exotic fish, a large eel loomed on the other side of the glass.

"That is a sentient being."

I turned to look at the man who had appeared at my side.

"He possesses karma," the man added, explaining that we must pray to alleviate the suffering of the eel. One day it will experience rebirth into a higher realm. Then it will have the opportunity to achieve enlightenment.

Thầy came and led me out of the fish room and away from the eel, down a narrow hallway, and into a back room that looked, of all things, like a miniature Tu Viện Hồng Đức. The only part that didn't surprise me was the small statue of Quan Âm. There she dwelled, completely laden with fruit and flowers and extending her helping hands to suffering beings. Thầy gave his dharma-talk that day about the abundant compassion of Quan Âm—compassion symbolized in her one thousand helping hands.

Whether manifest in the ordinary or the extraordinary, the chief principles of Mahayana Buddhism, compassion and wisdom, abound at Tu Viện Hồng Đức. This is what the people of the community taught me, most memorably from its serene and smiling leader, Thầy.

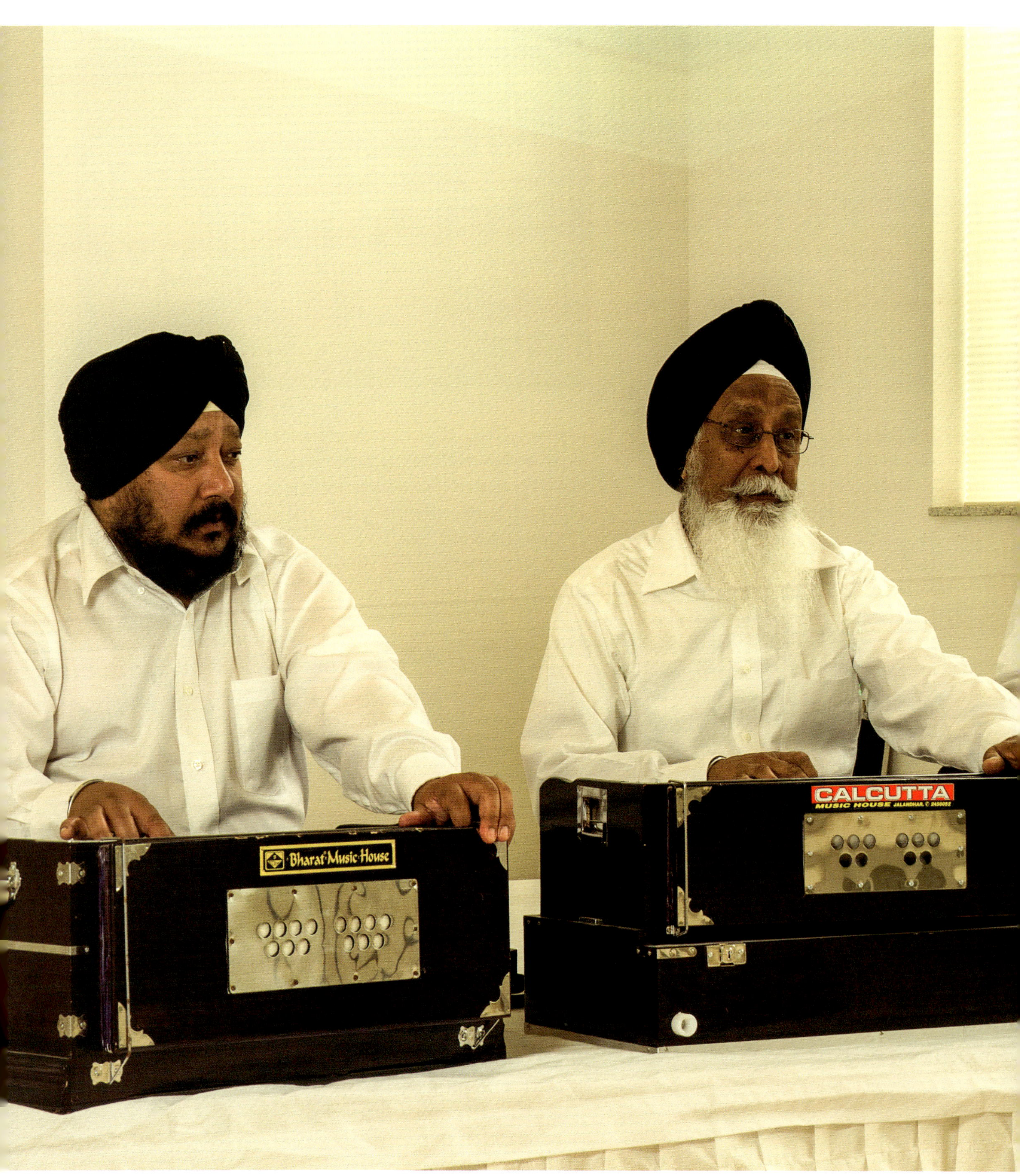
Bharat Music House
CALCUTTA
MUSIC HOUSE

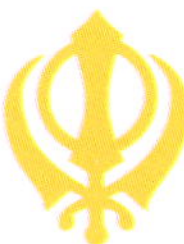

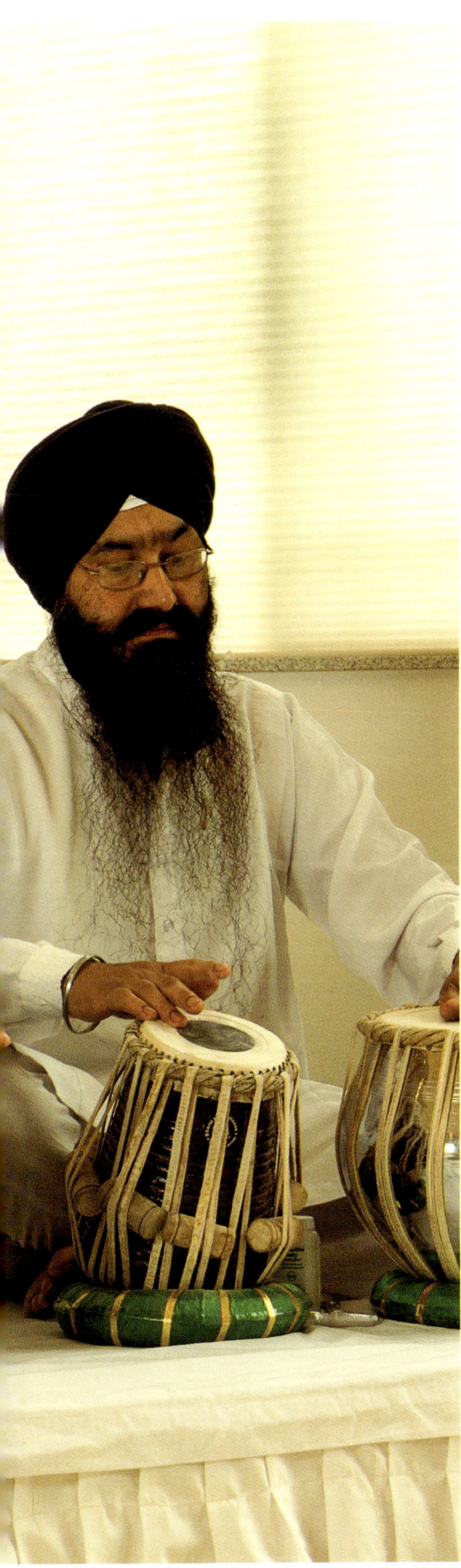

Sikhs of Iowa Khalsa Heritage, Inc.

Meghan Plambeck

HISTORY An ivory white dome peeks out from behind the crest of cornfields lining the suburban horizon of Johnston, Iowa: the dome of the *Gurdwara* of the Sikhs of Iowa Khalsa Heritage, Inc. You may not expect to find a thriving center for a religion founded on the other side of the world here in Iowa, yet the home of this Sikh faith community has been part of the heartland horizon since its establishment in 2009. Johnston residents pass by the *Gurdwara* on their daily commutes, often inquiring about the temple. Even before construction began on the physical building, Sikhs had established themselves in Iowa, back when only a few members gathered for worship on Sundays in each other's houses. Charting this community from these early beginnings to the Johnston *Gurdwara* helps to explain the depth of devotion that characterizes the "Sikhs of Iowa Khalsa Heritage Incorporated," or SIKHI.

Many members of SIKHI are immigrants from India with roots in the Punjab region. Each Sunday as members gather at the *Gurdwara*, Western and Eastern cultures combine to form a unique American entity of contemporary American Sikhism. Women arrive dressed in

Satpal Singh, Harkishan Singh, Lakhwinder Singh (left to right), playing harmoniums and *tabla* for *kirtan* at the *Gurdwara*

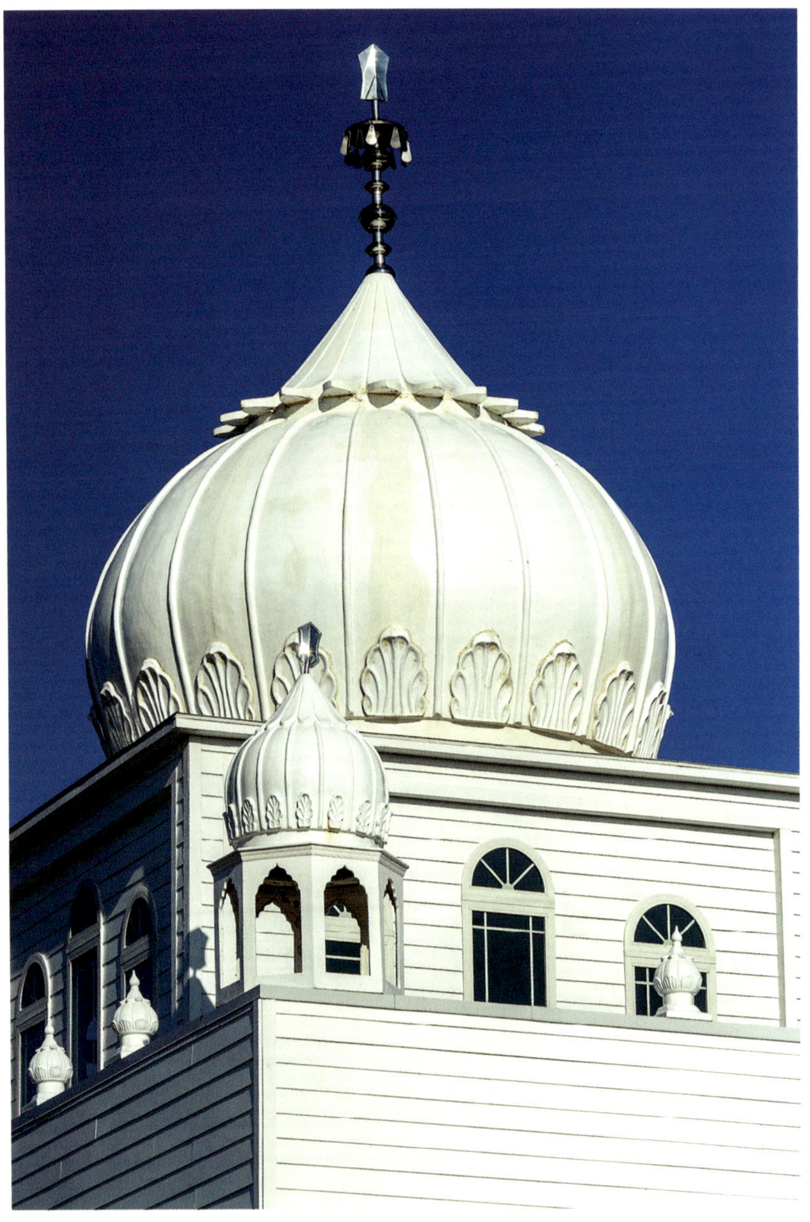

Central dome (*gumbad*) of the gurudrawa of the Sikhs of Iowa Khalsa Heritage, Inc.

bright scarves and *sarees* with intricate metallic detailing that compliments the gleams of iPhones and designer purses. Men of all ages come wearing traditional Indian Kurta Pajama garments, but they are outnumbered by those clad in Levi's or business pants with colorful polos. Most wear turbans, as well, in a rainbow of vibrant hues.

What started as a modest effort to build a temple in 2009 snowballed into a megaproject that grew way beyond the available means. However, as the caretakers of the *Gurdwara Sahib* would tell you, the benevolent Guru showered His blessings upon His followers and guided them to complete the project. "*Santaan ke kaarj aap khaloiya har kamm karaavan aaya Raam*"—The Lord Himself completed the task of His followers—cites one such caretaker, Kanwarpal Dhugga, from page 783 of the Sikh holy book, the *Guru Granth Sahib*.

Jasvin and Jasvinder Kakar have been part of the *Gurdwara* since the days when only a few members gathered for Sunday worship in West Des Moines. Originally, the couple moved from India to Iowa, an area that felt right to them not only because of employment opportunities but because of the warmth of the community. Jasvin explains that the Sikhs have been blessed by the growth of their numbers beyond the bounds of Des Moines' city limits. Eventually the Kakars were able to help fund construction of the Johnston *Gurdwara*.

Most of the congregation find other Iowans open-minded and welcoming. Now and then, people may stare at them or murmur, but Jasvin sees this behavior as arising from a lack of information, not from hatred or judgment. In fact, given the opportunity, Jasvin and many others at the Sikhs of Iowa Khalsa Heritage actually enjoy explaining why their dress and appearance is not necessarily typical Iowa style. Usually, people are delighted to learn more. Even the middle-school aged young people report that their classmates no longer see scarves, turbans, and Indian dress as strange; instead, they see them simply as aspects of their friends' culture.

Kanwarpal Singh Dhugga, a member of the Sikh community in Des Moines, immigrated to the United States at the age of 26. After completing his studies on the West Coast, he deliberately chose this area of the country. While acceptance and open-mindedness may not be the first traits others associate with the Midwest, 20 years into his life here, Mr. Dhugga is more optimistic than ever. "My fondness only keeps growing," he says. "People are so open-minded and willing to listen."

The name "Sikhs of Iowa Khalsa Heritage, Inc." forms the acronym SIKHI, which has great meaning for the faithful at this *Gurdwara*. "Sikhi" is the general word for a Sikh practitioner. "Khalsa," originates from *khalisa*, a Persian word meaning "pure," and emphasizes the community's purity of faith and practice. This faith and practice is outlined in a booklet entitled, "Sikhi: Faith and Followers," which members of SIKHI give to visitors to introduce their religion.

A bulletin board layered with articles from scholars and photos of visitors greets attendees upon arriving. The *Gurdwara's* Facebook page is filled with posts thanking high school and college classes for taking the time to visit and learn about Sikhism. This dedication to growth and outreach is one of the most important values held by the Johnston community.

IDENTITY In mid-April of each year, the *Gurdwara* bustles with activity as both locals and visitors gather to celebrate *Vaisakhi*, a Sikh New Year festival honoring the inauguration of the *Khalsa*. Though the event is formally celebrated only once each year, *Khalsa* values resonate through the *Gurdwara* all year long, permeating every aspect of worship and community life.

During *Vaisakhi* and throughout the year, Sikhs fly the *Nishan Sahib*, the Sikh flag. A double-edged sword known as the *khanda* in the center encircled by two curved swords or *kirpans* on each side together constitute the Sikh emblem that is pictured on the flag. It represents the warrior spirit of Sikhs, specifically that of *Khalsa* Sikhs who are known as "Spiritual Warriors." *Vaisakhi* honors Guru Gobind Singh, the tenth guru and founder of the *Khalsa* for inspiring Skihs' warrior spirit. "He taught that you cannot turn the other cheek forever," explains Mr. Dhugga. "Otherwise, you will go extinct. He said you need to stand up, but the only battles you will fight will be in self-defense."

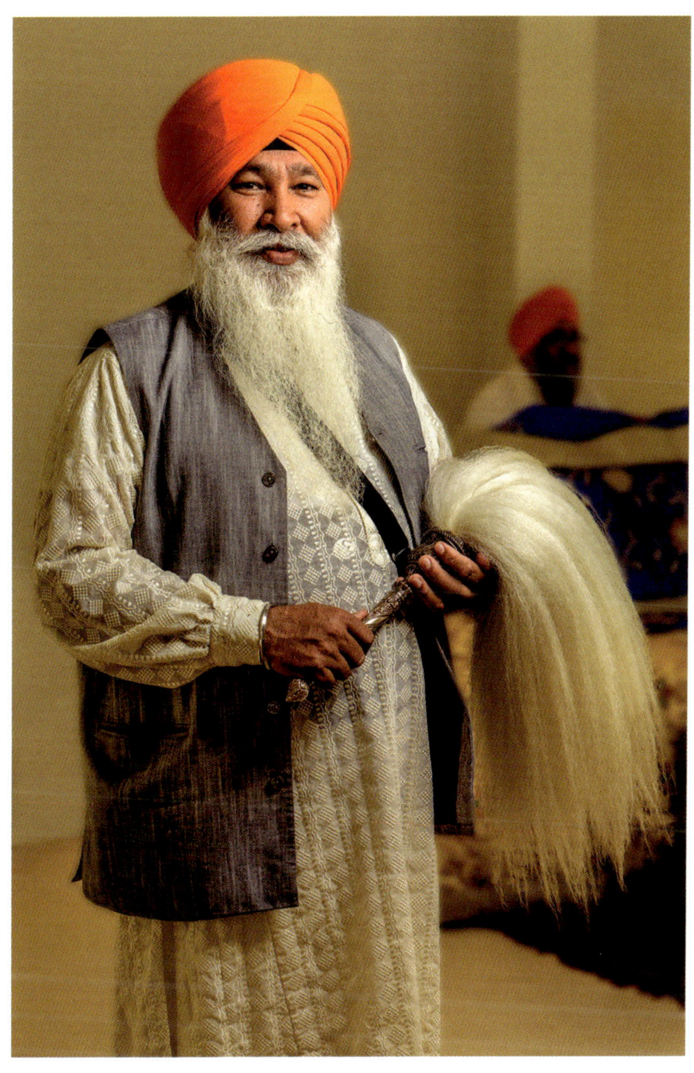

Satpal Singh, the gurdwara's priest (*granthi*), holding the fly whisk (*chaur*) that is waved over the *Guru Granth Sahib* as a sign of reverence and respect

For Sikhs, self-defense is historical. They suffered religious persecution and the killing of the fifth and ninth gurus under the Muslim Mughal dynasty, which ruled Northern India for many centuries beginning in 1526 and up through the British Raj in 1858. Dhugga draws parallels between the violent Sikh persecution of the late 1600s and the crimes committed by ISIS today. He himself didn't believe the extent of the horrors when he first learned the history, but seeing the violence still being committed in the name of religion today has made him believe "every word of it."

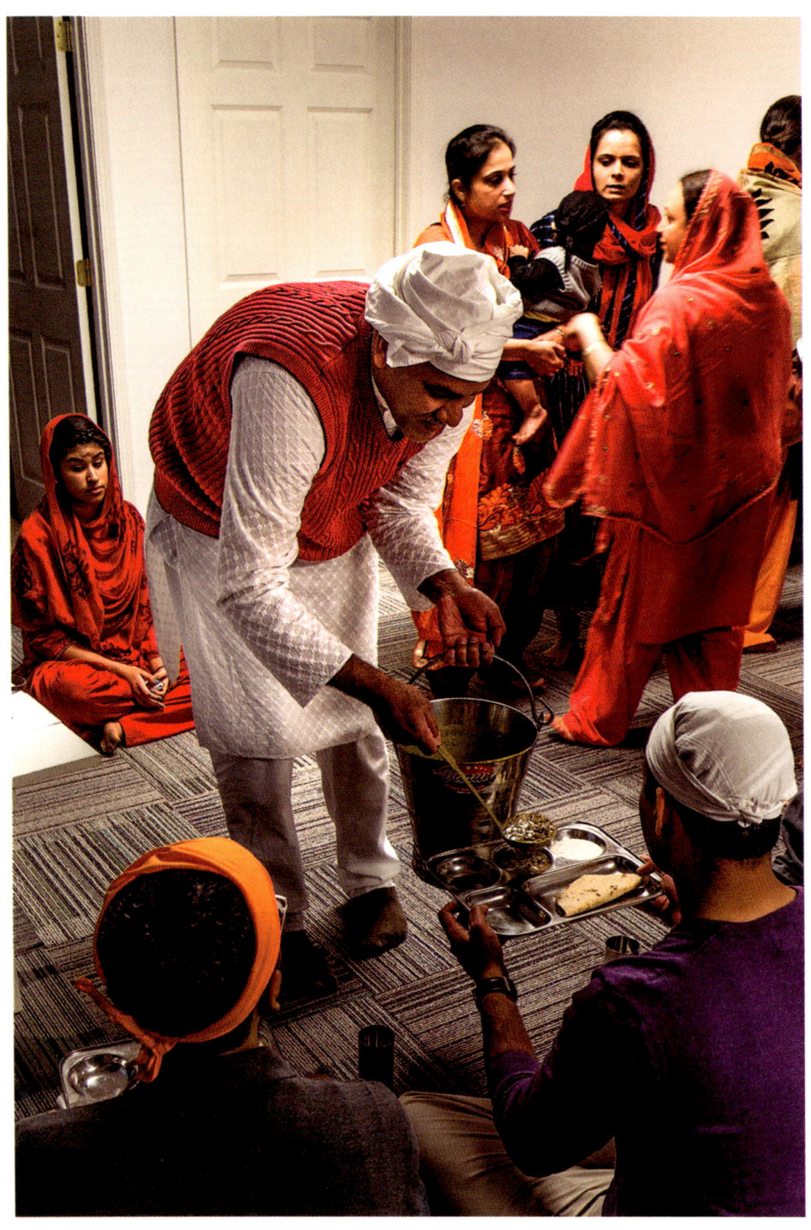

Hardeep S. Ballagan serves *langar* in the *langar* hall in the basement of the *Gurdwara*

Men slaughtered. Women kept as sexual slaves. He squeezes the fingers of his left hand together to model the shape of a blade and sets my wrist in the palm of his right hand. He begins at the first joint on my pinkie, grazing his bladed hand across the joint of each finger as he tells me the stories of how Sikh leaders would be captured and slowly cut into pieces, only to have their captors stop before their victims died. To prolong the torture, as an example, they were burned on red-hot skillets; then they were drowned.

Sikhs are not a violent people, Mr. Dhugga makes clear. They are warriors for the sake of justice and bravery. Now, centuries later, the present-day tradition of the 50-hour continuous recitation from the *Guru Granth Sahib* indicates remembrance of Sikhs of old, whose last request as they lay dying after the battles was to listen to the hymns from the Holy Book. Likewise, the *Chaur Sahib,* a ceremonial whisk waved over the Holy Book during prayer, reminds today's faithful of the little brush the warriors used to sweep clean the pages of the Holy Book. Fighting guerrilla warfare, the Sikhs of yore spent most of their lives on horseback. The Holy Book had its own tent, but the *Chaur Sahib* helped to whisk away the dirt and insects that collected during their 50-hour continuous recitation of hymns as they marched through the jungles. This has become the present-day tradition of the 50-hour recitation.

SPACE Inside the stark white lotus dome so visible to passersby from the road, the interior features of the *Gurdwara Sahib* are immaculate, including ivory colored ceilings, walls, and floors with virtually no adornment. Here, you find beauty in simplicity. This Sikh community wanted to build a place of worship that would embody their beliefs and provide a physical representation of the community, as well as their *sangat,* or spiritual family.

Until 2009, the Des Moines Sikh community worshiped at the *Gurdwara* in West Des Moines. Members who had been with that community when numbers were only around one dozen helped purchase the first Des Moines *Gurdwara.* Members were able to construct a proper *Gurdwara* in Johnston through donations from the *Gurdwara's sangat,* the greater Des Moines community, and even from India. *Gurdwara* translates as "doorway to the Guru." Since for Sikhs, the spiritual and temporal worlds are inseparable, they hold the

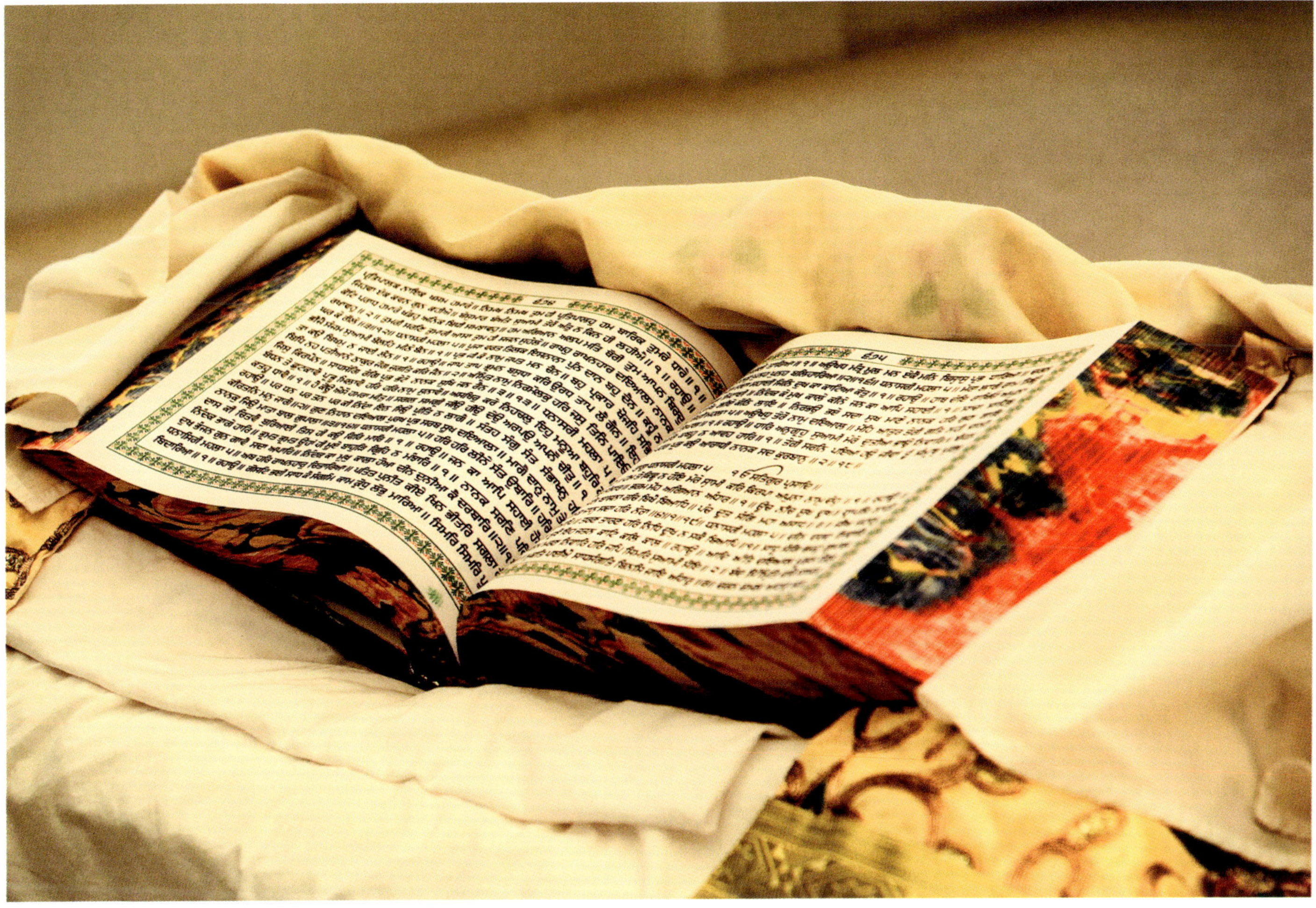

Guru Granth Sahib

physical *Gurdwara* in extreme regard. Their reverence for this place of worship is reflected in the architecture and upkeep.

On any given Sunday, the sun shines through the skylight in the dome of the *Gurdwara*, softly illuminating the sanctuary's golden canopy. The *Guru Granth Sahib* lies at the center of a raised platform called a *palki* dressed in decorated fabrics whose metallic detail catches the light.

The entire sanctuary has been constructed to bring focus to the Sikh Holy Book, which is studied both for its meaning as well as its use in practice. Perched atop an elevated stage and angled towards the main entrance, the Holy Book remains covered, but open, until the start of the prayer service. The Book is closed at night after evening prayers, wrapped in white fabric that is changed every evening, and taken to a side room where it is placed on a cushioned bed for the night. It is brought out again early in the morning, preferably before sunrise, placed on the small cot (*Peera Sahib*), and opened gently, with the two sides rested on small pillows. The very first composition on the left page is considered to be the order of the day. During services, hymns are sung and the prayers offered. Then the priest folds back the always elaborately designed dressings—these change weekly—and opens and reads aloud the text of the order of the day, bookmarked by a pure white cloth. Rippling swirls of watercolor decorate the margins, while the jet-black ink of the printed verses contrasts starkly with the pure white of its pages.

All attention falls to the Holy Book. Congregants face the book throughout services, taking care not to point their feet or backs towards the *Granth Sahib*. A single phrase fills the air many times throughout the service: "*Waheguru Ji Ka Khalsa, Waheguru Ji Ki Fateh.*" The *Khalsa* belongs to God. Victory belongs to God.

PRACTICE To symbolize their devotion to Waheguru, the *Khalsa* adopt five articles to be worn at all times:

- *kesh*, uncut hair
- *kangha*, a comb
- *kara*, a steel bracelet
- *kachera*, cotton undergarmets
- *kirpan*, a small ceremonial sword

The Sikhs who are baptized in the *Khalsa* are required to adhere to these five practices. As regulars and visitors gather to celebrate this holiday, the sea of turbans may be surprising since, due to social and political factors, turban wearing by Sikhs is on the decline on a global scale. This is not so with the Sikhs of Iowa Khalsa Heritage, many of whose members adhere strictly to the "five K's" of the *Khalsa*.

For Sikhs, physical symbols like the "five K's" bear significant spiritual weight. Many members of the Johnston community are *Khalsa* and raise their families to become *Khalsa*. *Miri Piri* represents a guiding ethical force that recognizes both the physical and spiritual aspects of life: *Miri*, the temporal, symbolizes the power of worldly existence and the physical world. *Piri*, the spiritual, symbolizes the internal, non-worldly aspects of life. In this community, the spiritual and the temporal are equally important. One must embrace each to understand the other.

* * *

Families flow into the central worship hall each Sunday from about 11:30 a.m. to 1 p.m. I'm greeted by pulsing music that ripples the ground as I enter. People are carrying donations for the upkeep of the *Gurdwara* and for funding of *langar*, the community meal that follows every service. Congregants greet one another and visit briefly as they make their way toward the *Guru Granth Sahib*. They submit their donations in the *golak*, or donation box, and then kneel to the Holy Book and touch their foreheads to the ground. Then they stand again to make a small donation to the musicians and seat themselves on the floor amongst the rest of the congregation.

Services begin with *kirtan*, the singing of hymns from the *Guru Granth Sahib*. *Miri* and *Piri* are evident as the community conducts typical Sunday worship. *Kirtan* parallels the songs of divine praise and sounds from the harmonium and *tabla*. It's not in English, but if you feel the pulse and movement of the verse, you will begin to understand the words.

After an hour or so of *kirtan*, the community rises for the collective prayer, known as *ardās*, at the conclusion of which *karah parshad* is distributed to the congregation. This mixture of wheat flour, butter, and sugar is prepared by the community in the *langar* hall and then carried upstairs to the main sanctuary. The small sword

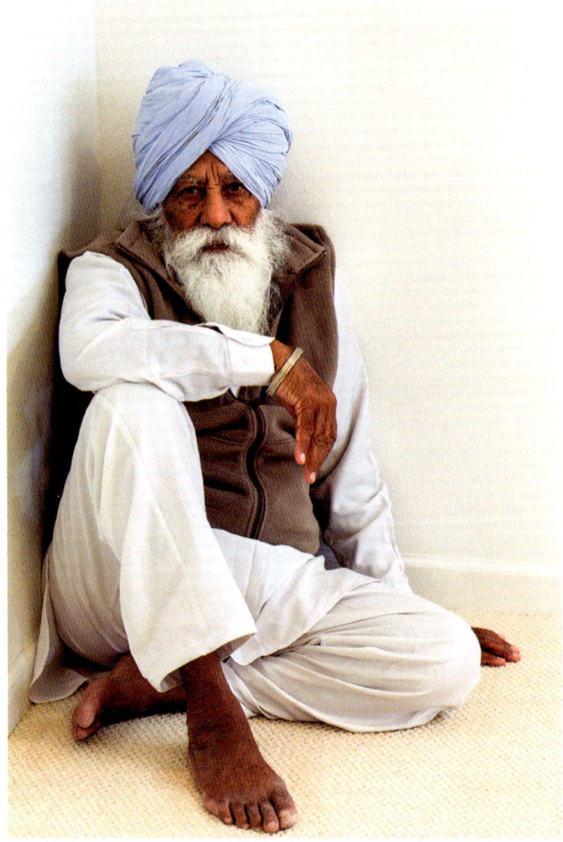

Sohan Singh leaning against the wall of the *Gurdwara* during *kirtan*

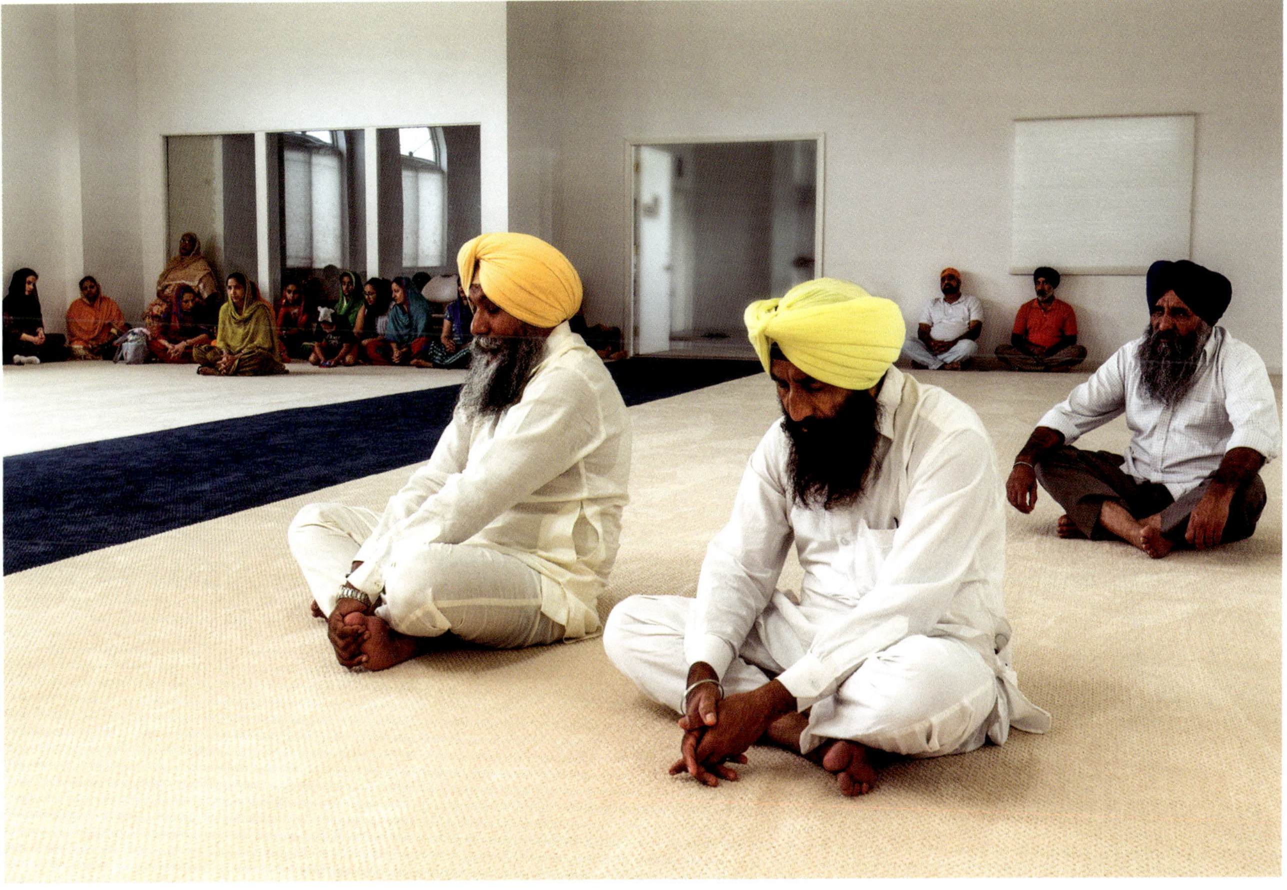

Members of the *Gurdwara* listen to *kirtan*

called the *kirpan* is used to sanctify the *parshad*, a tradition initiated by the 10th Guru. Then distribution begins: each man or woman, young or old, visitor or regular, receives the "Holy Pudding." After partaking, some members wipe their hands on the napkins handed out by younger members; others rub the oils left by the *parshad* into the skin of the hands and face in hopes that it will stimulate the growth of more uncut hair, the most visible mark of a *Khalsa*-observant Sikh. For the faithful, this offering is more than food: it's a gift from the Guru, a means of profound spiritual connection.

Satnam Waheguru—Gumukhi words molded of silver—are mounted above the *Guru Granth Sahib*, the only item in the entire *Gurdwara* resting on a higher plane than the Holy Book. The essence of this religion, *Satnam Waheguru*, connotes a single over-riding belief first emphasized by Guru Nanak in India in the 1400s that remains central to belief at the *Gurdwara Sahib* today: equality. During *kirtan* and *langar*, all who are able sit together on the floor, although chairs are available for those with restricted mobility. To understand the significance of this practice, imagine participants of all ages, sizes, and worldly status sitting together on the same plain wooden floor—doctors and ditch diggers, children and seniors, women and men.

Satnam Waheguru means "true name" and "wonderful Lord." Because Sikhs believe that all religions provide varying interpretations and means of connecting with a singular ultimate reality, these words remind Sikhs to have tolerance towards other faiths. Jagtar Singh, an active member and leader of the community, reminds me that no matter how we label ourselves, "we are all the same." *Satnam Waheguru* teaches that, "We are all united in our humanity. We are all united in our seeking of God."

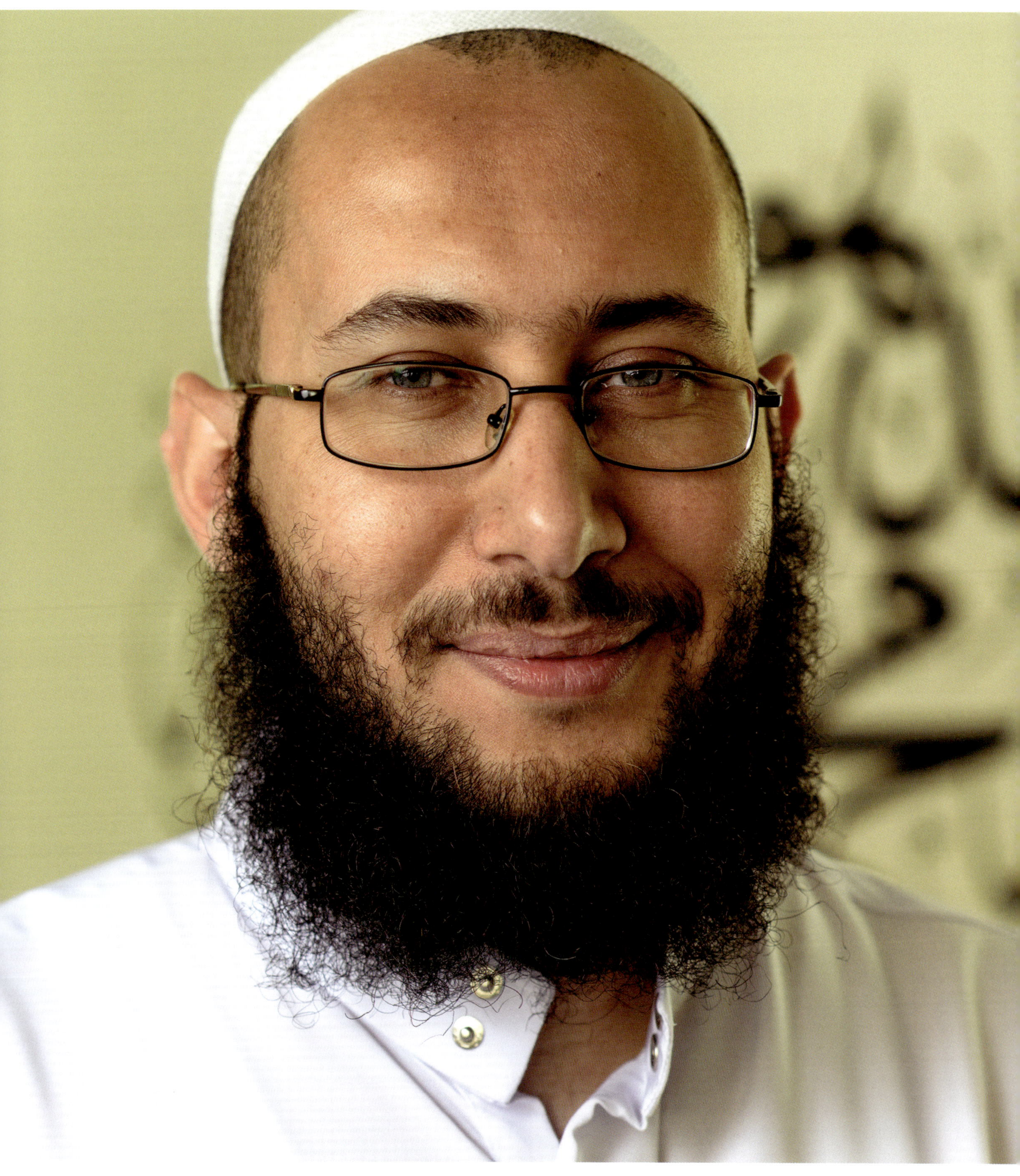

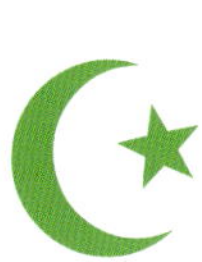

Islamic Center of Des Moines

Dustin Eubanks

PRACTICE It's Friday afternoon at the Islamic Center of Des Moines, and cars pack the parking lot. Some members arrived earlier for the *khutba,* a sermon given at the beginning of the *jumu'ah* service, but now cars overflow into the streets as the faithful arrive right on time for the prayer component of the service known as *salat.* According to the Prophet Muhammad, *peace be upon him,* Friday is reserved as a day of rest and reflection, making the *jumu'ah* essential to Islamic faith and practice.

The faithful file in through the doors as greeters smile and call out *"As-salamu alaykum"*—Peace of Allah be with you. Men wearing traditional, body-length *thawbs* chat with those clad simply in T-shirts and blue jeans; others arrive straight from work in their suits and ties. Women tug their young children into a separate prayer room from the one designated for men and older boys, as is tradition in Islam. The women's long flowing skirts and head coverings, known as *hijabs,* fill the room with color as all members of the Islamic Center gather to make *salat*—to pray. The first call to prayer known in Arabic as the *adhan* crackles over the speaker system, resonating throughout the mosque and bringing everyone to silence.

Imam Younes Ali Younes

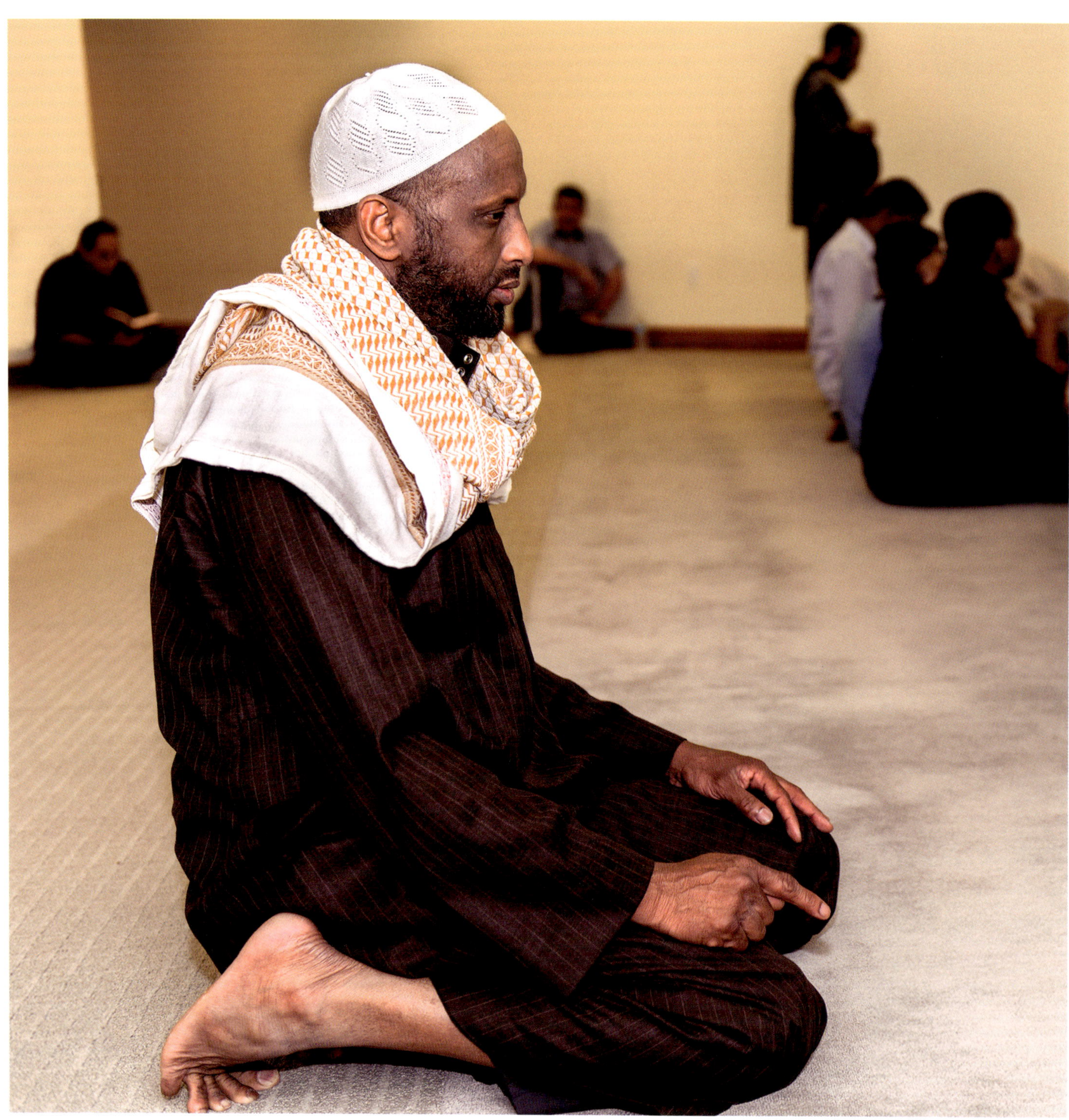

Members of the Islamic Center perform voluntary prayer before the nighttime prayer (*isha*)

In the foyer, a modestly dressed man in a plain button-down shirt and slacks removes his shoes and places them neatly on a shelf where they join a long line of tennis shoes, sandals, and loafers. He then begins to wash his face, followed by his hands and then his feet in ritual order in an ablution sink, performing *wudu*—cleansing. Ready, he steps, right-foot first, into the prayer room, placing his copy of the Qur'an on a small wooden pedestal before bowing his head and praying quietly to Allah. Outside, the sun has started to descend in the sky, casting a golden glow upon the man as he reads from his holy book. Submerged in prayerful connection, he is completely still save for his lips, which move silently to form the words of prayer.

Following this quiet time, the imam Yunnis Yunnis delivers an impassioned sermon addressing what it means to be Muslim in America. He encourages his congregation to engage in peaceful conversation with others in order to dispel the negative rhetoric surrounding Islam. "Minds will be changed upon seeing the great humility of Islam lived properly," he says.

The *muezzin* calls for the final prayer, involving a specific process of standing, bowing, kneeling and *sajda,* or prostrating, during which the faithful focus solely on the presence of Allah in their life and in the world around them. In Islam, prayer serves to acknowledge submission to Allah. It is a time to admire His greatness and appreciate the unity of all things in Him.

* * *

Fayiz Abusharkh, a former imam, is a knowledgeable and dedicated Muslim in the community. "I have to pray first," he explains when he arrives for our interview. He slips into silence, his copy of the Qur'an on the small pedestal before him. After praying, he eases into a chair and pulls from a plastic grocery sack a small notepad on which is drawn a sketch of a tree. The tree, according to Fayiz, metaphorically depicts the roots of Islam, the core tenets of the faith that serve as its basis.

"There is no God but Allah," he begins, "and Muhammed is the messenger of Allah." This statement is the Muslims' creed. Second, Allah created angels. The third tenet states that Muslims must believe in all of Allah's revealed books, with the Qur'an as the last and most important of His revelations. Fourth, Muslims believe in the Day of Judgment and in the prophets. And finally, Muslims believe in Allah's destiny for all. From these roots grows the tree—first, the trunk, which is the *Sunnah*, the sayings and doings of the prophet, Muhammad; then the branches: one for morals, and another for living the daily practices of Islam. The fruits that hang from these branches, hewn with ink on paper, represent the "rewards" for investing oneself in Islam with total mind and heart.

Fayiz also believes that Islam encompasses all religions in its roots. "There are many 'lords' or religions on this earth, but there is only one Allah," he says, a hopeful gleam in his gentle eyes. It is his belief that Islam encompasses all religious belief just as Allah encompasses all things in unity, creating a world where all people and all religions can live peacefully despite their differences.

Those unfamiliar with the teachings of Islam often have questions about Islamic doctrine, such as the differing gender expectations regarding clothing and conduct. The separation of men and women during prayer stems from an effort to make this time an intimate and private experience for each supplicant; as such, it is seen as beneficial to have men and women in separate spaces in order to avoid potential distraction.

The *hijab* is a traditional head covering worn by many Muslim women. It serves as a symbol of their submission to Allah, and it forces people to appreciate women for who they are rather than for the way they look. Many Muslim women find this liberating, including Niha, a Muslim student at Drake University. She wishes people would take time to see the "inside view" of Islam, rather than assuming that wearing the *hijab* is oppressive to women. Wearing the *hijab,* along with other doctrinal practices for both men and women, is an entirely personal choice made by each individual upon reaching puberty. Another member of the ICDM, Arabic professor Nahed Waly, affirms this sentiment: "This is my religion, and these are my clothes," Dr. Waly explains. "This is my face; this is my shape. You must accept me as I am."

SPACE Before the Islamic Center of Des Moines converted a former Christian school into their mosque in 1983, the Des Moines Muslim

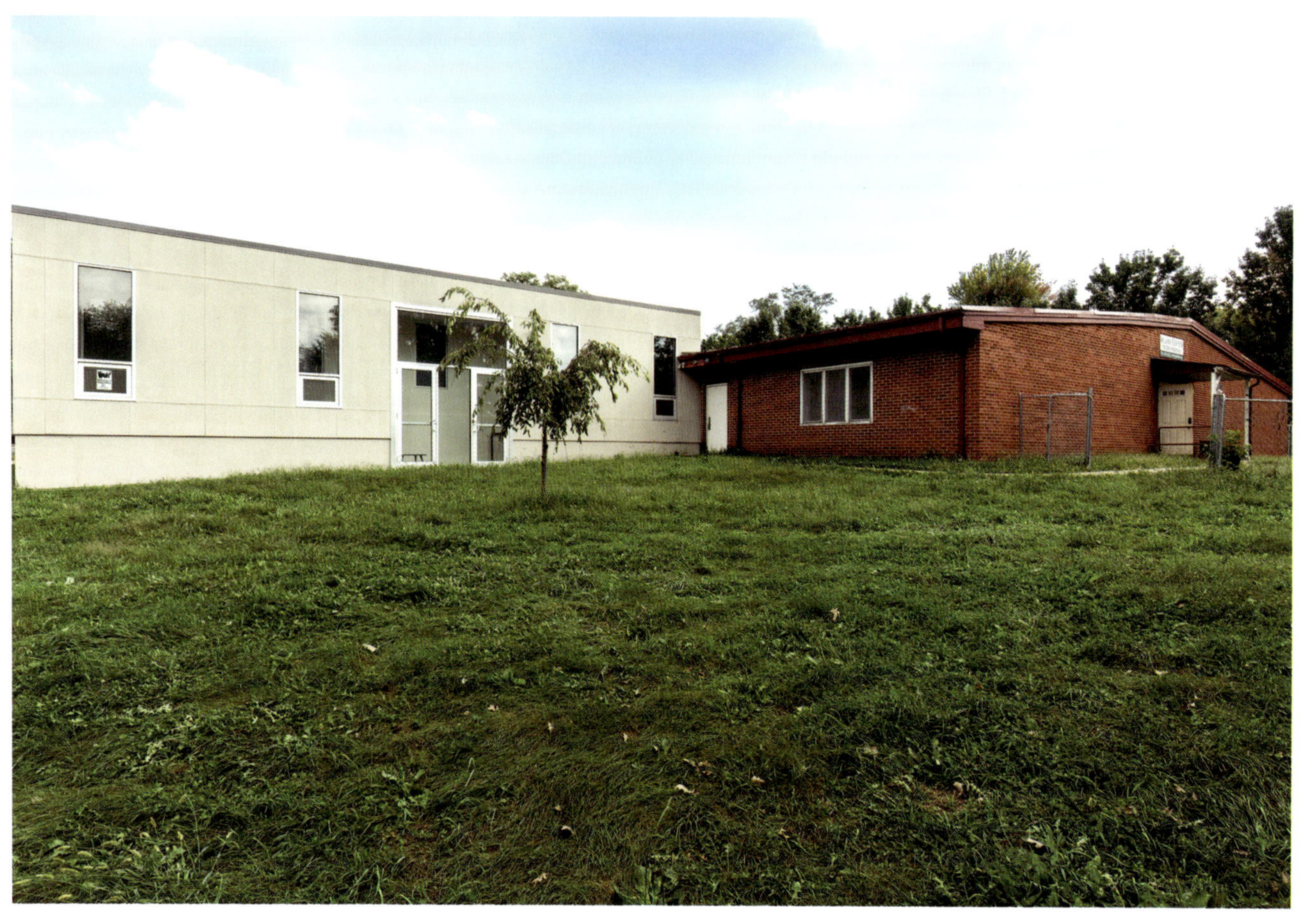

The Islamic Center of Des Moines

community hosted services in the suburban basements of Valley Junction. Their numbers were considerably smaller then, with about only 15-20 attendees. Now, ICDM is home to about 250 prayer-goers for Friday *jumu'ah* at their current Franklin Avenue location. Jamal Muhammad remembers praying on the second story of a house near the Drake Diner. Even after the current location was first purchased, the members of ICDM would continue to gather at a house on Clark Street for Saturday night dinners.

"This is the 'mother mosque' of Des Moines," explains Hamed Baig, alluding to *the* Mother Mosque in Cedar Rapids, the longest-standing mosque in North America. But ICDM is not the only center for Muslim community and faith in Des Moines. In early years, the *khubta* was given in three languages: English, Arabic, and Bosnian. Eventually, an increasing number of Bosnian Muslims started to form their own religious communities, building new mosques in several locations around Des Moines. According to Hamed, Des Moines is now home to nine mosques.

Through the eighties and nineties, Jamal and a friend hosted radio and TV shows that were aimed "towards understanding in Islam." They would take phone calls, fielding questions about Islam and informing the Des Moines community about Islamic practices. Five times a day, 89.3 FM would play the *adhan* between the newest tracks from Snoop Dogg and Tupac, so their Muslim listeners would know when to begin prayer. This effort of outreach was not without its problems, though. Conflicts arose after hiring a Christian host who refused to play the call to prayer in his time slot. Jamal, now the station engineer, requested that he still play it. Citing religious freedom, the host refused and was let go.

Though their radio presence started to disappear in the late nineties, the Islamic Center of Des Moines continued to grow. Educational programs for Muslim children served the rapidly increasing number of families in the area, and in 2004, the ICDM helped to launch Des Moines' first independent, non-profit Islamic school: New Horizons Academy. The two entities eventually parted ways, and today the ICDM runs its own educational programming. These changes and more have shaped the ICDM into the institution it is today, one that continues to adapt to accommodate the city's diverse Muslim community.

HISTORY "The door [to Islam] is open to everyone," Salih Kocher tells me through the steam hovering over his cup of coffee. The *masjid* takes great pride not only in its diversity, but also in its role as a welcome station offering immediate resources and a sense of belonging for immigrant families in central Iowa.

"If you're an immigrant and you're looking for people to help you out, ICDM can definitely be that place for you," says Yousuf Shamsie, a third-year medical student at Des Moines University, who splits his attendance between ICDM and Masjid an-Noor, another prominent Des Moines mosque. He attributes the mosque's character, like much of the community, to its broad acceptance of nationalities.

Dr. Nahed Waly, who came from Egypt five years ago, now takes part in a *halaqah,* a "circle" of sisters at ICDM that welcomes new women in the community for discussion of the *Qur'an.* Her daughter, Mai Nasr, who also attends ICDM, remarks on the growing international Arab presence in Des Moines. In the past, separate Arab nationalities might have kept to themselves, Mai explains. Now, a simple *"As-salamu alaykum"* is enough to start a conversation in the grocery store. At a typical gathering at ICDM, Pakistanis, Afghans, and Iraqis say hello to each other, pray in the same lines, and converse in the parking lot, regardless of their country of origin. They want to know how a sister's children are doing, or how a new job is treating a brother.

Gathering for lunch one Sunday afternoon, a group of young men from the mosque discuss their faith and their connection to the Islamic Center of Des Moines. They all met when their families arrived in Iowa and began attending ICDM. Some of their friendships date as far back as their "Sunday School" years, when children take Sunday religion classes to learn about the Muslim faith. One member of this brotherhood, Bulland, will soon finish his medical exams and intends to return to his home state of New Jersey to practice medicine. His hands flutter lightly across a keyboard, a proud grin spreading across his young face. On the screen, the ICDM is the

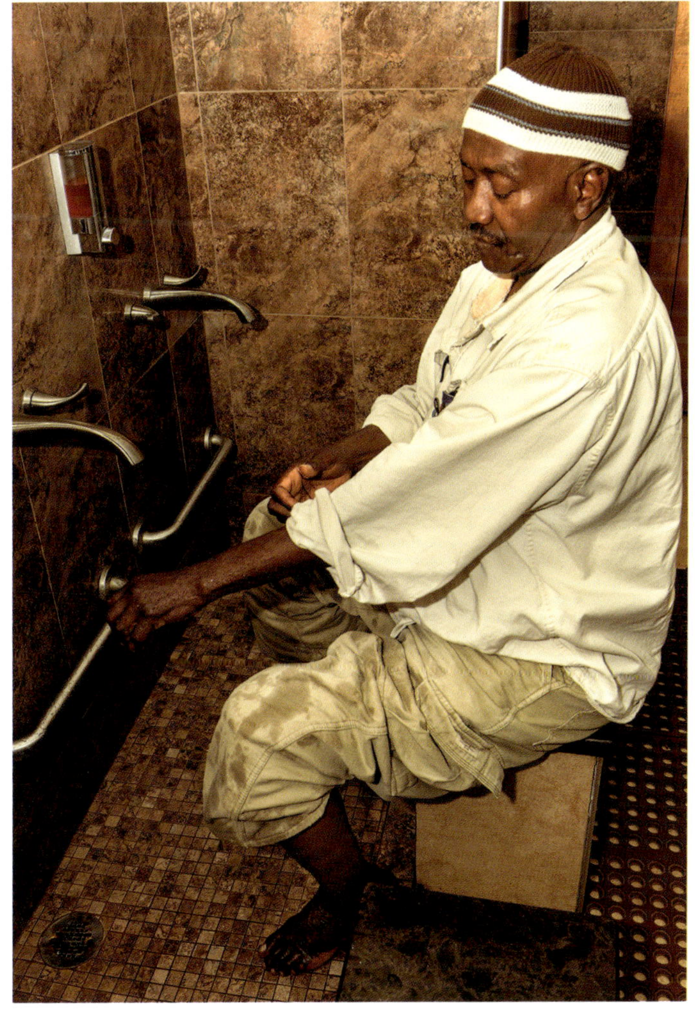

Muhammad Basheer performs his ablution (*wudu*) before the nighttime prayer (*isha*)

first search result on Google for "Des Moines mosque," a clear indication of its popularity in the area. Because he knows that other mosques might not be so diverse, he already anticipates how much he will miss the welcoming community of ICDM. Not that other mosques would turn anyone away—to do so would defy the entire idea of unity, which is so important to Islam. Still, ICDM is defined by its inclusivity, a "house of God" for everyone.

IDENTITY Before heading to the main prayer room to observe the service, Professor Tim Knepper meets Fayiz in the overflow prayer room. Humbly and not without humor, Fayiz explains the commonalities among Judaism, Christianity, and Islam. Religion scholar Dr. Knepper is now the student, learning about the Muslim principle of unity—*tawhid*—and its application to the different faith traditions.

Bob Blanchard, a photographer and Professor Knepper's partner for this project, captures shots of congregants as they leave the *jumu'ah* service. Kids running up and down the wheelchair ramp eye him curiously. "I like taking pictures, too," a budding young photographer announces to Bob, thus forging a friendship between the professional and his kindergarten-aged protégé.

"As-salamu alaykum!" Jamal and Abdullah call to us, their hands wrapped around cups of hot tea. His camera slung and ready, Bob moves quietly in the background as Jamal tells a story about Gabriel, from the Qur'an. The "Qur'an is the cure for any disease a person has in their heart," he says, his eloquence and use of dramatic pauses drawing a rapt audience. The ICDM is a place of welcome, a stimulating and joyful atmosphere regardless of one's faith.

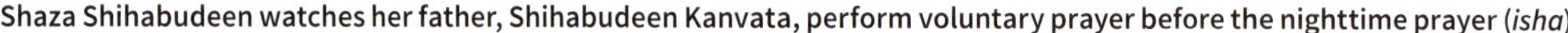

Shaza Shihabudeen watches her father, Shihabudeen Kanvata, perform voluntary prayer before the nighttime prayer (*isha*)

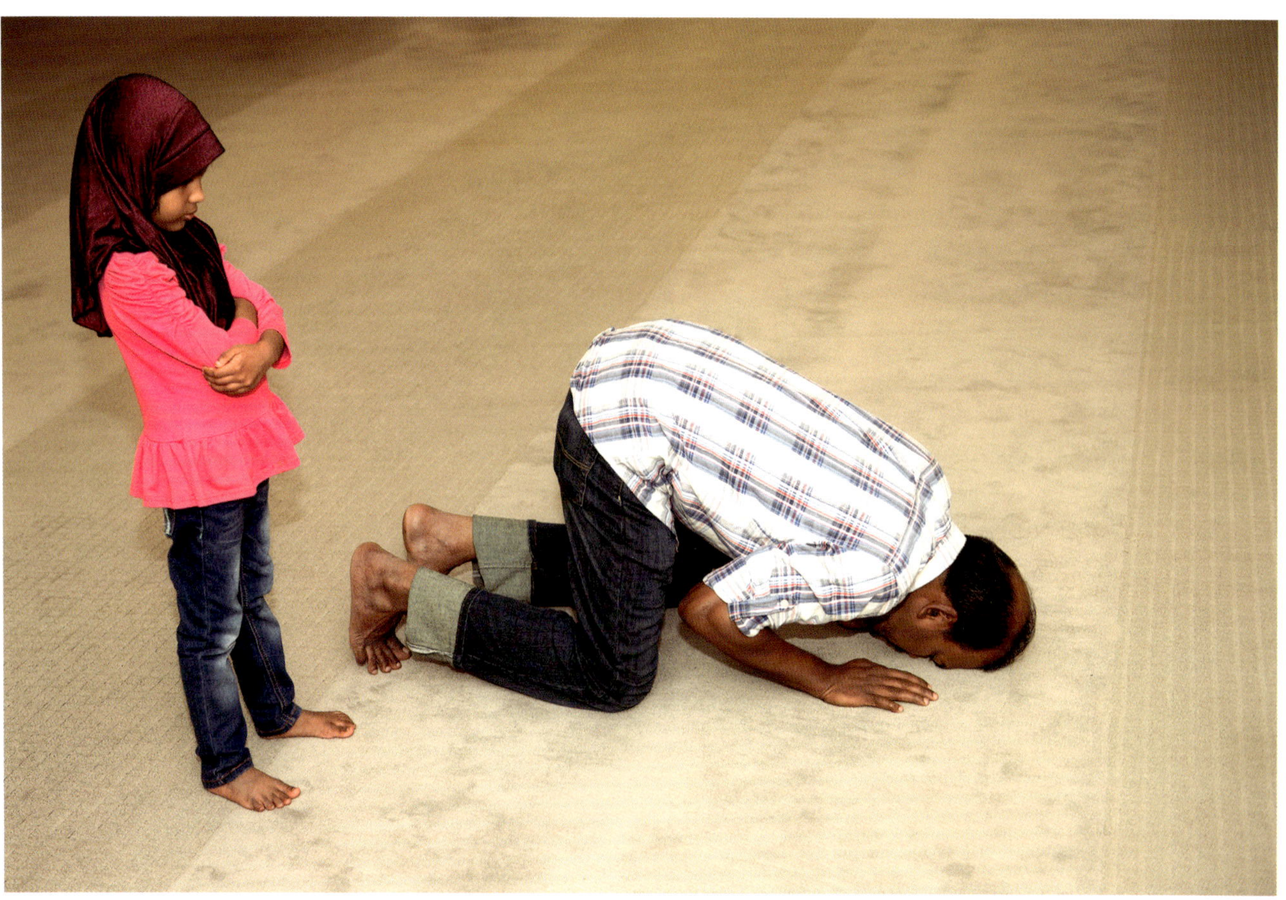

ICDM makes a point to dispel ill-informed assumptions about Islam. Yousuf Shamsie notes that the negative media and perceptions of Islam are as new to Muslims as they are to non-Muslims. "You find yourself talking about it," Yousuf says, "even though you don't understand it." Moments of "humiliation" cause the most difficulty, with TSA searches at airports reducing American citizens to stereotypes just because they wear a *hijab* or are otherwise deemed suspicious-looking to officials. The immediate association of "Muslims" with "terrorists" is difficult to address. And yet, American Muslims want to undo the damage peacefully. At the ICDM, members happily answer questions that non-Muslims ask about the faith. They host public discussions about Islam in America and seek out interfaith events in the area that encourage dialogue and resolve disputes.

Each week, at the in-house Islamic School at ICDM, children complete lessons from a workbook on Islam—how to incorporate their faith into their daily life, what friendships with non-Muslims look like, and stories about Islam's great teachings and the rewards of living a life of faith. Assignments on American history are also taught because as important as their devotion to Islam is, the teachers want their young people to be proud Americans as well.

The level-five class—populated by the oldest children, ranging in age from eleven to fifteen—is keenly aware of the influence of the media. Some came with their families from other nations, but some, like 14-year-old Ramla, who describes herself as "Minnesotan," have lived in the United States their entire lives. They have not experienced much discrimination in Des Moines and feel generally respected by their non-Muslim classmates at school.

But they're not immune, either. Upon finding out she was Muslim, one of Ramla's classmates tried, respectfully, to express her concerns. "No offense," her classmate said, "but I think the refugees are carrying bombs." In other words, politically charged conversations are a matter

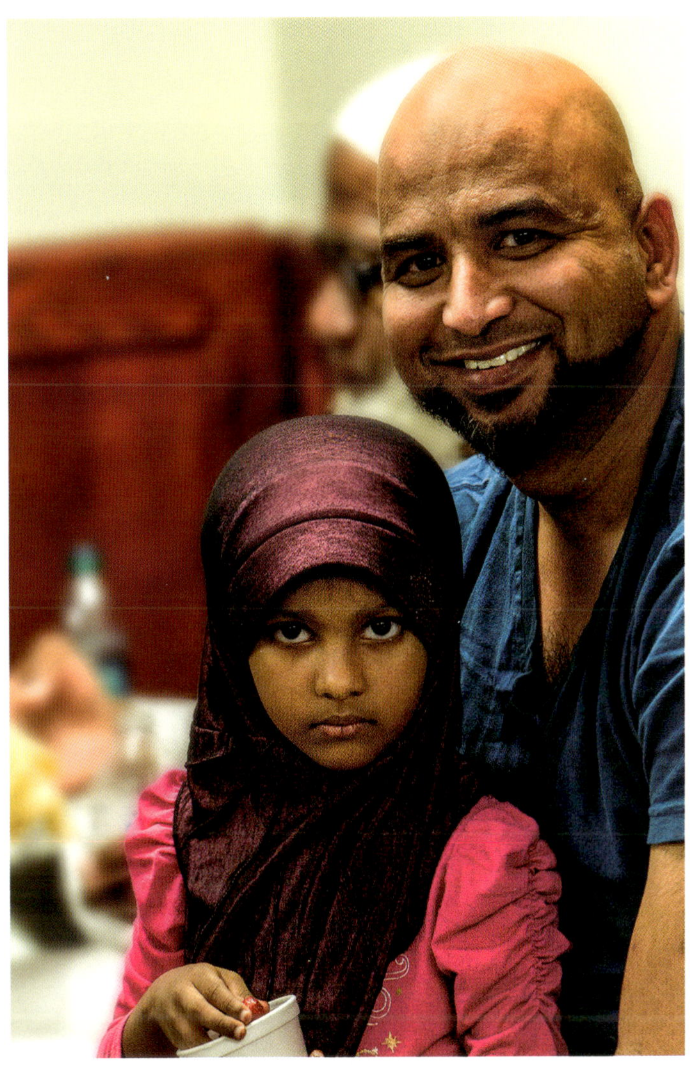

Jaffer Mohamed-Ali and his niece, Shaza Shihabudeen, at the breaking-of-the-fast meal (*iftar*) during the month of Ramadan

of course. Omran, a 12-year old student born in Baghdad, raised his hand to ask me how I felt about Presidential candidate Donald Trump. A prolonged conversation ensued on the perceptions of Muslims in America. Despite the serious tone of the topic, the students' optimistic laughter filled the room.

The members of ICDM are gentle people. They are citizens of Des Moines. They are black and white and brown. They are Muslims from birth and converts. They are business-owners and teachers, professionals and workers. They are Egyptian, Palestinian, Somalian, Afghan, Pakistani, and more. They are our neighbors, colleagues, and friends. They are American.

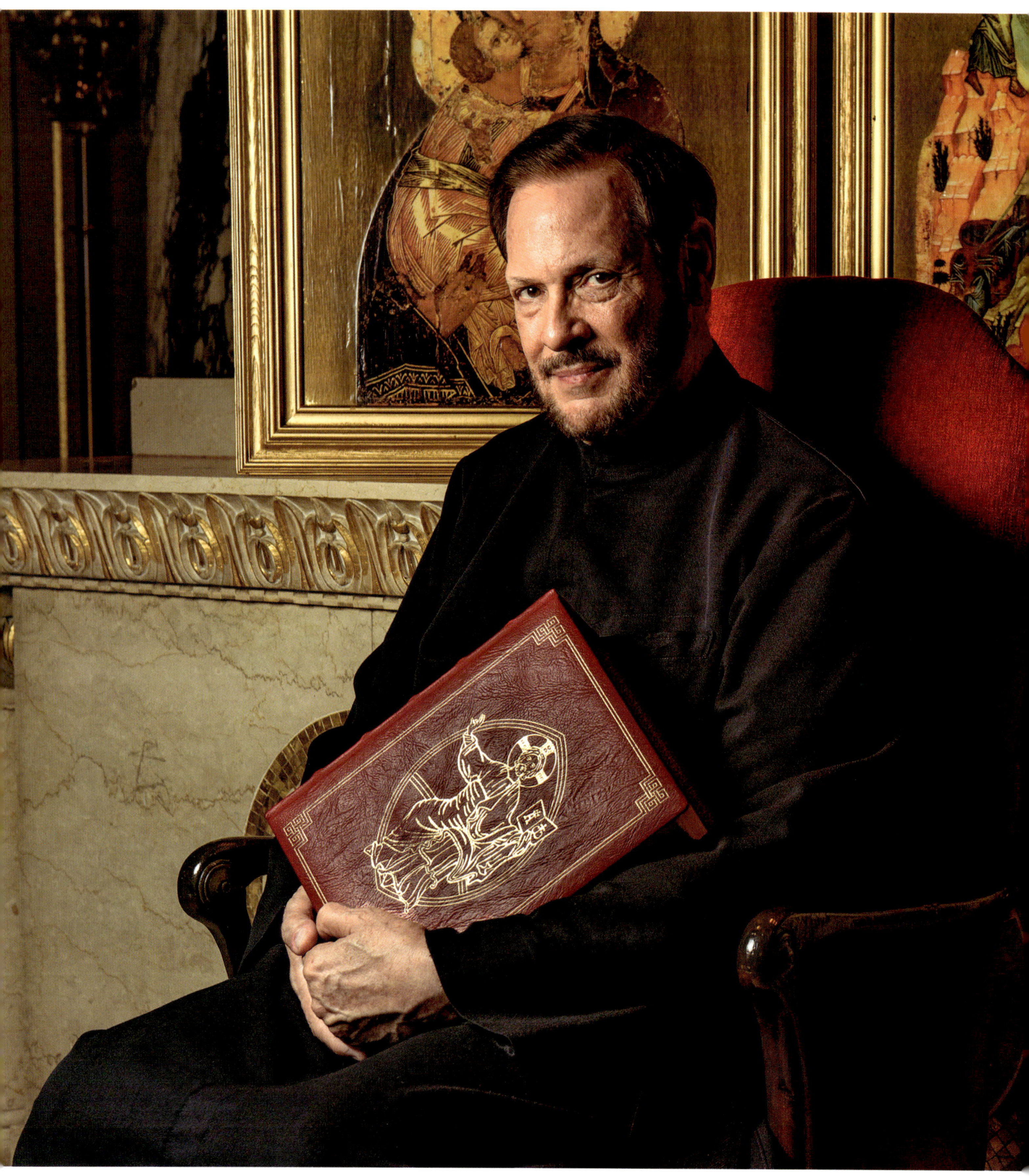

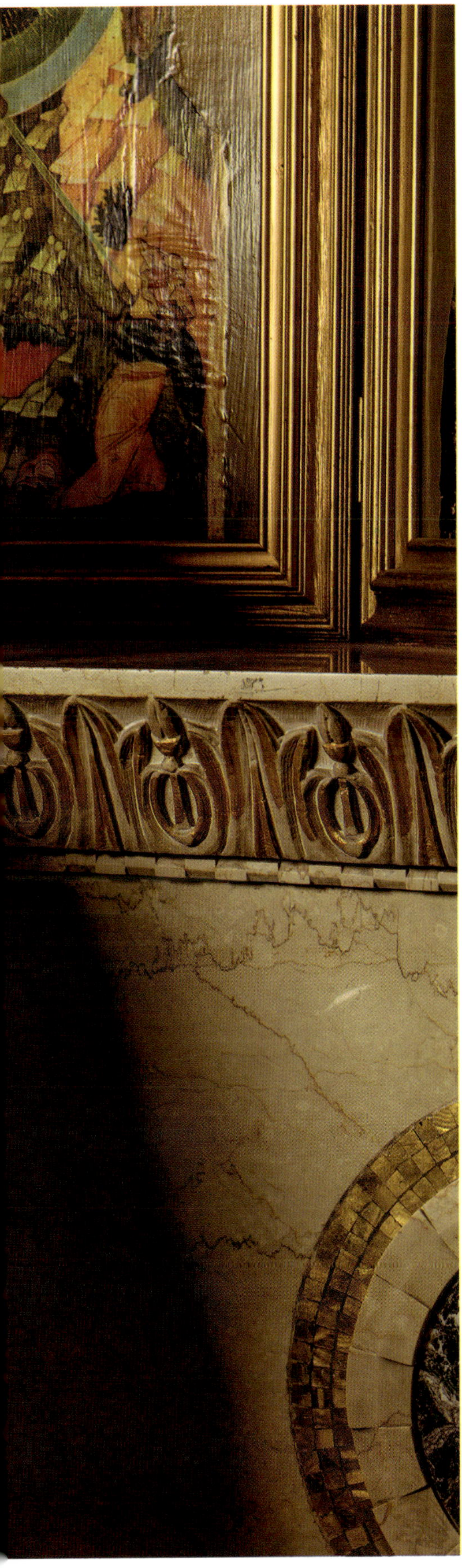

Basilica of Saint John

Tierney Grisolano

SPACE Up a flight of stairs to the vestibule in the Basilica of St. John, three sets of wooden doors mark the entrance to the main sanctuary, or nave. I push through the center set, my jaw dropping at the magnitude of this space. The click of my heels reverberates down the long, marbled aisle and through the expanse around me like a booming metronome. It feels like an eternity before I finally take my seat on one of the dark, wooden pews. Then I look up.

The steeply arched ceiling, composed of a pattern of squares laced in glittering gold, creates the appearance of a tall dome. Stained-glass windows are inlaid at intervals along the base, and underneath those, a series of discs made from varieties of marble from around the world represent the universal reach of Catholicism, which, itself, means universal. Sweeping columns line the pews. The columns are adorned with squares of gold and rise all the way to the ceiling, merging with the arches that stretch to the very top of the sanctuary. (One of the nuns, Sister Mary Claire, says that if there were ever another flood, the church would be transformed into an ark, turning upside down to save the congregation.) The gleaming elegance of the architecture is diffused in a mixture of warm gold

Father Aquinas M. Nichols

and cool blue-green hues as beams of sunlight stream through the stained-glass windows.

In the expansive silence, one's gaze falls naturally on the altar—this, too, made entirely of marble. At its center, a table topped with a white cloth is laid with four tall candles in golden receptacles, two on each side. Behind the table a Presider's chair upholstered in bright red seats the priest. Towering over both chair and altar, four columns arch and ascend to form a point over which rests the roof of a huge canopy called a baldacchino, which symbolizes the tent that housed the Ark of the Covenant during the time that the Israelites wandered in the desert. Like the tent that protected the Ark where God's presence resided, the baldacchino stands over the host where the presence of Jesus dwells.

But there is a twist. Typically, the sacramental bread and wine that are transformed into the body and blood of Jesus Christ during the ritual of Communion are kept under the baldacchino. However, because St. John's Basilica enjoys the distinction of being listed on the National Registry of Historical Places, many visitors come through the church daily. The sacramental bread and wine were moved to a chapel adjacent to the northeast corner of the nave so that parishioners can venerate the Holy Sacraments undisturbed. In contrast to the palatial, glittering sanctuary, this smaller space, called the Blessed Sacrament Chapel, is relatively unadorned. Still, it is St. John's most sacred space according to the Basilica's head priest, Father Aquinas M. Nichols: here, the Blessed Sacrament is reserved.

HISTORY Sunlight now cascades through a stained glass window that had remained covered for construction during my many weeks attending St. John's. Now, patterns of blue, red, and yellow light fall on the parishioners and pews. A newly installed elevator is further evidence of recent building improvements, enabling more direct access for disabled parishioners than the previous series of ramps at the back of the church, which were exposed in all weather. Now St. John's Basilica can say it provides truly universal access to Catholicism.

The elevator installment is the latest example of the effort to include all people in the church's long history of welcome. Purchased on June 7, 1905, the Basilica complex originally stretched across a full fourteen lots. By Christmas Day that same year, St. John's held its first service in its partially finished school. Construction on the church itself didn't even begin until August of 1913 and wasn't officially completed until September of 1926. The cost of construction was approximately $480,000; not even seven million dollars would achieve that feat today.

St. John's was always an inner-city church. In the early years, members of St. John's came largely from its surrounding neighborhoods in the central west and northwest parts of the city near the Drake University campus. As its parishioners steadily moved further out to the suburbs, however, the church became more geographically diverse. Nowadays Father Aquinas's flock drives in from towns like Newton, Indianola, Earlham, Ames, and Ankeny.

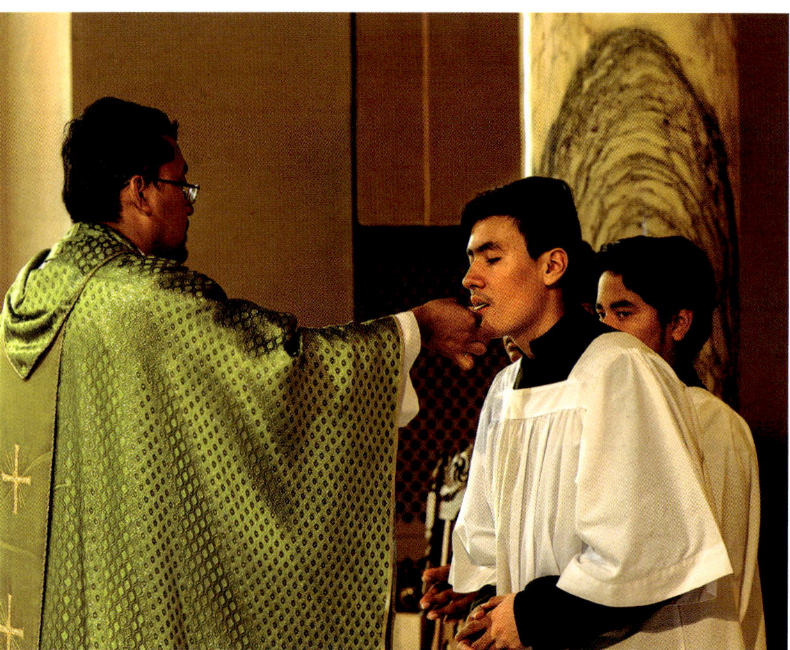

Revered Reynaldo serving Eucharist to an altar boy

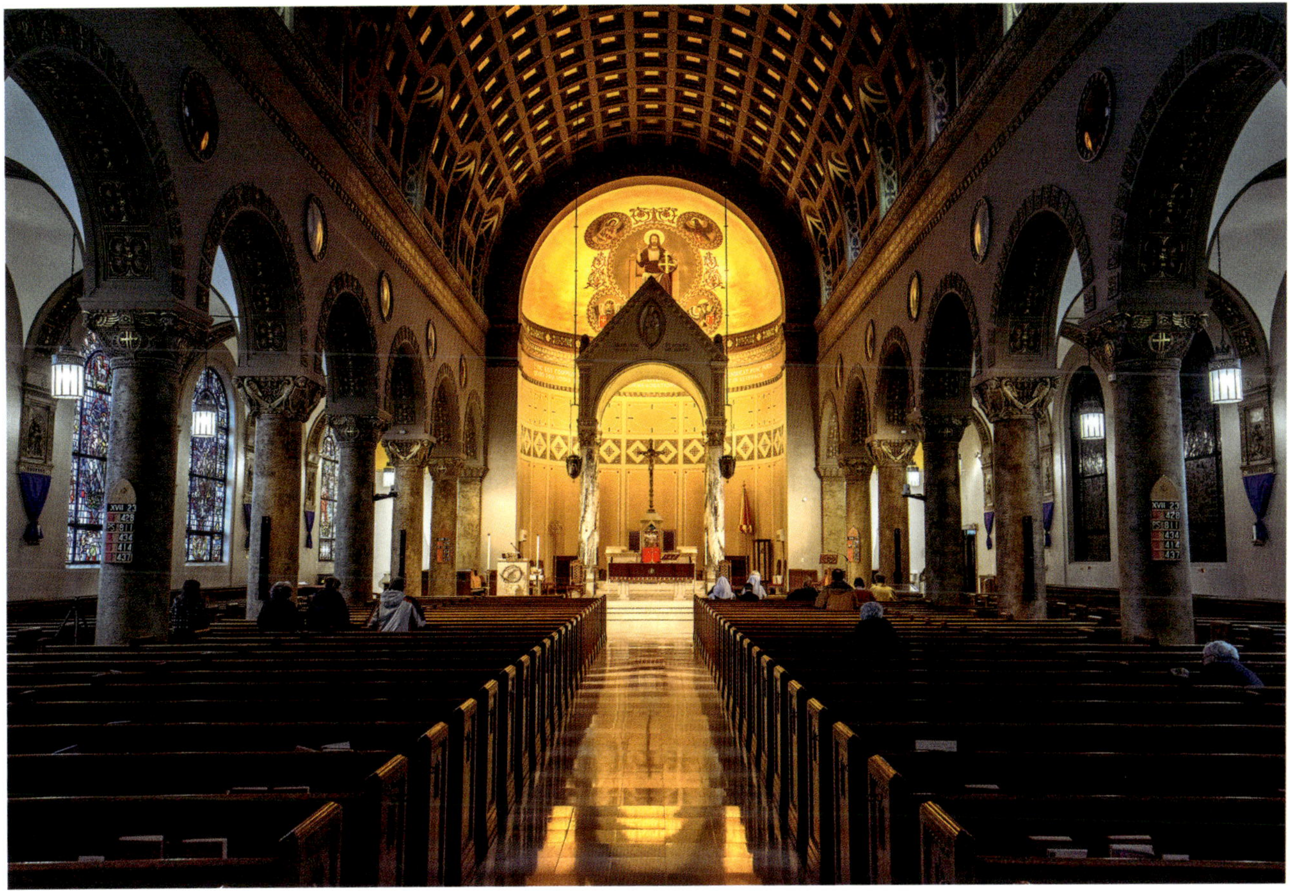

Sanctuary of Basilica of Saint John

Unlike many Catholic churches in the diocese, the Basilica has enjoyed continual growth, most of it by young families, many of whom home school their children. Father Aquinas Nichols notes that this growth in particular and the congregation in general is remarkably diverse.

This diversity is evident at the Basilica's many masses, attended not only by Latin and European Americans but also by a growing contingent of Africans and a significant remainder of Vietnamese. Although Des Moines' Vietnamese Catholics now have their own church—St. Peter, on the east side of town—the Basilica was their primary church from the 1980s up until 2009, when many Vietnamese refugees lived in the St. John's neighborhood. Former St. John's deacon, Quan Tong, remembers this era well. In 1991 he and his family were resettled from Vietnam to the Basilica neighborhood of Des Moines. Fifteen years later, Quan was ordained and appointed St. John's first Vietnamese deacon. In this role, he provided assistance not only to Vietnamese refugees but to Latin Americans and Africans as well. Although Deacon Quan followed the Vietnamese community to St. Peter's in 2009 (and from there to St. Ambrose in 2012), his heart has remained with the first American church that welcomed him.

Six years ago, Reverend Jose Reynaldo Hernandez was called from his home in El Salvador to serve as the first Spanish-speaking priest in the Des Moines diocese, first at Our Lady of the Americas and in the past year at St. John's. He conducts a Spanish-speaking mass on Saturday evenings. For Reverend Reynaldo, the Basilica is unique in the way it "combines together" so many different people. Everyone is welcomed at St. John's. And Sister Mary Claire, one of two Franciscan Sisters of the Eucharistic Heart of Jesus who attends the Basilica,

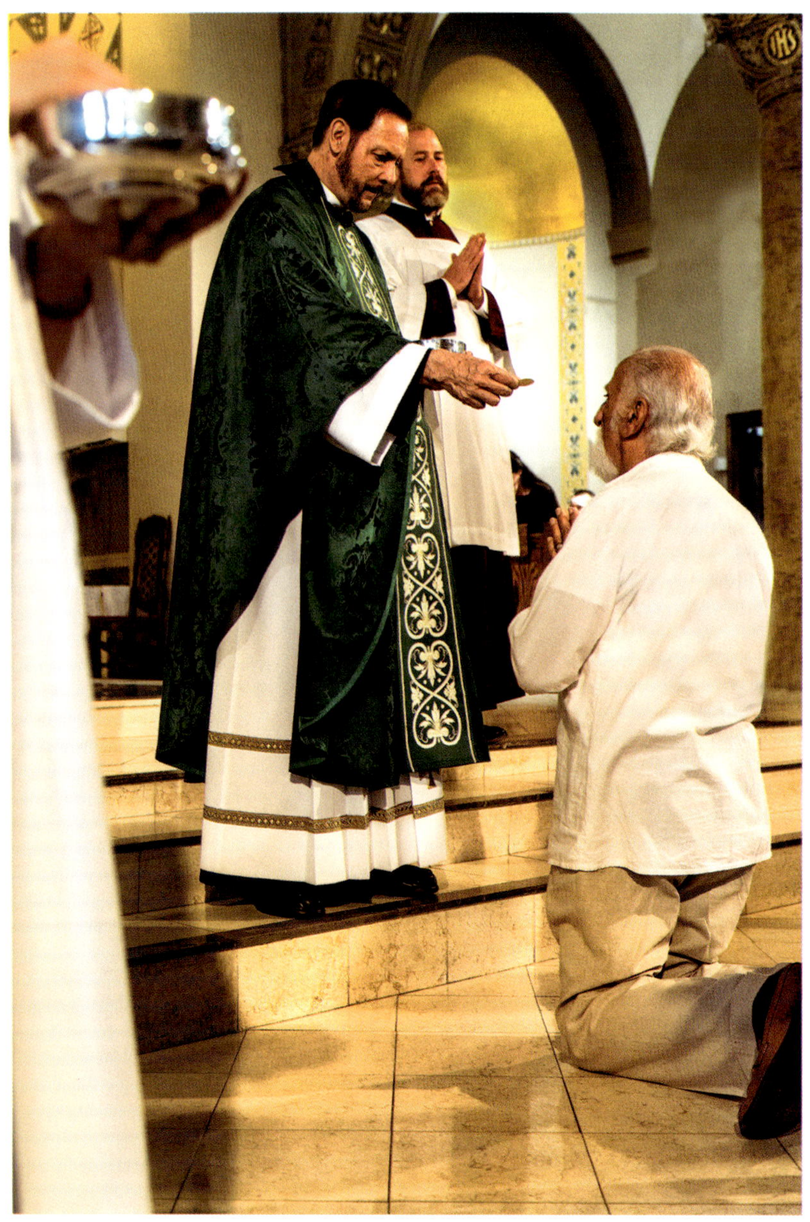

Father Aquinas serving Eucharist to a parishioner

agrees wholeheartedly. For her, St. John's is a welcoming community unlike any other. In her words it is "the only parish around here that has felt like home."

Every Sunday, the Basilica's cantor, Carolyn, peers out at this diversity from the choir loft—so many different faces, such diverse attire. But she also hears these different voices join together in singing the hymns of the holy Catholic Church each week, seamlessly uniting their voices into one melody. This, for her, is one of the most important things about being Catholic: "It's so universal that it doesn't really even matter what your ethnic community is; you always will come together to worship and take part in the mass."

Leading all these English-speaking masses is Father Aquinas Nichols. Although priests tend to be moved from church to church every six years, Father Aquinas has served at the Basilica for sixteen years and was recently appointed for six more. Because Father Aquinas was a Benedictine monk—then serving at the Vatican as Secretary to the Abbot Primate of the Benedictines—the Bishop knew St. John's would benefit from his knowledge of traditional liturgy. Indeed, this is what the parishioners of St. John's seem to admire most about Father Aquinas—his fidelity to tradition and monastic spirituality. In Deacon Quan's words, Father Aquinas is also "a shepherd caring for his parish as if they were his own children." He has a tender side, shares Sister Mary Claire, which is exemplified best in the time that he spends blessing newborn children and hugging their parents after many a service. "He loves to hold those babies," she exclaims, later adding that she has seen him moved to tears during many a mass. Indeed, Father Aquinas is very grateful to be at St. John's. He loves the parish and its congregation for many reasons, among which he singles out their spirit of dedication to Christ in applying their deeply held Catholic values to their lives and their community.

IDENTITY "Welcoming, friendly, and unified" in their faith are the words Rosemary Sloss uses to describe the congregation of St. John's. A member of the Basilica's Adult Faith Formation and RCIA, or the Rite of Christian Initiation of Adults, Rosemary adds that the congregation is also very diverse. When asked what visitors should know about them, she replies, "Well, we are a very conservative church"—orthodox in its services, which enact the same liturgy as that of the Pope's church, Saint Peter's Basilica in Rome.

"The Pope's church" is proud nomenclature for St. John's parishioners. It means their church is one at which the Pope could take part in the liturgy exactly as he would do at his own church. St. John's didn't start out with this distinction, however. That happened on December 31st, 1989 when Pope St. John Paul II approved the request of the priest there at the time, Father Chiodo, to have St. John's named as a minor basilica.

To qualify for this honor, a church must maintain certain key features: architectural antiquity and dignity, historical significance, and devoted mission and worship. St. John's is very much a basilica—one of only some sixty in the country—and its parishioners are proud that their tradition maintains liturgical fidelity to Rome.

Carolyn takes deep pride in the liturgy, the music, and the Basilica. But what makes her proudest of all is the heritage of Catholicism itself whose roots can be traced back to early Christianity. That means that Father Aquinas stands in a succession of priests leading "all the way back down the line to the Apostles and St. Peter." As a Catholic, she knows she can receive the same sacraments and participate in the same Catholic faith no matter which church she attends. At the same time, the basilica serves an important function in obliging the many requests for information about the Catholic faith. As such, questions from both its own parishioners as well as from the wider community are welcome. That's the whole point of religion as Father Reynaldo sees it: to help us live in peace with others who are different from us, to love others—all others.

* * *

St. John's has been specially designated by the Bishop as one of three "Doors of Mercy" locations in Des Moines. Currently, this is one of its most important forms of outreach. Related to this distinction is Pope Francis's declaration that 2016 is a Year of Jubilee. According to the Old Testament, Jubilee years happen at the end of seven cycles of *schmita*, or sabbaticals, which translates to every 50 years. During this period, debts were forgiven and slaves and prisoners freed. In the Roman Catholic tradition, however, the Year of Jubilee has a more spiritual meaning—it is a special time of mercy from God for the forgiveness of sins. The first such Jubilee Year dates back to 1300; since then they ordinarily occur at intervals of 25 years.

Sometimes, however, special circumstances call for "Extraordinary" Years of Jubilee. One such circumstance occurred last year. Although the next official Jubilee had been set for 2025, Pope Francis wanted, in Rosemary's words, to "elaborate on God's mercy." Thus, he declared the period from December 8, 2015 until November 20, 2016 an "Extraordinary Jubilee of Mercy."

One walks through the "Door of Mercy" as if walking through Christ to the Father, thereby realizing the mercy of the Lord. Specific prayers accompany this action: "Our Father," "Hail Mary," "Glory Be," and the Nicene Creed followed by a celebration of the Eucharist and Reconciliation. Walking through the door enhances one's spiritual faith through self-examination; one resolves to change through recognition of God's love and mercy.

When we cross the threshold, says Father Reynaldo, we are met by Jesus Christ who pardons our sins and gives us His mercy and strength. Then we can begin again, trying to be more merciful like Jesus.

PRACTICE Before mass one evening, a mother and father lead their family into the pew. Like their parents, the children first kneel on the cushioned rail before crossing themselves. As the parents bow their heads in reverent silence, their eldest girl does her best to teach the little ones to do the same, just like mom and dad.

A typical Roman Catholic Liturgy has two parts: the Liturgy of the Word and the Liturgy of the Eucharist. The Liturgy of the Word includes readings from the scripture and the sermon, while the Liturgy of the Eucharist includes the offering, the Eucharistic prayer, and Communion. The high point of the service is the Holy Eucharist. Father Aquinas blesses the wafer

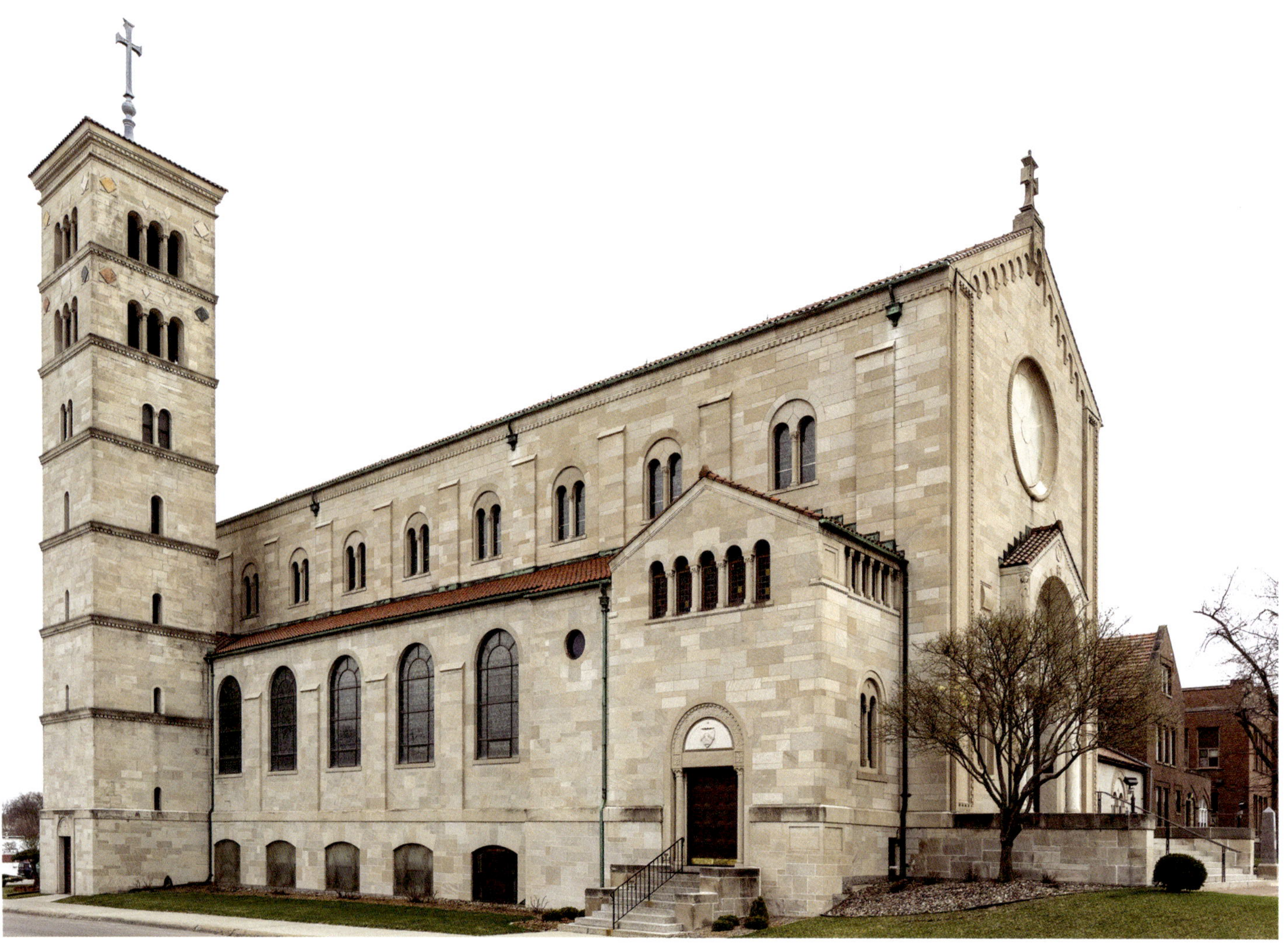

Basilica of Saint John

and wine, which are transformed through the ritual of trans-substantiation into the actual body and blood of Jesus Christ. One by one, the faithful come forward to kneel or stand at the altar as Father Aquinas and his deacons serve the Holy Sacraments—the body of Christ from a precious metal platen and the blood of Christ from a precious metal chalice.

One of the holiest of seasons for Christians is the 40-day period in early spring called Lent, which leads up to Easter Sunday. On this day, Christians celebrate the resurrection of Jesus Christ. Prior to Easter, the faithful reflect on Christ's withdrawal into the desert where he fasted for 40 days, and on His sacrifice on the cross which atoned for the sins of humankind. Many Christians observe this period by giving up certain foods or performing other tests of self-discipline. Good Friday, three days before Easter, is the one day that doesn't include the Liturgy of the Eucharist because on this day, Jesus died. The altar, typically covered by a cloth colored to represent different stages of the Lenten season, remains bare. The altar statues are covered, and the red candle that represents Jesus' presence is unlit.

During this service, Father Aquinas proceeds down the aisle where he prostrates himself in the likeness of Jesus on the cross. The congregation waits in silence for some time—silence meant to underscore the solemnity and importance of the day and the manner in which Jesus died. Father

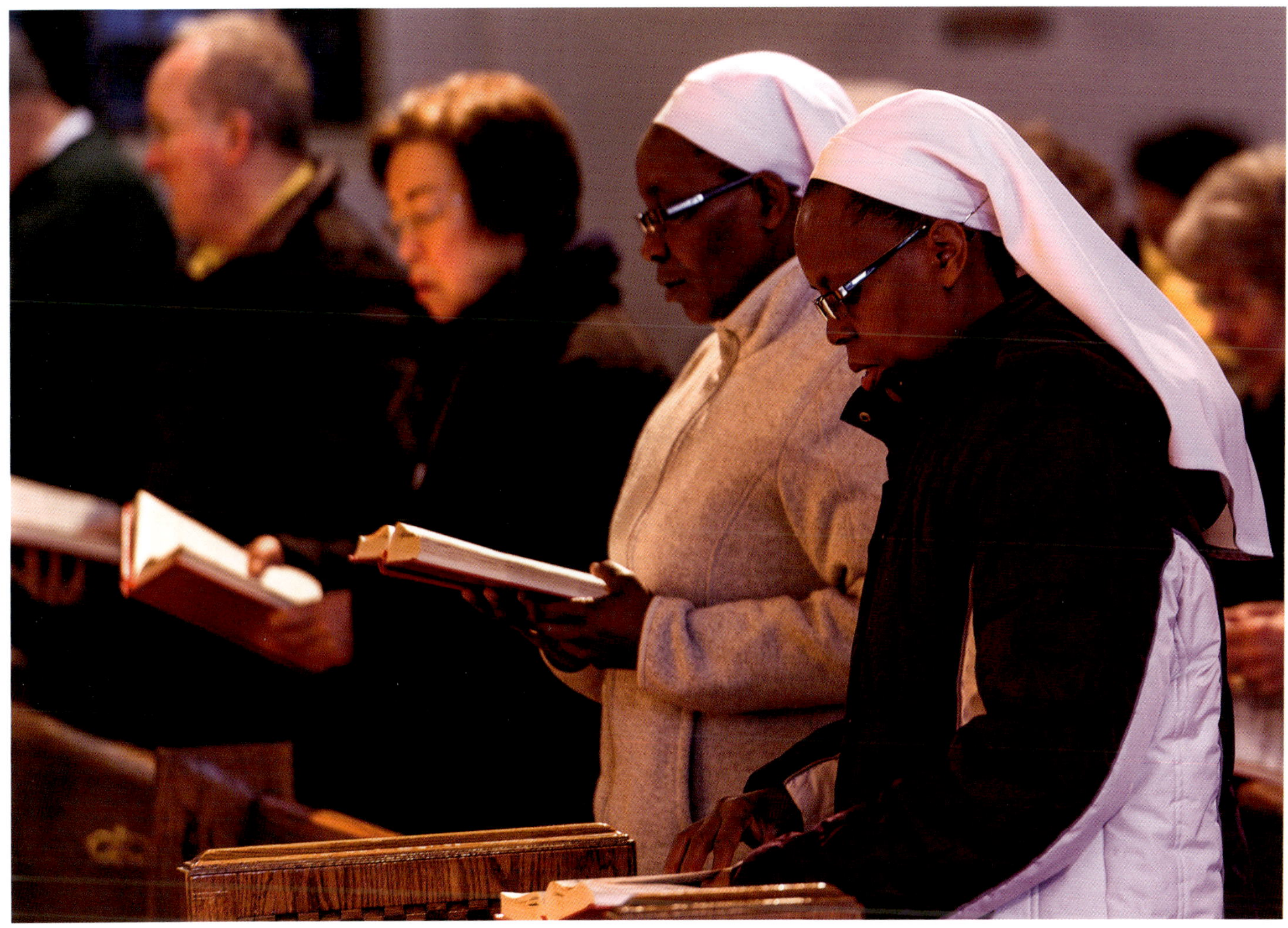

Members of St. John's Basilica singing hymns

Aquinas eventually stands, and the story of Jesus' crucifixion is sung. At the end of the aisle, he uncovers a cross, kisses it, and then walks it to the high altar where the faithful are invited to come up and repeat the kiss.

One special mass—the abundantly musical "Festive Sung Mass" on Sunday mornings at 10:30—is conducted exactly like the mass at the Pope's church, Saint Peter's. It was this mass that moved me more than any other in my several weeks of attendance—surely because of its splendor, but also because I realized that I no longer felt like an outsider. No longer was I waiting for the cues about when to stand or sit or kneel, nor did I wonder any longer what these actions meant. No longer did I need to wait to hear what page the hymn was on or have to ask about the parts of the service, or communion, or the altar. Instead, I could focus on what the services meant for me.

Silence. There is something so peaceful about the services at St. John's. Although we are active and responsive throughout the service, what I'll remember most are the moments of profound quiet. Silence, as the faithful lean in to the singing of the hymns, the recitation of the psalms, and Father's sermon. Silence, as Father Aquinas prepares the Holy Eucharist. Silence, as the faithful participate in sharing the body and blood of Christ. It is a depth of tranquility, full and complete, that moves inward, stilling the soul.

As Deacon Quan describes it, above all, St. John's Basilica provides sacred spaces and times for its diverse parishioners to be at peace.

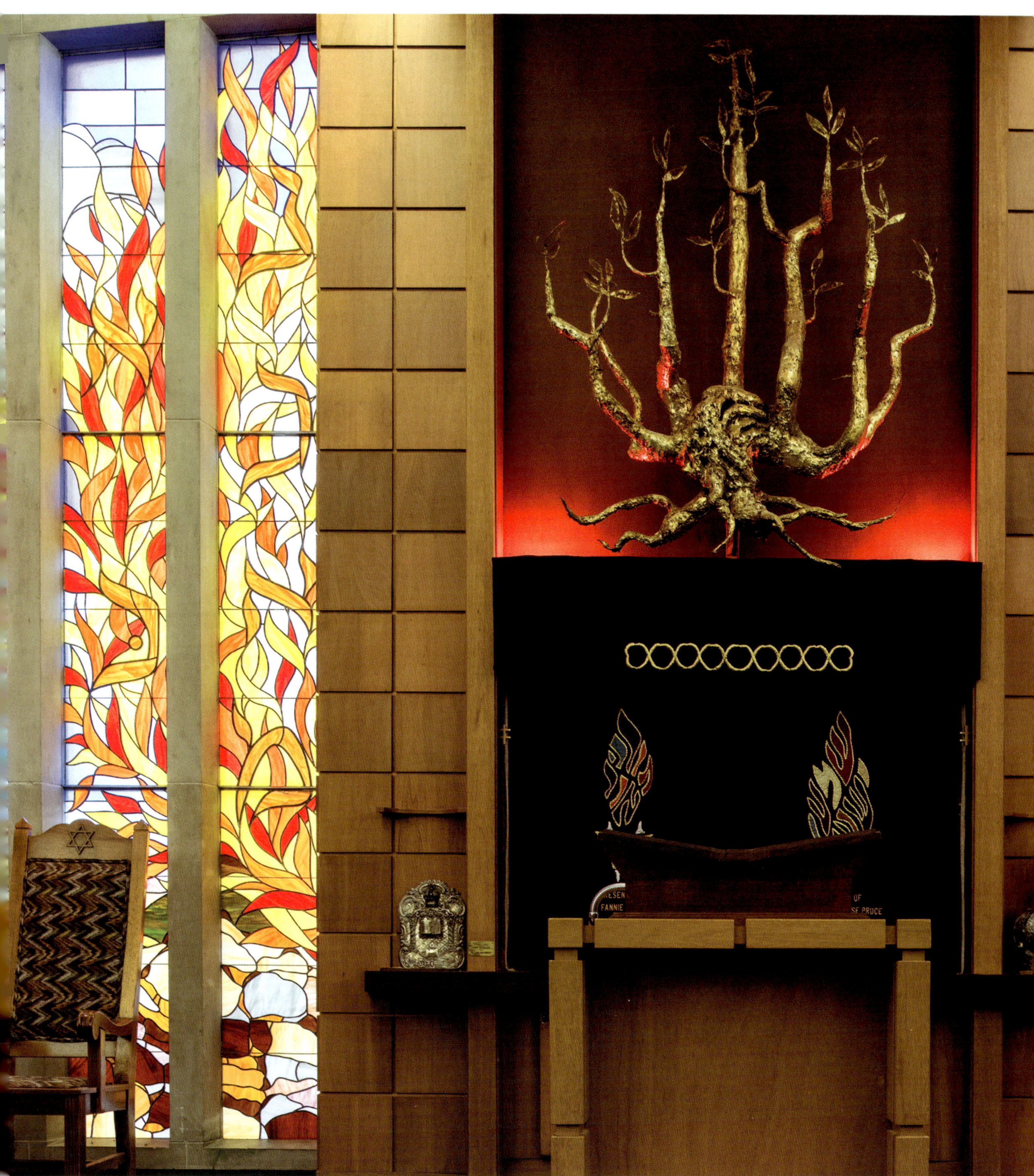

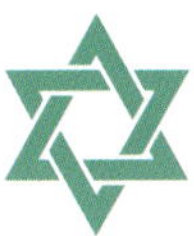

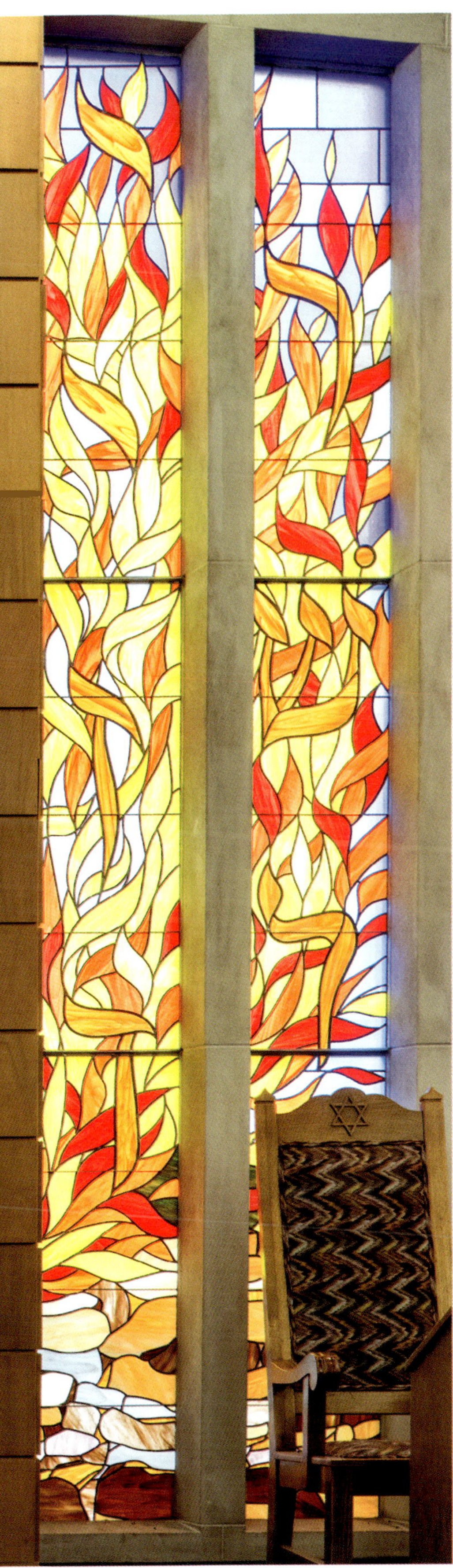

Beth El Jacob Synagogue

Isaiah Enockson, with Tim Knepper

HISTORY Tucked away in an idyllic neighborhood on Cummins Parkway lies the place that Des Moines' Orthodox Jewish community has called home since 1957, the synagogue of Beth El Jacob. Each Saturday, you'll find many members walking to and from the Cummins Parkway location instead of operating a motor vehicle on Sabbath, or Shabbat—in observance of Jewish law (*halakah*). But it may not be this way for much longer. Due to the rising cost of upkeep, the community must now confront the issue of moving to a new location. The seventy remaining families can no longer support a 32,000-square-foot synagogue, explains the synagogue board's president, Sidney Jacobson. And their nearly six-year rabbi, Leib Bolel, recently assumed a new rabbinate in Scottsdale, Arizona, so that his children could take advantage of a traditional Torah education. Still, the community is resolved to maintain its identity, even if this means moving. Meanwhile, this is home for now.

For over one hundred years, since 1881, Beth El Jacob has offered a welcoming atmosphere and supportive community for those who wish to practice and participate in the Orthodox way of life. This is no small feat, for while Orthodox Judaism is the dominant branch of Judaism in

Beth El Jacob's Torah Ark (*Aron Kodesh*)

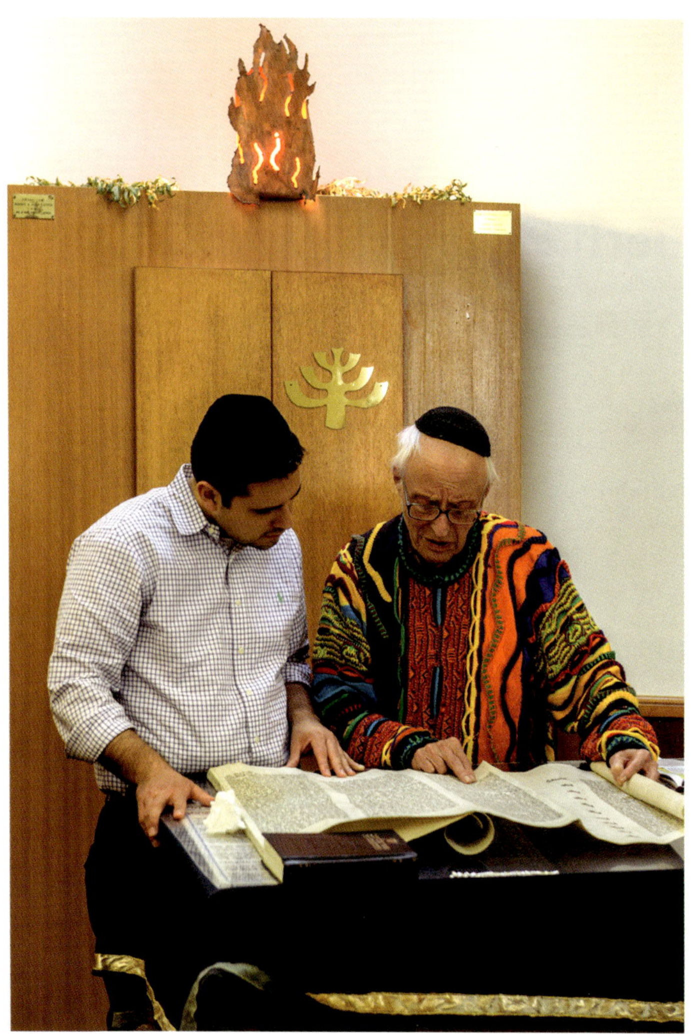

Yosef Garcia and Rabbi Emeritus Berg, reading from a Torah scroll in the chapel

Israel, it is dwarfed in the U.S. by both Reform and Conservative Judaism. Orthodox Jews comprise just 7% of the Jewish population in the Midwest.

As a Modern Orthodox synagogue, or *shul*, members of Beth El Jacob strive to observe traditional Jewish laws and traditions but live in the modern world. G-d's revelation to Moses on Mount Sinai constitutes the Torah—the first five books of the Hebrew Bible—which contain the 613 commandments, or *mitzvot*, that bind Jews in covenantal relationship with G-d. Orthodox Jews believe that alongside this "Written Torah," G-d also revealed to Moses instructions for implementing and interpreting these *mitzvot*. This "Oral Torah" was passed on from generation to generation until it was finally written down in the first millennium of the common era in several forms, one of the most important of which is the Talmud.

Modern Orthodox Jews do not alter these laws and traditions to accommodate modern values; still, they strive to understand and implement them in a modern world. This distinguishes Modern Orthodoxy both from Ultra-Orthodox Judaism, which does not always strive as ardently to integrate Jewish law and tradition into the modern world, and from Conservative and Reform Judaism, which sometimes adapt Jewish law and tradition to fit contemporary values or mores.

Beth El Jacob observes the traditional within the modern. The *shul* contains Des Moines' most established kosher *mikvah*—a supply of natural water used for rituals. And Beth El Jacob's rabbi has traditionally overseen Des Moines' *Chevra Kaiddisha*, a group dedicated to preparing the bodies of the deceased in the traditional Jewish manner. Given the importance of education within Judaism, the *shul* also hosts a variety of programs and events geared towards the education of children and adults alike, from its Hebrew Supplement Program for Children to a variety of adult education classes, such as a business ethics class that applies the principles of Judaism to the modern business world. Also notable is Rabbi Bolel's establishment of Jewish Students on Campus (JSOC), which through outreach at local universities and colleges has educated and encouraged many Jewish students in more traditional forms of practice. For former Rabbi Bolel, it is distinct educational opportunities such as these that reveal the quintessential character of Beth El Jacob.

SPACE A prominently positioned sign greets those who enter Beth El Jacob's social hall. The sign, which came through the congregation's affiliation with the Union of Orthodox Jewish Congregations of America, details how to

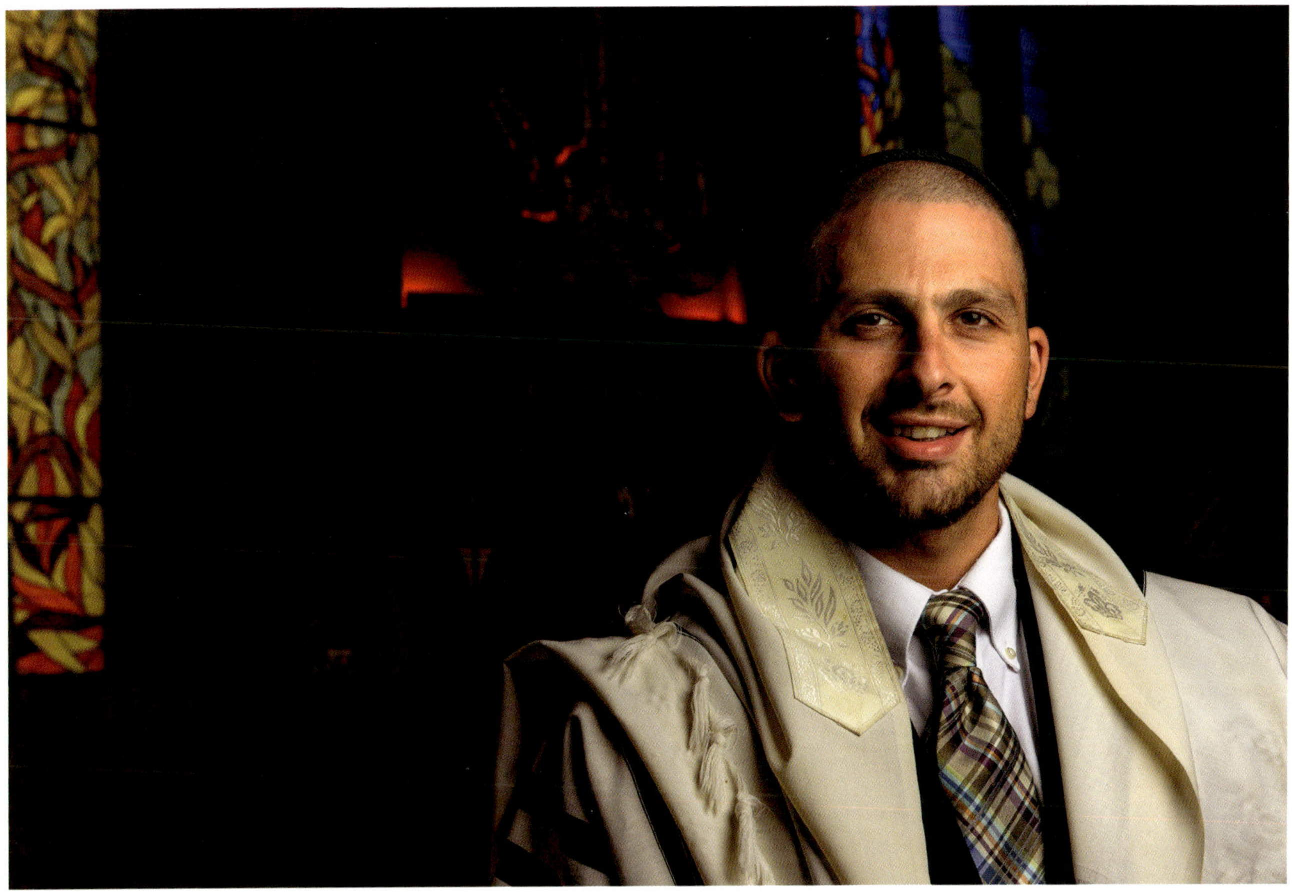

Rabbi Loeb Bolel

advocate politically for the Nation of Israel. As is the case with most Orthodox communities, Beth El Jacob's strong support of Israel is fueled by certain viewpoints, yet it also transcends political ideology and partisanship. For Jews, Israel is the Promised Land, given to them by G-d thousands of years ago.

Marble plaques, engraved with the names of those who made significant contributions to build the *shul*, line its main hallway. These plaques stand in remembrance of Lithuanian immigrants who were integral to the initial success of this community over one hundred years ago. Many current members have been connected to Beth El Jacob since birth; some families date their ties back to the very beginning of this community. A long line of small tapestries dedicated to former members also decorates the social hall.

Inside the main sanctuary, a large wooden sculpture commands the eye—the burning bush through which G-d commanded Moses to lead the Israelites out of captivity in Egypt. Floor-to-ceiling stained glass flames flank this sculpture, which stands just above the sanctuary's Ark of the Covenant. Inside that vessel, G-d's covenantal relationship with His people is written on the Torah scroll. Deliverance by G-d and relationship with G-d: these are the legacies that found Beth El Jacob.

At Beth El Jacob, most services are held in the smaller chapel rather than in the sanctuary. Here, as well, a representation of the burning bush stands above the Ark. As in the main sanctuary and in accordance with Orthodox practice, a *mechitza*, or long divider, separates men's and women's seating areas. Lining the chapel's walls, *yahtrzeit* boards memorialize departed members of the congregation with names inscribed next to tiny bulbs lit in remembrance. History shines forth in these lights.

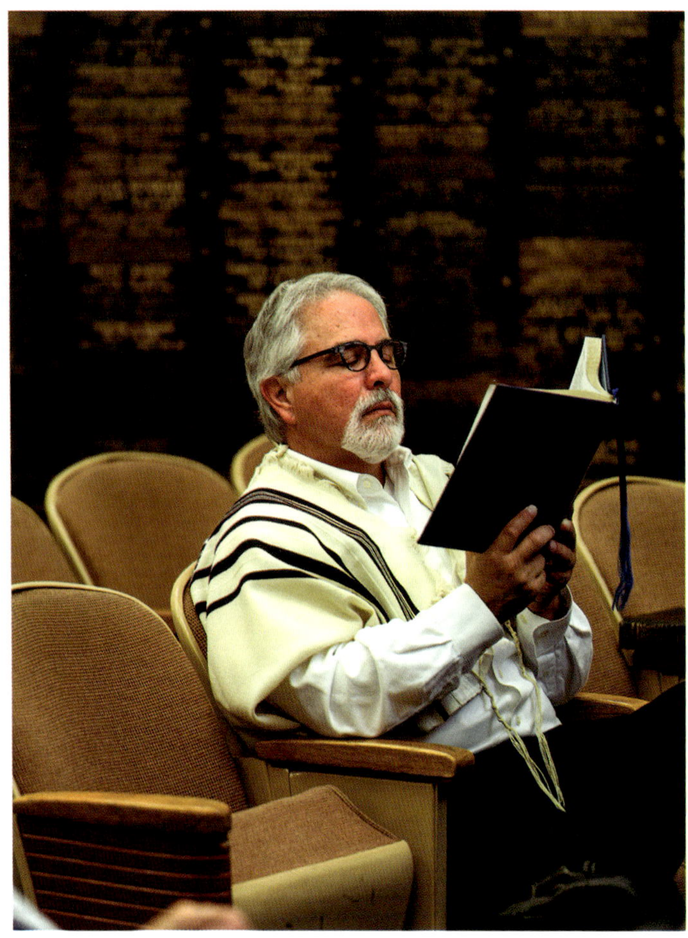

Daniel Dunn, reading from a prayer book (*siddur*) in the chapel

At the same time, the synagogue's classrooms and social hall, library and gymnasium indicate that belief is alive in every aspect of daily life at Beth El Jacob.

PRACTICE As we rise for the *Amidah*—the Orthodox prayer of nineteen blessings recited three times daily, facing Jerusalem—a little dog named Lady, the service-dog of one of the attendants, nuzzles hands and brushes against legs in search of affection. She found plenty during the beginning of the Shabbat service. During that first hour, congregants typically trickle in, wandering the chapel to greet and catch up with one another, and, of course, taking time to pet Lady. During *Amidah*, however, Lady has to wait.

This mingling of strict adherence to Jewish law and casual informality is characteristic of the people of Beth El Jacob. During the service, for example, men wear their yarmulke, *kippah*, and prayer shawl, *tallit*, observing a formal order of readings and prayers. Still, a relaxed and conversational atmosphere reigns.

Communal prayer and Torah study are the main objectives of these Shabbat services. The prayers, psalms, and blessings recited throughout the service are deeply familiar to congregants because, as observant Jews, they view these elements as part of daily life. But certain aspects of the service, such as the *Amidah* prayer and reading from the Torah, can only occur if there is a quorum (*minyan*)—ten males over the age of 13.

Each morning, men gather at the synagogue to pray and study the Torah. They strap small boxes, *tefillin*, containing important Torah passages to their forehead and left arm during morning and evening prayers. Every Friday at sundown, women light the Shabbat candles in their homes, ushering in the week's day of rest. As an Orthodox community, Beth El Jacob places great importance on following these and all *mitzvot* in accordance with the totality of *halakhah*. It is this fidelity to law and tradition that Sidney Jacobson appreciates most.

Keeping kosher. The separation of men and women during services. Maintaining the vital presence of the *mikvah* bath. Refraining from driving a vehicle during Shabbat, even if it means spending the night at the home of a family that lives closer to the synagogue or observing Shabbat at home. These *mitzvot* have always guided the Modern Orthodox Jews to a deeper relationship with G-d, and always will.

* * *

The Jewish calendar is full of annual holidays, one of the most important being the springtime observation of Passover, *Pesach*, celebrating G-d's deliverance of the Hebrews from slavery in Egypt. *Seder*, meaning order or arrangement, occurs on the first night of *Pesach*. This highly ordered meal can take several hours when properly executed.

Rabbi Bolel praying with his *tallit* and *tefillin*

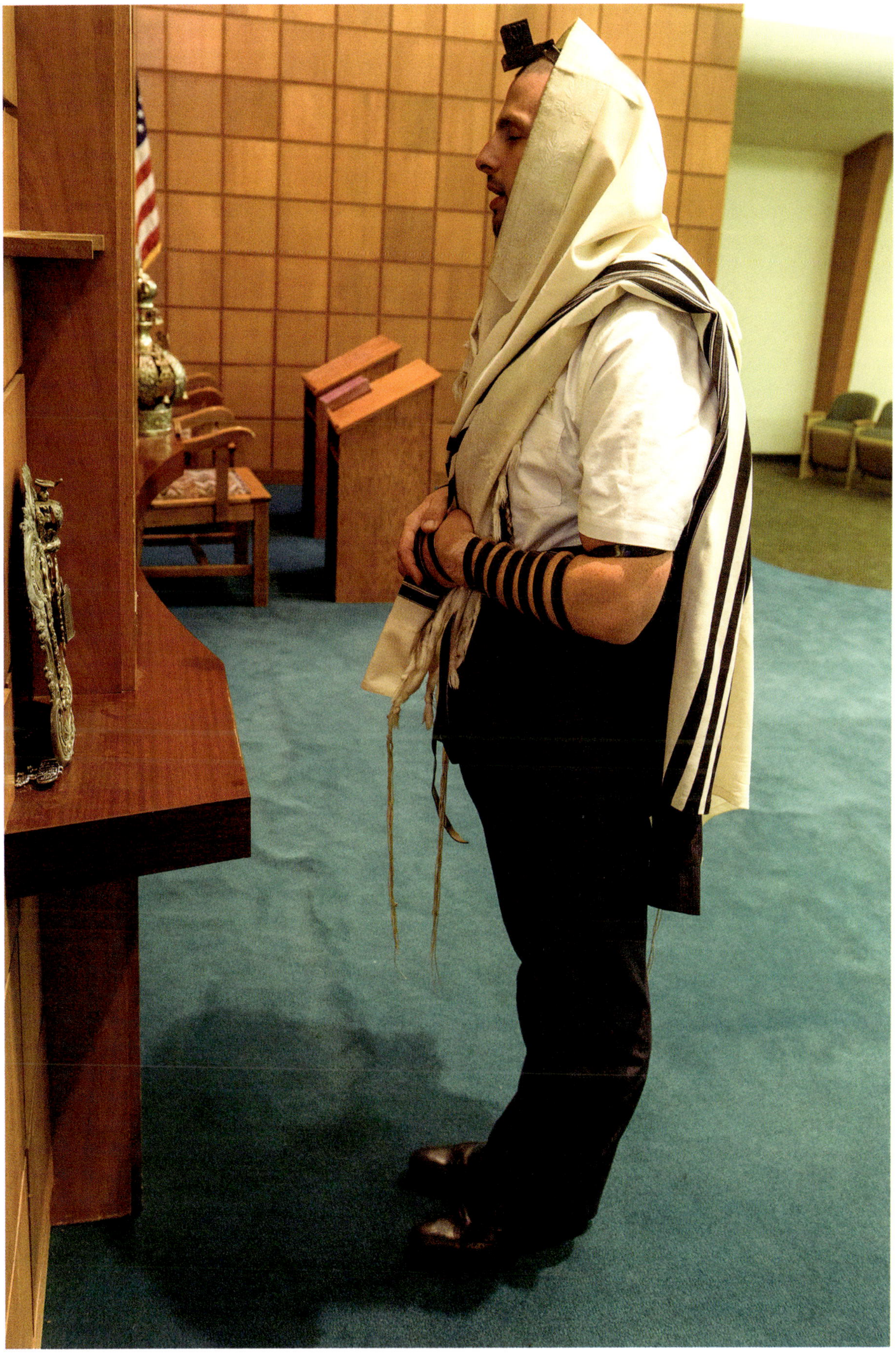

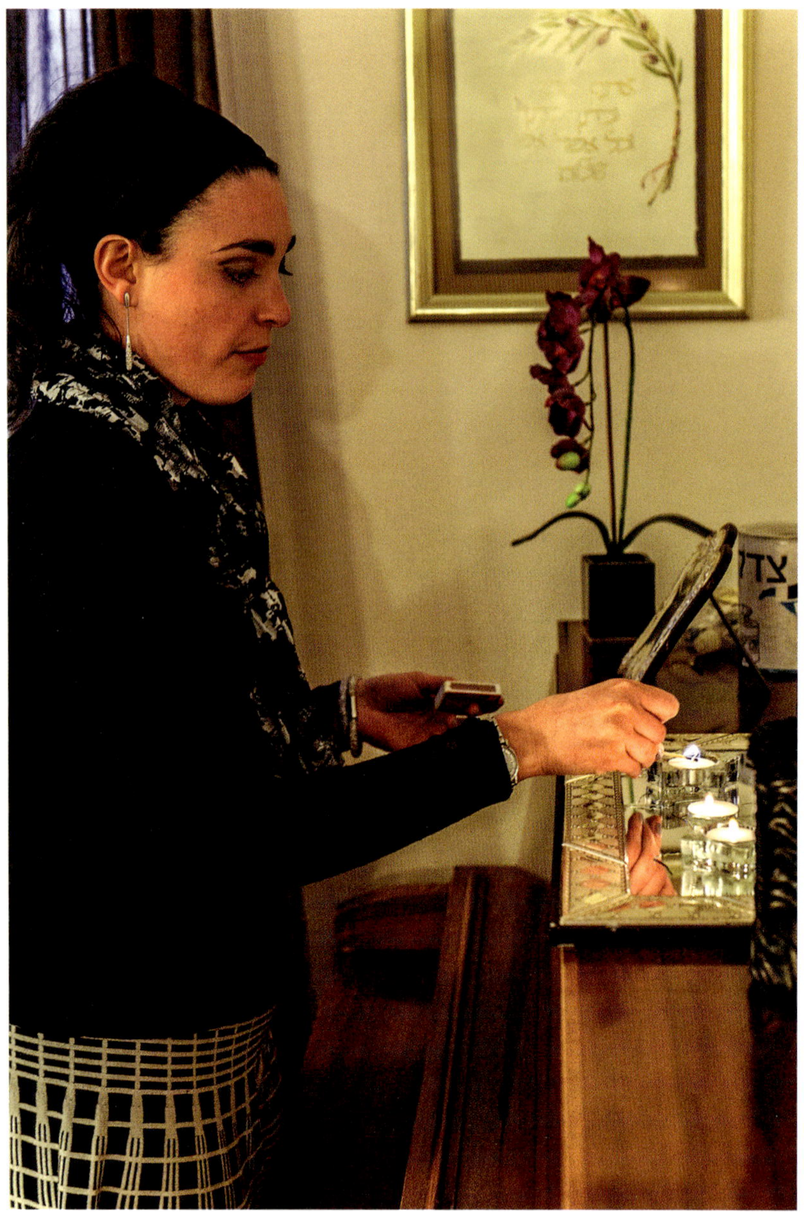

Rabbi Bolel's wife, Devorah, lighting the Shabbat candles in their home

Children are integral to the meal. Traditionally, the youngest will ask the "Four Questions."

- Why is it that on all other nights during the year we eat either leavened bread or matzah, but on this night we eat only matzah?
- Why is it that on all other nights we eat all kinds of vegetables, but on this night we eat bitter herbs?
- Why is it that on all other nights we do not dip [our food] even once, but on this night we dip them twice?
- Why is it that on all other nights we dine either sitting upright or reclining, but on this night we all recline?

A children's song, the *Had Gadya*, ends the meal: a goat is eaten by a cat, which is bitten by a dog, which is beaten by a stick, and so on and so forth, until man is killed by the Angel of Death, who is ultimately defeated by G-d. Through this seemingly perplexing song, G-d's awesome power is revealed. He alone stands untouched by any force of nature or divinity. He alone is the end of all things. That is why, as Rabbi Bolel put it, our worship must focus entirely on G-d.

A "mock Seder" held before *Pesach* gives adult members at Beth El Jacob a chance to look more deeply into the elements of the Seder so as to better teach their children and grandchildren. This gave me the chance to learn more about the meaning behind the *Had Gadya*. The intersection of Orthodox Jewish tradition and everyday modern life became clearer to me. The Seder creates an educational opportunity for all. It's a time when the community of Beth El Jacob gather to experience a mix of spiritual seriousness along with joyous celebration. The first *Pesach* Seder took place thousands of years ago, but its significance has not diminished for the members of Beth El Jacob today.

IDENTITY Among some of the more notable, older members of Beth El Jacob is David Wolnerman, one of the last Holocaust survivors living in Iowa. He is, in Rabbi Bolel's words, "the epitome of the staunchly faithful Jew." Asked how he survived one of Hitler's concentration camps, David Wolnerman's frequent refrain is "it was G-d."

Non-ethnic Jews who have converted to Judaism also find a religious home at Beth El Jacob. One notable character, Chaim, has tattooed arms and hands that immediately signal he is not Jewish by birth, since tattoos are strictly forbidden in Orthodoxy. Displaced after Hurricane

Katrina, Chaim found his way to Florida where he decided that he wanted to convert to Judaism. This wasn't easy: the conversion experience lasts three years—converts have to mean it. In Chaim's case, his rabbi in Florida supervised his conversion process early on.

When Chaim later moved to Des Moines in order to help his family, it was Beth El Jacob that extended its characteristic hospitality and support, and it was Rabbi Bolel who picked up where Chaim's rabbi in Florida left off. In the end, the place where his process began is, for Chaim, his *true* community. But Beth El Jacob welcomed him when he needed a faith home. For now at least, Beth El Jacob is that home.

My very first visit to Beth El Jacob featured a hip-hop and rap artist from the West Coast, Nissim Black. This 29-year-old African American man converted to Orthodox Judaism after a violent childhood and a long search for spiritual belonging. Dressed in the traditional Haredi Orthodox garb of black pants, shoes, and jacket, with a white dress shirt and a black, broad-brimmed hat, the Jewish rapper spoke of his turn to Orthodox Judaism. For Rabbi Bolel, Black's message is vital, in part because he can help to "break the stereotype of Jews as white." But the rapper also holds a commitment to educating youth. As he shares on his blog, "The main thing is that a person has a REAL connection to G-d that they can give over and instill in their children."

Nissim Black's appearance is just one example of Beth El Jacob's outreach to young adults. The most important is Rabbi Bolel's ongoing work with JSOC at central Iowa universities and colleges. Drake graduates like Ethan Siegel and Randy Kane had never been as invested in the Jewish faith until they encountered the community at Beth El Jacob through JSOC. Thereafter, they began to study it and live it.

From serving as a decades-long faith home for survivors of the Holocaust to welcoming the energy of young believers like Chaim and Nissim

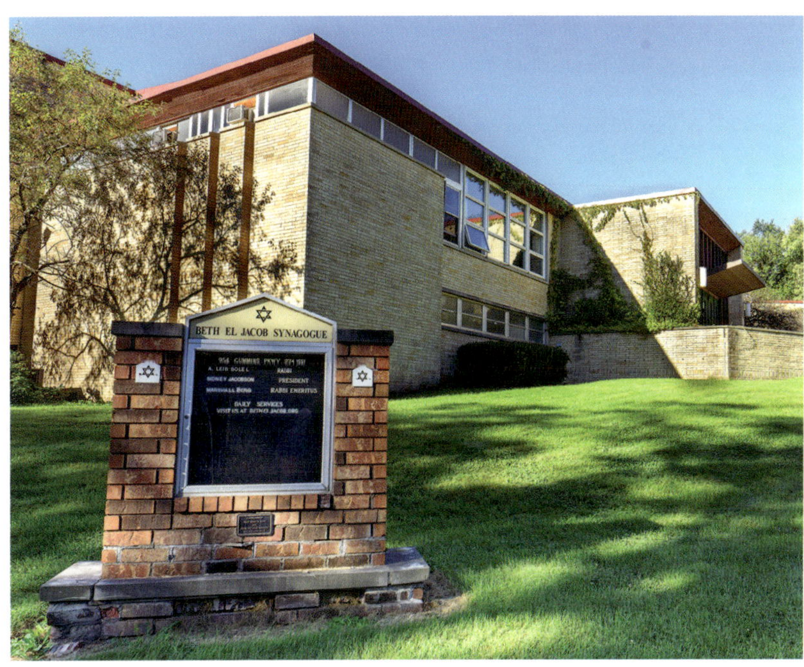

Beth El Jacob Synagogue

Black, Beth El Jacob achieves its educational mission in sometimes unexpected ways.

The centrality of learning became especially clear to me one early Saturday morning as I arrived for Shabbat service. Emeritus Rabbi Marshall Berg, who led the *shul* from 1970 to 1999 and now serves as its Torah leader, greeted me warmly. Ever the rabbinic sage and teacher, Rabbi Berg immediately launched into an impromptu Hebrew lesson about the meaning of my name. "Isaiah" means "salvation of the Lord," he explained, while "Daniel" means "divine judgment" and "Enoch" means "education." He didn't stop there. According to Rabbi Berg, my last name gave me a burden in life—the burden to become more educated. Being in college wasn't enough, he told me. I must go even further. I must always aspire to become smarter.

Education matters greatly at Beth El Jacob. I'd witnessed that throughout my experience there. It's no surprise that the *shul's* own "Philosophy and Mission Statement" accentuates this value best of all: *Love everybody and work together through the guidance of the Torah to become better human beings... and then teach that to our children.*

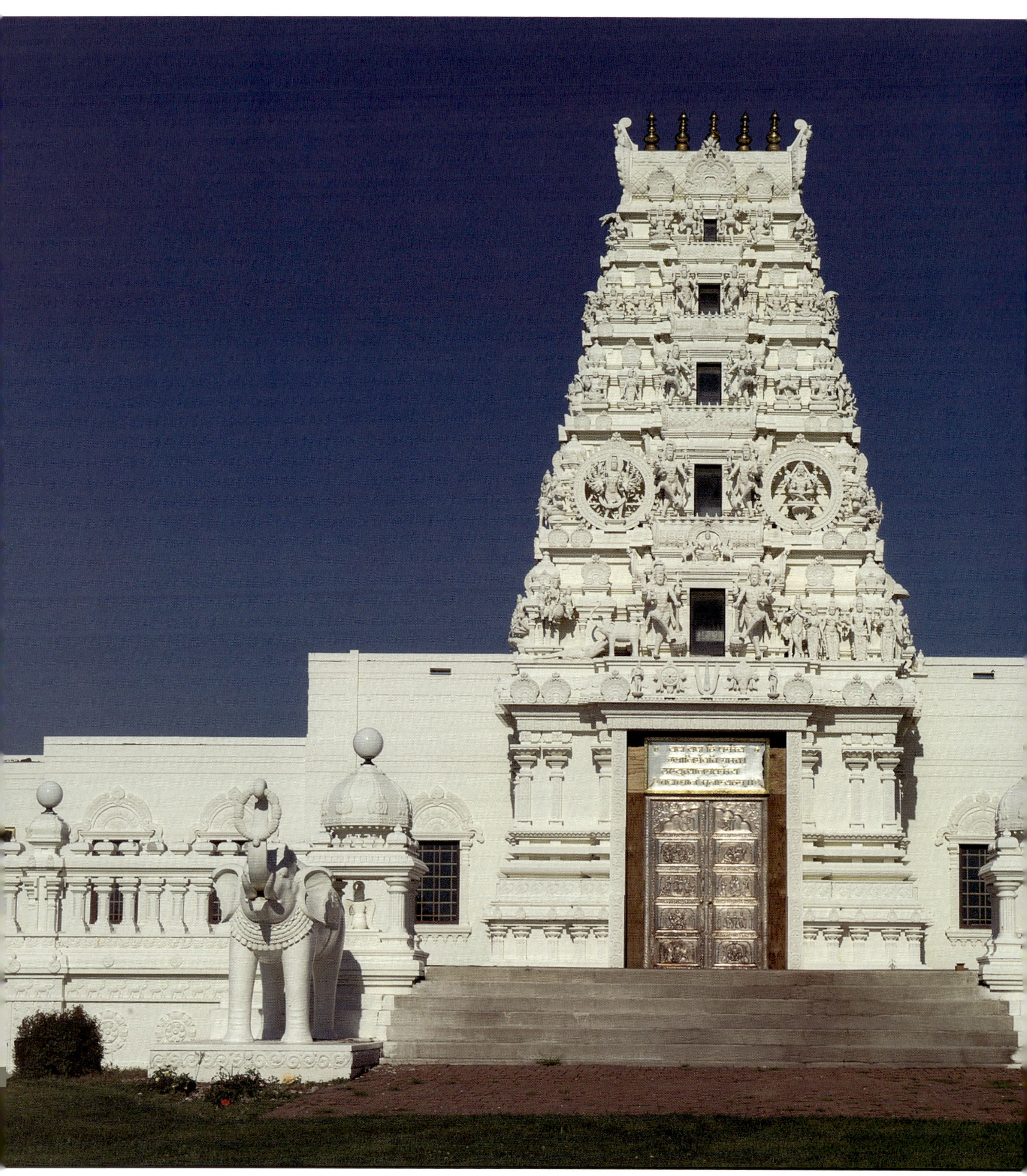

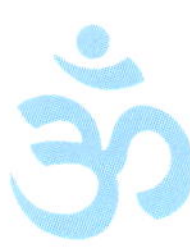

Hindu Temple and Cultural Center of Iowa

Hanna Howard

HISTORY Rising above fields of corn and soybeans in Madrid, Iowa, the white, ornately carved tower of the Hindu Temple and Cultural Center signals to passersby that the world has come to rural Iowa. This parcel of land just across from the Des Moines River along Highway 17 seemed auspicious—which matters deeply to Hindus—for its proximity to flowing water, a sacred source of purity in the Hindu faith. It allows the Temple's two priests, Dr. Khimanand Upreti and Pundit Vasudevakumar Narayanam, to take *murtis*, the carved statues of Hindu deities, to the riverbanks for devotional practices such as *abhishekam*, the ritual bathing of *murtis*.

From its very groundbreaking in 2002, the space designated for the Temple was considered sacred. Members housed their main deity, Sri Venkateshwara, the god Vishnu, in a nearby room while the Temple's *sanctum sanctorum*, the innermost sanctuary of the Temple, called the *garbhagriha*, was under construction. Meanwhile, artisans from India carved the intricately detailed sanctuary alcoves that would house the other deities, all of which were hand-carved and imported from India. Designed to reflect the architectural styles of both Northern and Southern Indian temples, the alcoves accentuate

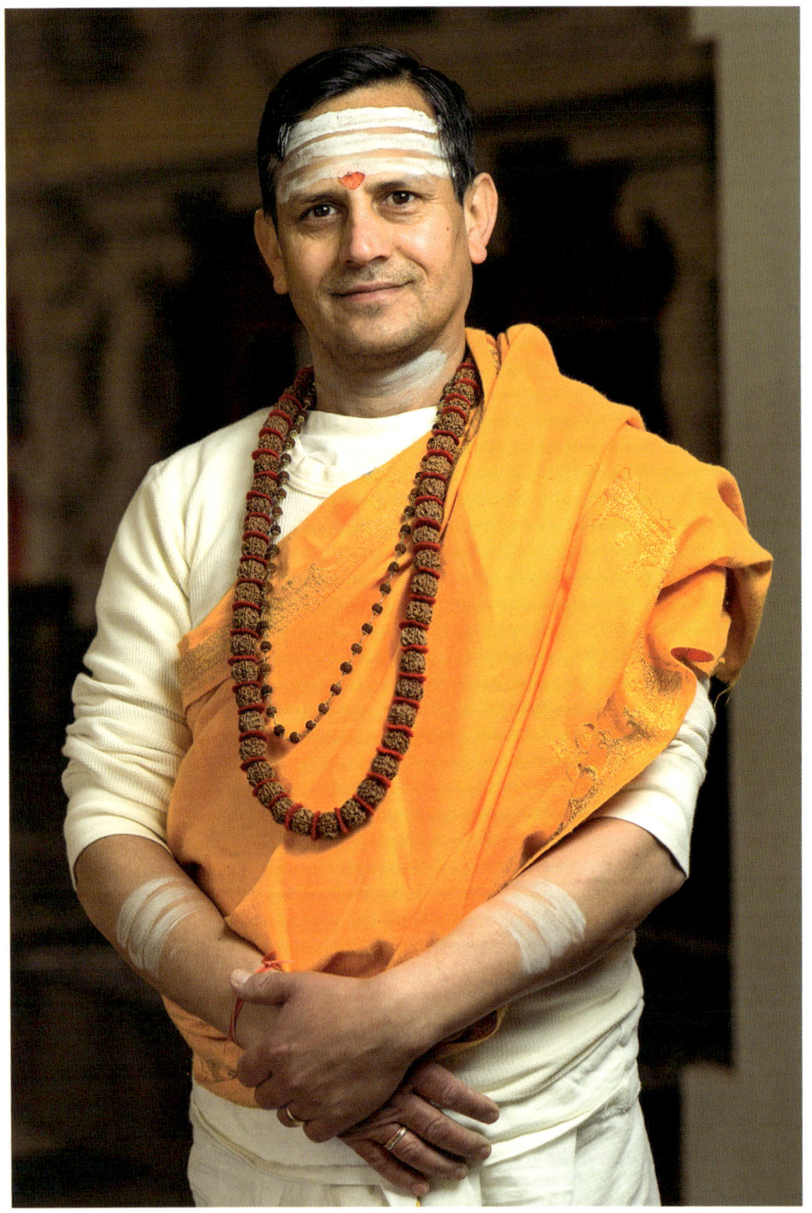

Dr. Khimanand Upreti, the temple's Shaivite priest

the diversity and complexity of this growing Hindu faith community in Des Moines.

The heart of the Temple—its members—existed long before work began on the structure itself. Back in 1956, just a handful of families made up the central Iowa Hindu community. One of this group, Dr. Prem Sahai, dreamed of a place of worship that Hindus could call their own. But Dr. Sahai also dreamed of a cultural center that could "decrease misunderstanding between religions and educate the community or the state as a whole in terms of what the different religions are and what the common grounds are." He knew it would require a decades-long labor of love. Sadly, Dr. Sahai passed away just before temple construction began without seeing his thirty-year dream realized. Dr. Sahai's nephew, Dr. Navin Gupta, called it "a big project in his mind," one that Dr. Sahai's sons were determined to help make a reality.

Dr. Anil Sahai, Dr. Sahai's younger son and the temple's first chairperson, provided the guidance and support to unite the Hindu community around the Temple's construction and many other projects. On weekends he put in long hours, his dedication extending even to mopping floors or encouraging the children to pick up litter in the hallways. In the words of the Temple's religious coordinator, Manjunath Lakshmipathy, Dr. Anil Sahai's "humbleness knew no bounds."

Three years after groundbreaking in June 2005, the Temple celebrated *kumbhabhishekham*, the dedication ceremony inviting the deities to dwell in the individual *murtis* created for them. Priests from Hindu communities in Chicago and Omaha came to partake in the seven-day celebration and still return annually for 2-3 days of summer anniversary celebrations. "It's like a renewal," one community member put it. Everyone comes together to remember the reason they built this sacred space and the people, like Dr. Sahai, who helped create it.

SPACE An earthy scent of incense and camphor greets the senses as you cross over the threshold into the sanctuary of the Temple, or *Mandir*. Here await many of Hinduism's deities—all of them manifestations of a single, ultimate God. If you circle the space clockwise, your gaze falls first on the southern wall, to the *murtis* carved in the smooth white marble customary of northern India. First, you encounter Durga, the goddess of war; she is a fearsome aspect of the great divine feminine energy, Shakti, or simply, "the Goddess." To Durga's right awaits Sarasvati, the goddess of wisdom and music. She is popular with younger members of the Temple, who often invoke her name just before an important exam. With one more step to the right you encounter Swaminarayan, a 19th century guru believed by his devotees to be an incarnation of the deity Vishnu. Photos and drawings of the man himself litter the *murti's* marble feet. Last on this side is Laxmi, her feet covered in offerings of coins and bills, as suits the goddess of wealth.

Two divine couples flank the *garbhagriha* at the back of the *Mandir.* On the left are Rama and Sita accompanied by their faithful servant, the monkey-god Hanuman, and one of Rama's brothers, Lakshmana. Rama and Sita are referred to as the model king and queen, while Hanuman and Lakshmana represent good subjects. It is customary to depict these four as deities, but Rama had two more brothers, Bharatha and Shatrugna, as well. The lives of all six are narrated in the Hindu epic called the *Ramayana,* or Life History of Lord Rama, who was the seventh incarnation of Lord Vishnu. On the right of the *garbhagriha,* you find Krishna and Radha. Krishna, the eighth incarnation of Lord Vishnu, is credited with the quintessential Hindu scripture, the *Bhagavad Gita,* which contains over 700 verses about attaining salvation through different paths, preferably devotion.

Poised between the two couples, in the *sanctum sanctorum,* is Sri Venkateshwara, flanked by his two consorts, Sri Devi and Bhoo Devi. Sri Venkateshwara, otherwise known as Sri Balaji, is commonly worshipped in Southern India because, according to myth, over five thousand years ago, He came down to earth in search of his consort, Lakshmi, and then married her incarnations, Sri Devi and Bhu Devi. At the end of an era, he then turned to stone at the foot of the mountains near the city of Tirupati in the Indian state of Andhra Pradesh. Today, Tirupati is home to one of the most resplendent temples dedicated to Sri Venkateshwara, called Tirumala, which dates back to 300 C.E. Because many Hindu Temple and Cultural Center attendees claim Southern Indian ancestry or have moved to the United States from Southern India, many have visited Tirumala, often for important rituals. One young woman said her family has traveled there several times in the past few years, once for a family wedding and another time for a significant rite of passage in her brother's life—his *upanayana,* or thread ceremony, when young men are given sacred cords to wear forever as a symbol of entering the first, or student, stage in their spiritual journey.

Sri Venkateshwara's central location designates the Temple as Vaishnavite, dedicated to the worship and service of the god Vishnu, the preserver. Vishnu is responsible for keeping the world peaceful. Despite this designation, Hindus who have not dedicated their practice exclusively to Vishnu are not turned away. Rather, the Temple welcomes and caters to worshippers who have devoted themselves to the other two prominent forms of Hindu devotionalism—worship of the Goddess, in this case in the form of Durga, and of Shiva, whose family populates the northern wall.

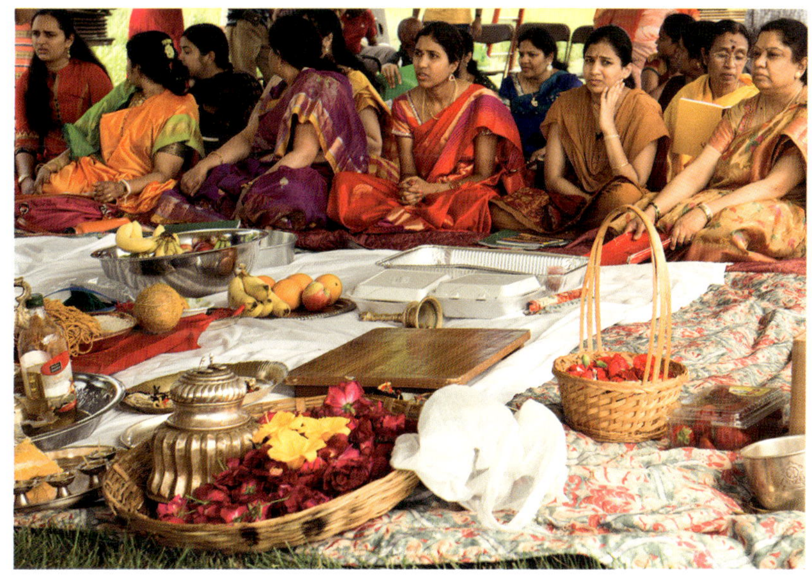

Members of the Hindu Temple and Cultural Center participating in the *Balaji Kalyanam*, a wedding ceremony for Lord Venkateshwara (Balaji) and Goddess Padmavati

Along this wall the *murti* craftsmanship common in Southern India is on display, most notably the black granite from which the *murtis* are carved. You first encounter Shiva, god of destruction and procreation, represented as a lingam, or a symbolic phallus, within a symbolic vulva called a yoni. To the right is Parvati, wife of Shiva and goddess of love, beauty, and fertility. Temple patrons commemorate the marriage of Shiva and Parvati each year by observing *Maha Shivarati* in February or March, during which praying and chanting last long into the night. Next to Parvati is Ganesha, her son by Shiva. Ganesha is the elephant-headed god of good luck and new beginnings. Myth tells us that Shiva himself beheaded Ganesha in a fit of rage and misunderstanding. Only when Shiva replaced his son's head with that of a baby elephant at Parvati's request was order restored. Another son of Shiva and Parvati, Kartikaye, the god of war, sits next to his brother and completes the clockwise circle of worship around the *Mandir*. Father, mother, and sons are often depicted together and form a moral core in many Hindu myths that provides a model for the ideal family.

A woman worshipping in the temple sits in lotus position facing the *murti* of Sri Venkateshwara. You sit and follow her example, scanning the perimeter of the *Mandir*, in awe of the pantheon's diversity. In quietness, the woman closes her eyes. Gods and goddesses surround the mandir. You close your eyes, too. Hinduism is a religion populated by towering figures, human and divine. But it is a faith capable of contrasting modes and depths—now majestic and immense, now intimate, reflective, and personal.

PRACTICE Temple members gather in the lotus position on ornate carpets lining the floor of the *Mandir* to witness and participate in the Venkateshwara *abhishekam*, as they do on the first Saturday of each month. They face the *murti* for the *abhishekam*, the ritual bathing of the statues in libations of milk, coconut water, honey, or *ghee* (clarified butter). Manjunath Lakshmipathy, the Temple's religious coordinator, chants passages of Vedic text as Dr. Khimanand Upreti and Pundit Vasudevakumar Narayanam answer his chants in call-and-response style.

Now ritually cleansed, the *murtis* glisten in the light. After about an hour, the priests spread a paste made of ochre and vermillion onto the statues until they are nearly covered. The chanting subsides and the faithful rise from their lotus positions. Bells sound inside the *garbhagriha* as Khimanand Upreti and Vasudevakumar Narayanam resume chanting—now joined by everyone standing in the *Mandir*. A large bell at the center of the worship space rings in tandem with those of the priests. Chanting and ringing reach a pitch that reverberates through your body. Finally, Khimanand Upreti brings water, which he pours through a decorative metal sieve over the statues of Venkateshwara, Bhoo Devi, and Sri Devi, washing them clean.

As the chanting and bell-ringing subside, Dr. Upreti and Pundit Narayanam seal themselves behind a huge set of doors inside the *garbhagriha* with the *murtis*. In the meantime, the men

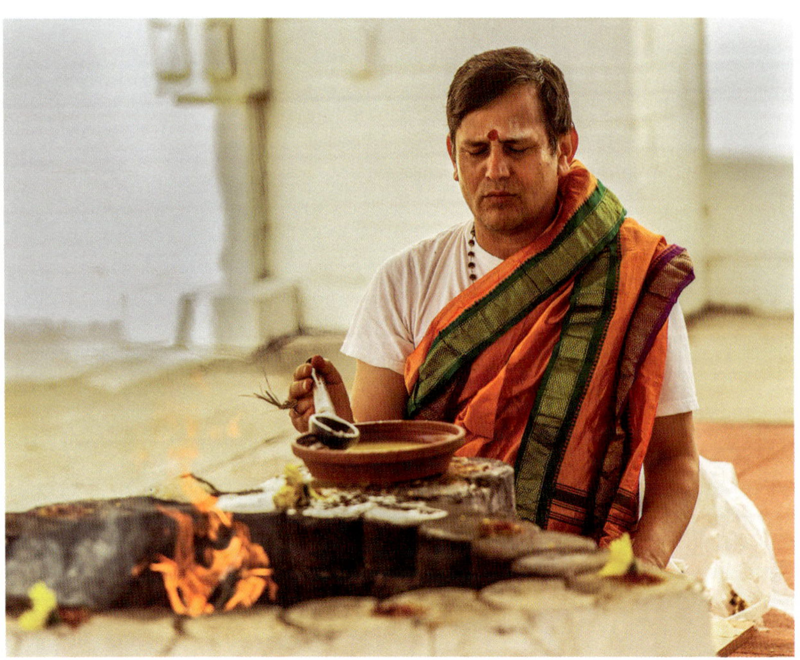

Dr. Upreti performing a special fire ritual (*homam*) during the temple's anniversary ceremonies.

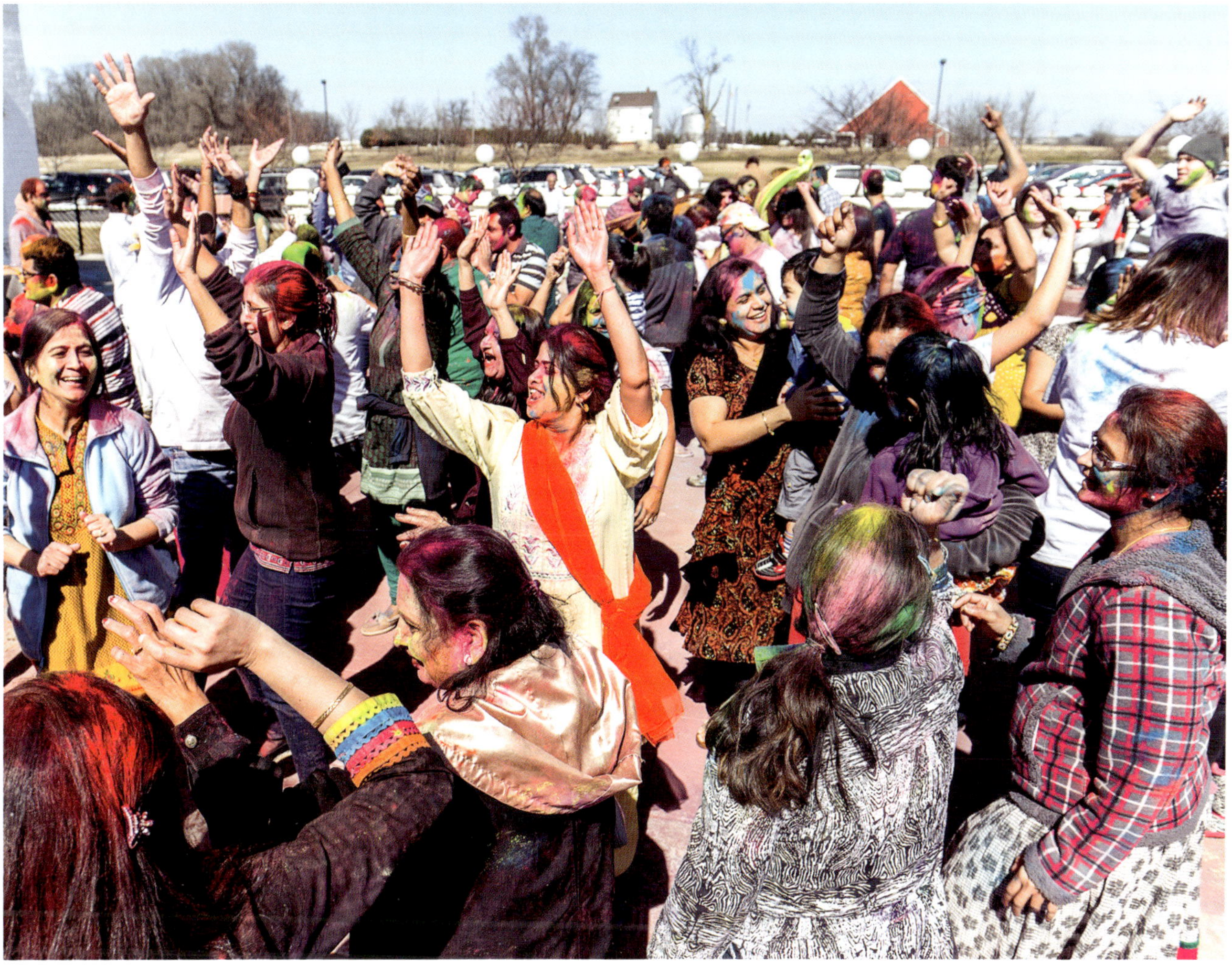

The celebration of *Holi*, the "Festival of Colors," outside the temple

in the room begin polishing the armor that Venkateshwara will wear when the doors are reopened. Women's voices raised in song rise and fall, rise and fall, echoing off the high ceiling. An hour later, the doors re-open. The deities are revealed, now dressed in fine clothes and adorned with wreathes of flowers, with offerings of fruit at their feet. Manjunath resumes chanting, joined by the patrons. The bells sound again as the chanting and ringing echo through the worship space, reaching a feverish climax.

The very next moment, all sound ceases. The abrupt silence is deafening.

This moment is the end of one of many regularly scheduled rituals and services the temple offers to its patrons. *Puja*, or acts of worship, and, more specifically, *abhishekam* ceremonies take place throughout the week. The Temple is open to practitioners and visitors throughout the day, even outside of scheduled services. In a custom that reveals the dichotomous communal and individualist nature of Hindu devotion, individuals and families are welcome to come and go as they please. While some find peace in sharing their faith with other members of the Temple community, others reflect upon their faith privately, personally—either at the Temple or in their homes.

* * *

For Pragnya, the dance teacher, sacred dance is another form of spiritual connection with God. She now teaches two dance traditions she learned

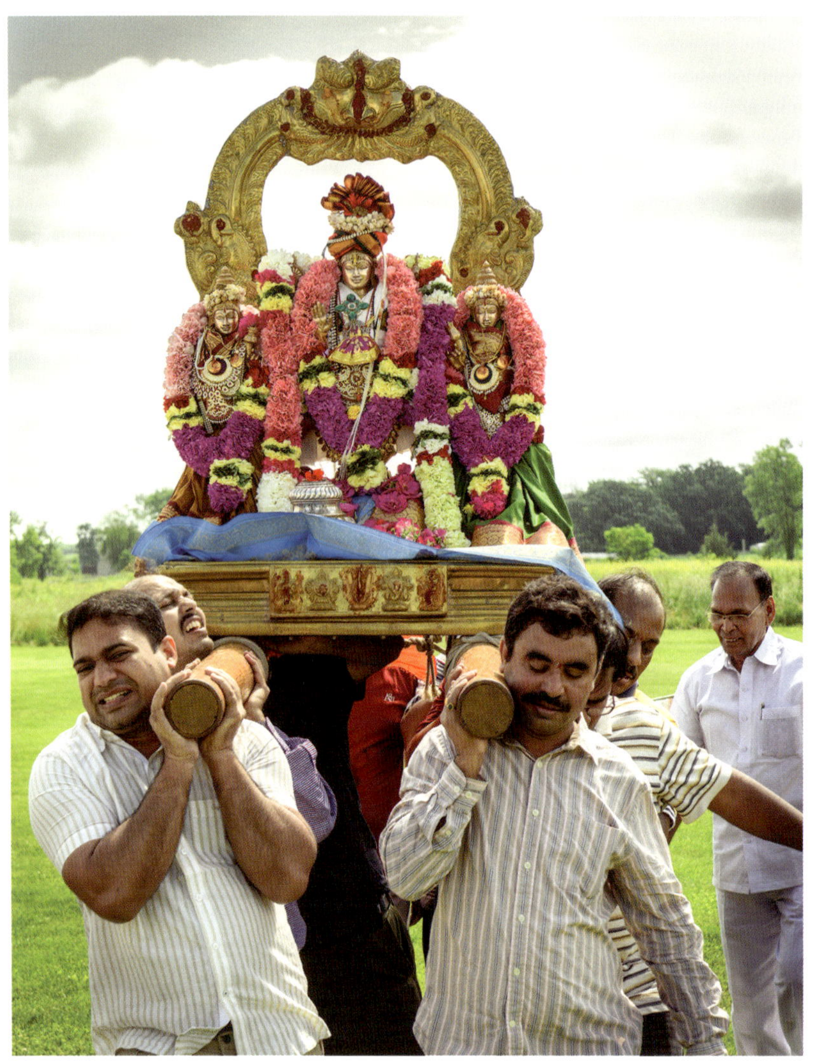

Sri Venkateshwara, flanked by Sri Devi and Bhoo Devi, are carried to the Des Moines River for the temple's anniversary celebration

as a child growing up in India—*Bharata Natyam* and *Kuchipudi*—to about forty students, children and adults alike. The two styles have many similarities, but in *Bharata Natyam*, the dancers tell the stories of the gods and goddesses, while in *Kuchipudi*, dancers assume the character of the gods. In *Kuchipudi*, "you *become* the Krishna," Pragnya explains. Dancers become one with the gods and goddesses, and because the deities themselves actually danced, "It becomes dear to you."

The Temple community serves as extended family for many, especially during times when the faithful gather to celebrate their connection to God. Here, festivals happen on a grand scale, helping to maintain ties "back home" with India as well as strengthening community ties. Here in Iowa, says Pragnya, you may not have the time or resources to make a meal like those you might share with your community in India if you're celebrating only with your immediate family. That's why celebrating at the Temple makes her happy—"because I don't feel I'm missing any big festival back in India."

Several parents who attend temple services are immigrants from India or other South Asian countries, and for them the Temple is much more than a place of worship. Because her own children were born in the United States, Pragnya explained, there is "no need" to educate her sons about American culture; they have been immersed in it all their lives. What they have not been as exposed to is their parents' cultural heritage. That's why children get instruction in Hindi language classes and in *bala-vihar,* which imparts the moral lessons and Hindu teachings that characterize their community. Each class begins with fifteen minutes of yoga and meditation, followed by discussion of the gods, goddesses, and morals. For many temple parents, this is a crucial way for their children to "keep in touch with our culture."

IDENTITY "When there's nobody here I normally just kick them off," Pratyusha Bujimalla says, rounding the corner to the shoe room where, today, she doesn't bother with the formality of the shelving unit. Pratyusha has attended temple services since she moved to the Des Moines area with her family in 2005. Now a second-year student at Johns Hopkins University, she lives most of the year in Baltimore, Maryland, but was able to meet with me at the Temple to share about her faith. Completely at ease in her traditional Indian saree made of swaths of silver-threaded lime green and royal purple fabric, Pratyusha shows me into the *mandir.*

"This is Kartikaye," she explains, gesturing to one of the *murti.* "He and his brother, Ganesha, were once in a competition to win a necklace from their father, Lord Shiva. Lord Shiva promised his necklace to the son who could run around the Earth three times the fastest." Indicating a small statue at the *murti's* feet, she adds, "Kartikaye's animal vehicle was a peacock, so he knew he could easily outrun Ganesha, whose animal vehicle was a mouse." Ganesha knew there was no way he could win. So, instead of attempting to ride the mouse around the world even once, Ganesha went to his father and mother, Lord Shiva and Parvati, and walked around *them* three times. When Kartikaye returned from his third trip around the world, Ganesha was given the necklace—"because your family should always be the center of your world," she said.

Going to temple as a child was something Pratyusha's family always did together. "I'm sure my parents loved to expose me to the culture that they grew up with," she explained. Now, she also wants to "get the word out about the temple and encourage people"—both Hindus and those of other beliefs—"to come visit and explore the immense cultural and religious experience that it offers."

Pragnya echoes the desire for outreach and greater cultural understanding. As a "cultural ambassador" for a local educational non-profit called CultureALL, she regularly visits Des Moines area schools to "spread the word about Indian culture." Pragnya and her husband chose to make their home in Des Moines after moving from Bangalore, India because they sensed people here have respect for and interest in other cultures. India is a long way away, though, and it can be difficult to reconcile your first home with starting a new life in Iowa, Pragnya explained. That's why "coming here and *not* being together as a community doesn't make any sense."

Dr. Navin Gupta moved to Des Moines in 1977 from his native India. He had family in the greater Des Moines area, so he attended and graduated from Drake University. According to Dr. Gupta, "the Temple was a thought that the Hindu community had for a long, long time."

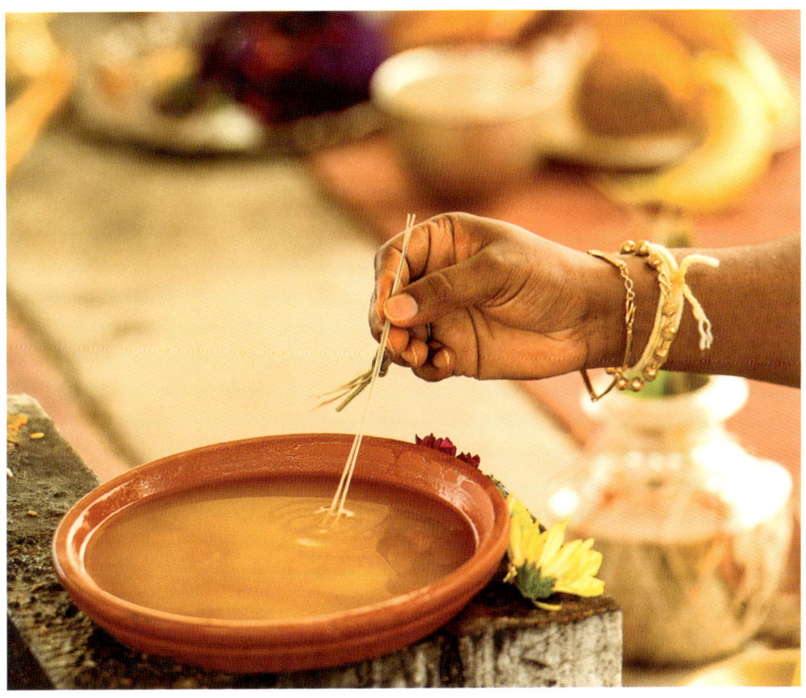

Saucer of *ghee* (clarified butter) used by Dr. Upreti in a fire ceremony (*homam*)

When Dr. Gupta first moved to Iowa, there were not many Indian families here. Now, the Temple's community flourishes. Its families are all religious-minded, especially the younger generations who have moved here for jobs and education. Being so far from their extended families, children do not benefit from the cultural upbringing that grandparents and great-grandparents can provide. Thus, the Temple takes on that role, providing a vital place of worship and a center of learning for the community.

Seeing his uncle's "brainchild" brought to fruition matters deeply to Dr. Gupta. He can uniquely claim his role as a part of the family that started the Temple, and he still attends temple services and engages with the community. "A place where the doors to your heart and mind are opened," Dr. Gupta says of the Hindu Temple and Cultural Center. It is a place to "look inside yourself," to "open your own mind to the Lord, the Supreme Being, and answer the three most important questions of life: Who am I? Where do I come from? Where am I going?"

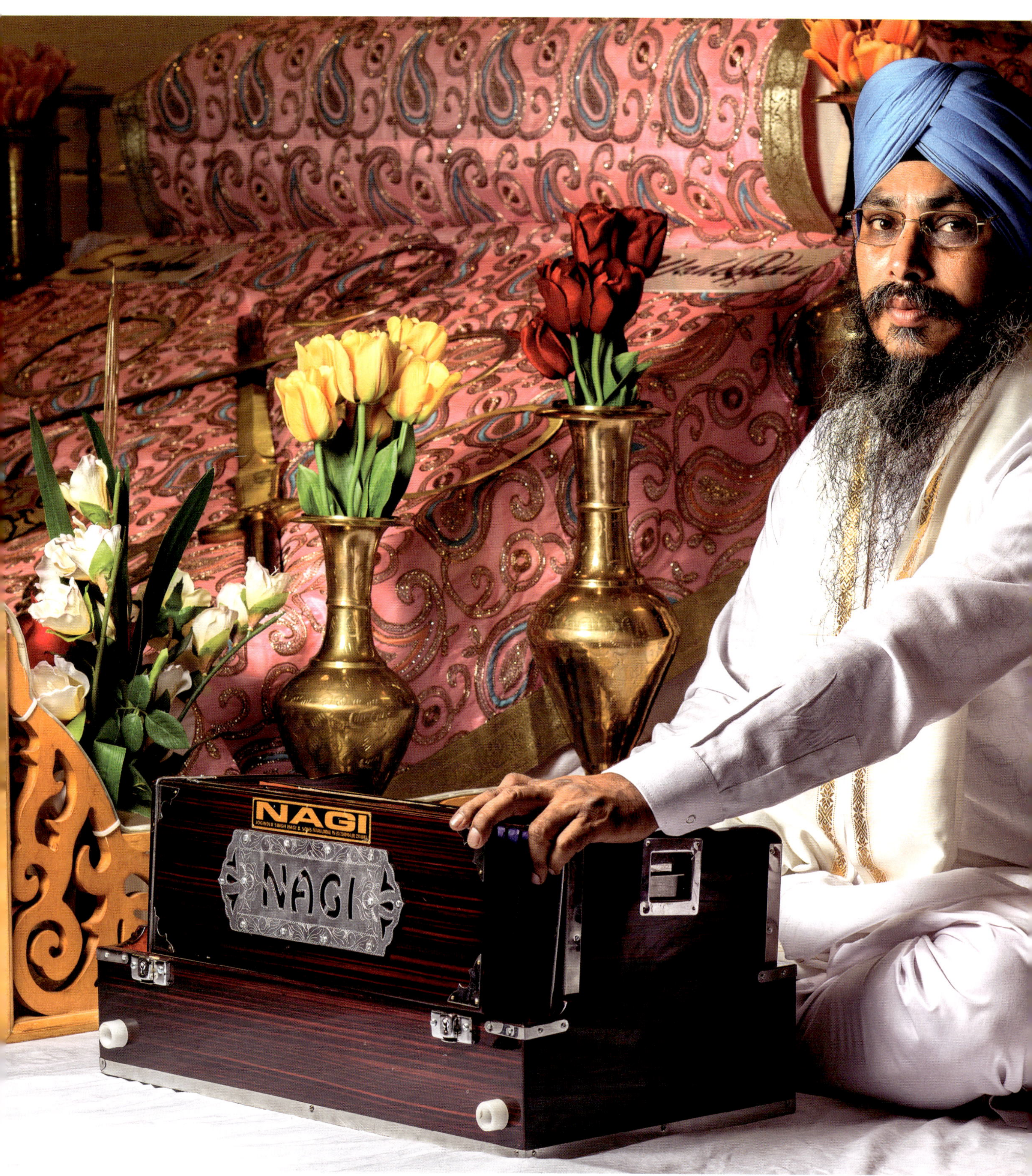
NAGI
NAGI

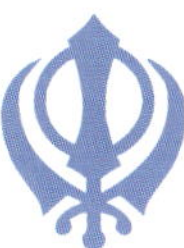

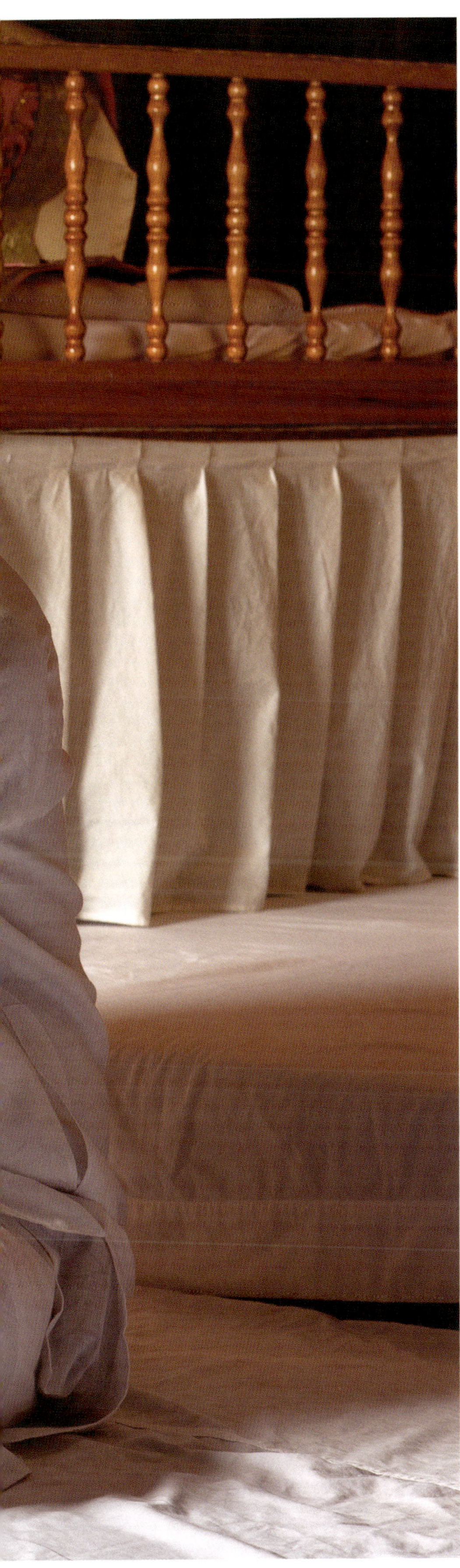

Iowa Sikh Association

Benjamin Weinberg

IDENTITY Wrapping the microphone wire around his wrist, the *granthi* stands at the front of the prayer room at the Sikh *Gurdwara*, or temple, tucked away in a West Des Moines neighborhood with only a tall saffron-colored flag to mark its location. The *granthi*, or priest, recites the *ardās*, a prayer performed all around the world at the conclusion of Sikh services, praising God for His guidance and protection throughout the five-hundred-year history of Sikhism. The *ardās* is the clear link for the Des Moines community to their fellow Sikhs around the world, as it brings people together in a common religion despite distance and culture. Most of the practitioners at the Iowa Sikh Association come from the Northern Indian region of Punjab, but no matter their origin, they all share Sikhism as the basis of their identity.

The *granthi*, Giani Chandanpal Singh Ji, concludes the *ardās*, and the assembled seat themselves cross-legged, bowing towards the Holy Book, the *Guru Granth Sahib*. The *granthi* chants, "*Waheguru*," or "Wondrous Lord," three times, and one by one each Sikh joins in to express glory to God, the Sikhs' ultimate Guru.

Giani Chandanpal Singh Ji, the priest (*granthi*) of the Iowa Sikh Association

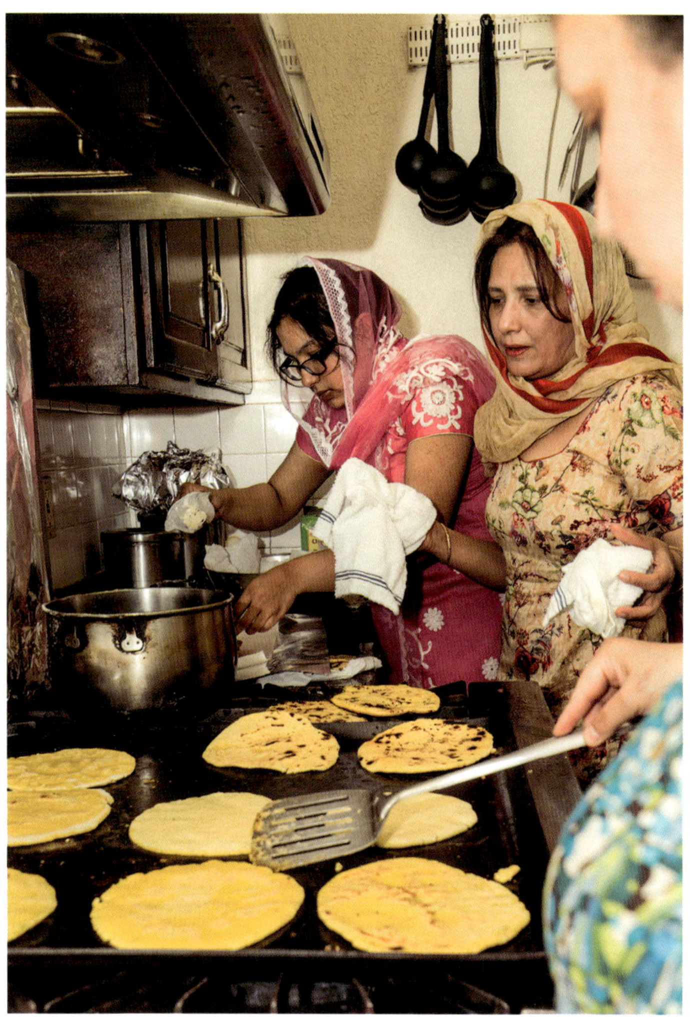

Apurba Kaur (left) and Gurmeet Kaur (right) cooking *chapatis* for *langar*

Sikhism's first human Guru, Guru Nanak, founded the Sikh religion over five-hundred years ago. Growing up in the Punjab during a time when the Muslim Mughal Dynasty ruled much of India, Guru Nanak witnessed the apparent exclusivism of Islam and the polytheism, ritualism, and classism that pervaded Hinduism at that time. He hungered for a simpler and purer path to God. One day in 1499, while bathing in a local river, Nanak disappeared, leaving behind his clothes on the riverbank. After spending three days in the court of God, Nanak returned, remaining silent. A day later, he broke his silence, proclaiming words that would inspire Sikhs for centuries to come: "There is neither Hindu nor Muslim, but only human. So whose path shall I follow? I shall follow God's path. God is neither Hindu nor Muslim and the path which I follow is God's." With these words, a new religion was born.

At the temple, the *granthi* continues his chanting. Members pass around a steel bowl containing *karah parshad*, a sacred pudding made from butter, sugar, water, and whole wheat flour. At the close of the service, all practitioners partake in this sacramental offering. The pudding is traditionally made by those who intend to share their joy or sorrow with the community. "When a person is feeling happy, they share it with the community and they feel more happy," explains Baljit Singh Virdi, a regular attendee of the Sunday service. "When a person is feeling sad, they share it with the community and they feel less sad. Happiness shared is doubled and sadness shared is halved." Today, money is donated by several members of the assembly to provide the ingredients for the delicacy. "The same feelings apply though," Baljit explains. It is an atmosphere of compassion.

While *karah parshad* occurs in Sikh temples across the world, the small gathering in West Des Moines provides a more intimate and profound connection. Vikram Singh Chouhan, a father of two young sons, has been a part of many Sikh communities in the past, particularly in Chicago and in Dayton, Ohio. But the West Des Moines *Gurdwara* is where he has found the most close-knit community. "The smaller a community is, the closer it is," he says. He was welcomed at this *Gurdwara*, where the two roots of the word literally mean door (*dwara*) to Teacher (*Guru*), with open arms. It's a doorway to a Teacher's house.

PRACTICE Whole wheat flour coats my skin as I roll out the chapati dough, my younger hands in stark contrast to Harinder Kaur's worn fingers as she sits beside me rolling the same dough. Rolling out 200 pieces of chapati bread is just another week for her. "Rest if you need to, *puttar*," she says

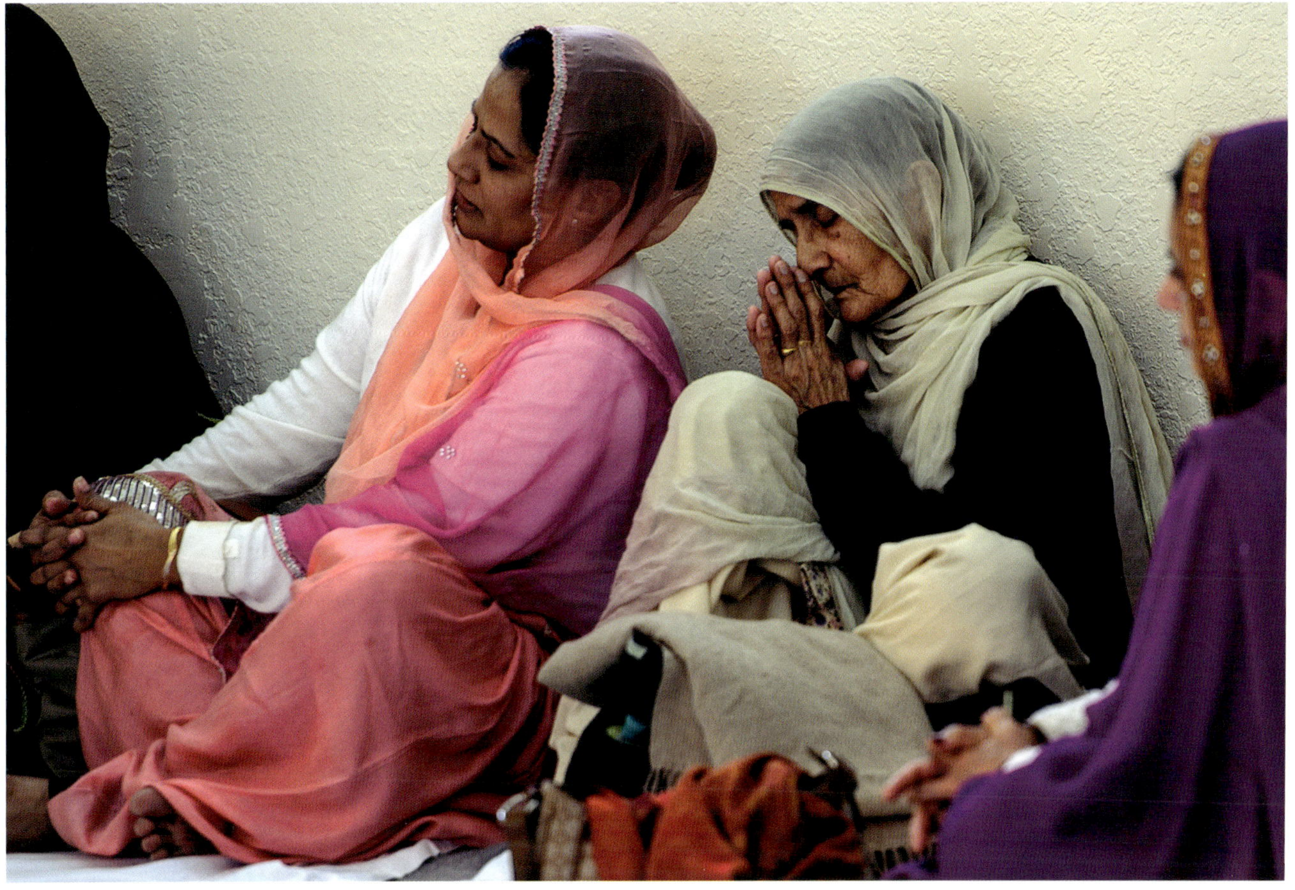

Harinder Kaur (left) and Tirlochan Kaur (right) listening to *kirtan*

with an affectionate tap on my wrist. The other volunteers, primarily women, working in the kitchen of the Iowa Sikh Temple speak Punjabi blended with sporadic, broken English. Though Harinder dubs me *puttar*, or son, the others interact simply through sweet and encouraging smiles.

In Sikh temples all over the world, when services conclude, the community kitchen brings everyone together to share a free meal, known as *langar*. Each week, a different community member graciously donates the majority of the food for that Sunday's *langar*, while the *chapati* is made fresh in the *Gurdwara's* kitchen every Sunday morning. Harinder ensures that enough food is prepared for those attending the temple. This is part of her religion; indeed, it is part of all Sikhs' religion—to share and consume together. Along with meditation on God's name and honest work, it constitutes one of the "three pillars" of Sikhism.

I arrive about two hours before the regular prayer service begins to help prepare *langar*. As I peel sweet potatoes, the *kirtan* music begins to play within the prayer room, and I know Baljit Singh Virdi is busy setting up his video camera to record his son playing the harmonium. Around 11:30 every Sunday morning, the harmonium and drums, also called the *tabla*, begin their gentle twang, and the musicians sing a hymn (*shabad*) as people trickle in. Eventually, Harinder leaves her post in the kitchen and joins those gathered within the prayer room, seating herself on the ground, legs crossed and back against the side wall. She listens as the *granthi* and his son and daughter lead the *kirtan*. Elder members of the community sing along, chanting "*Waheguru Ji Ka Khalsa, Waheguru Ji Ki Fateh*"—*Khalsa* belongs to God, Victory belongs to God—at the end of each *shabad*. In the few minutes of silence between

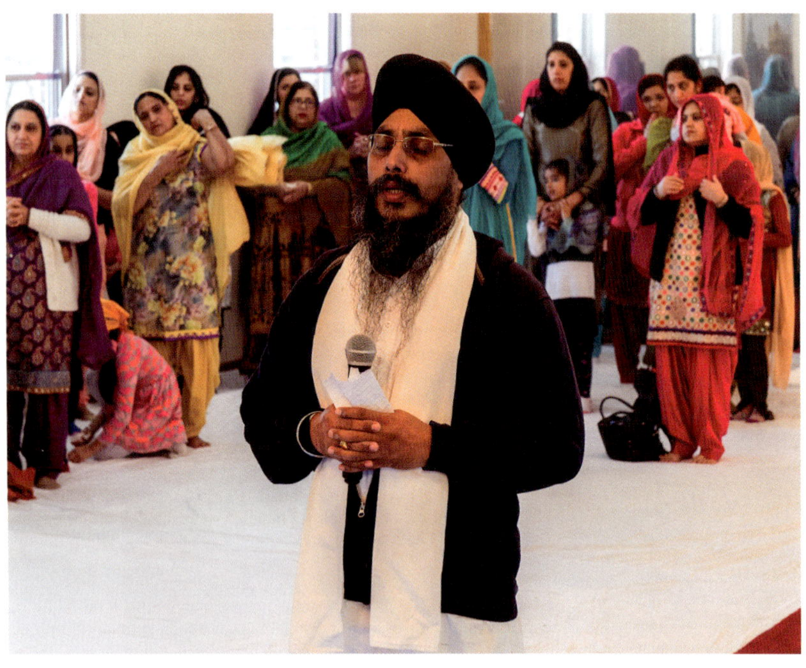

Giani Chandanpal Singh Ji leads the congregation in the *ardās* prayer at the end of *kirtan*

shabads, the *granthi* delivers a short sermon called a *katha* based on what he perceives as the needs of the community. After the *kirtan* has been played, the *granthi* opens the smooth leather cover of the *Guru Granth Sahib* and delivers a longer *katha* based on the *hukamnama*, literally the "royal decree" of the day, which is randomly selected every morning at the Golden Temple in Amritsar for all Sikhs.

The *Guru Granth Sahib* serves as the spiritual successor and embodiment of the teachings of the ten Gurus. According to Sikh tradition, the tenth and final Guru, Guru Gobind Singh, transferred all power to the Holy Book upon his death, making it the final, living Guru. The *granthi* is the protector of and provider for the *Guru Granth Sahib*, and it is his responsibility to uphold the practice of reading from its weathered pages each week.

To close the service, the *granthi* stands and recites the *ardās*, the final prayer. After recitation of the *ardās* the congregation rises and forms straight rows facing one another—men on one side, women on the other—in preparation for the *langar*. Here, there is no distinction of social class or caste. All are equal, partaking of the same food as their neighbor—yet another core principle of Sikhism. Throughout the week at the *Gurdwara*, a simple vegetarian meal is available for anyone in need. The first Guru, Guru Nanak, transformed the monotonous task of rolling chapatti dough two hundred times every week into a meaningful practice through his belief that no person should ever go to bed hungry. At *langar* on Sunday, a communal feel arises like the steam from the freshly baked Indian bread that is broken and shared all around, making Harinder's role here one of great worth and purpose.

SPACE Gurwinder Singh Kapur locks his affectionate gaze on his son, JJ Singh, as the musicians play *kirtan*. JJ quickly scrolls through translations of the *hukamnama* to find the daily hymn from the *Guru Granth Sahib* which has been randomly selected that morning. Only a sophomore at Valley High School, the young man is already a leader within his religious community. "If JJ gets this, I will have done well," Gurwinder whispers. JJ locates the translations for the Punjabi text and projects them onto a screen for the entire room to see. Gurwinder smiles proudly and explains that JJ is able to find the translation even though he isn't very familiar with Punjabi.

Many in the community do know and speak Punjabi well, like JJ's grandfather. Due to poor health, he is seated in the back of the room on a chair and not on the floor with the rest of his family, but this doesn't stop him from chanting through the service along with everyone else. This family of three generations, each with different backgrounds, has experienced the welcoming embrace of a *Gurdwara* to call their own.

But it was a long time coming.

For Harinder Kaur, finding her way to Des Moines in 1993 started with a flood—not the famous flood city residents remember from that year, but the flood that happened across the globe in the Punjab region, prompting her immigration to the United States. She remembers fleeing with her young son to the home of a neighbor and climbing the stairs as the rising waters swept beneath her feet and across her homeland.

Starting in the 1960s, a small Sikh community in Des Moines met for worship not in their own *Gurdwara* but in people's basements and living rooms. The flood of '93 in both the Punjab and in Iowa emphasized the reality of impermanence for Iowa's Sikh community. As the Sikh community grew, the small but vibrant group faced the frightening realization that they might never find a place to call their own. They began a search for a permanent place of worship in Des Moines.

Over the next five years, they scouted locations and raised money to purchase a suitable building. Families gave all they could. With the aid of prominent Sikhs from around the Midwest, the Sikhs of Des Moines were able to purchase a former Jehovah's Witness Kingdom Hall and set about renovating it for their needs. In went a kitchen to prepare *langar* and serve those in need. Out went the chairs and benches so that members could sit cross-legged on the floor and worship as equals. Streamers, flowers, and balloons now festoon the beige walls, bringing the spirit of joy and festivity to a once somber space. Children dart around the room, dodging and weaving between elderly Sikhs as they are led towards the altar. Time and history meld here, as an older generation ushers in the new. Those who helped to establish this sacred place and those fortunate to have grown up within it both reap its rewards. More than a place of worship, the *Gurdwara* is a place to call home.

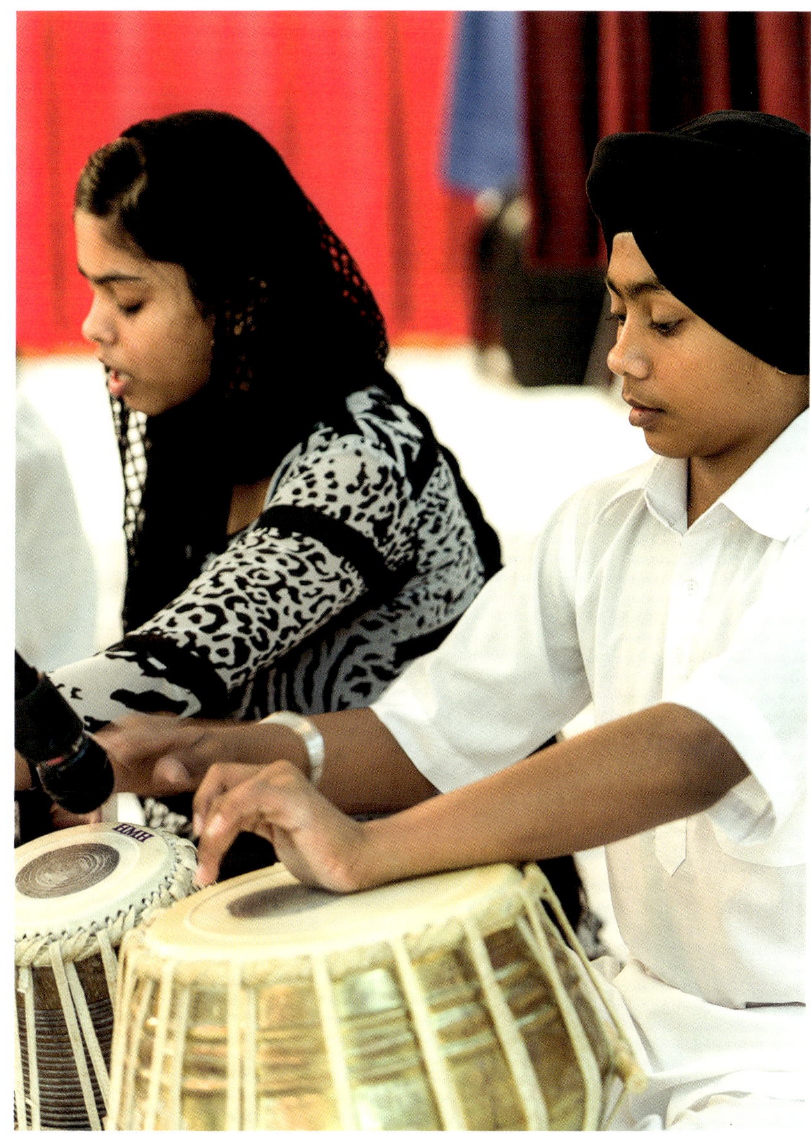

The *Granthi's* children lead *kirtan*, with Daljeet Kaur on the harmonium and Amrik Singh on the *tabla*

HISTORY "Why milk and not water?" a little four-year-old asks, tugging relentlessly at his mother's dress. Eight men adorned in saffron turbans surround the tall flagpole outside of the *Gurdwara*. Chanting fills the air, "*Waheguru, Waheguru, Waheguru*," the atmosphere as bright as the large flag rustling in the wind. The men have cleansed the silver pole with milk and are rewrapping the flag that hung in honor of *Vaisakhi*. "Because that is what we do as Sikhs," the boy's mother answers. Milk is used to wash sacred objects in Indian religions because it is considered pure.

The tall saffron flag, his mother continues, acts as a prominent feature or guiding beacon. It represents all Sikhs. "In India," she tells her son, "the flag pole can be seen from miles and miles away." This is not the case in Des Moines, however, where city regulations limit flag height. Although the orange banner still carries the

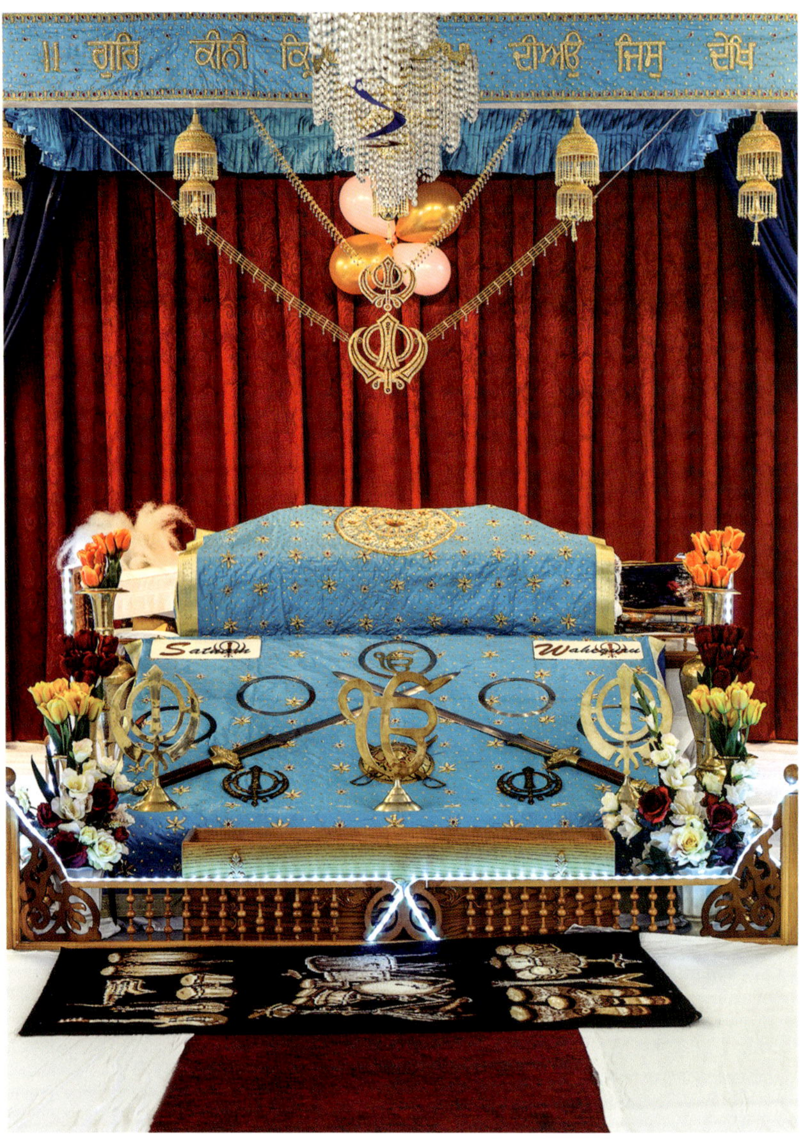

The *Guru Granth Sahib* rests on top of the altar (*palki*), the front of which is adorned with swords that symbolize the *Khalsa*

deeper meaning of the Sikh religion, it can't be seen past 12th and Walnut Street.

Vaisakhi commemorates the founding of the *Khalsa*, an association of Sikhs who pledge a special devotion to their religion. When the *Khalsa* was established in 1699 by the last Guru, Guru Gobind Singh Ji, it served as a fighting force to protect Sikhs and their religion from persecution by the Mughal Dynasty in Delhi. These days, the *Khalsa* symbolizes the utmost in dedication and commitment: *Khalsa* Sikhs stringently follow all five of the practices known as the "5 K's"—*kesh*, uncut hair; *kangha*, a comb to hold the hair in place; *kara*, a metal bracelet; *kachera*, special undergarments; and *kirpan*, a short sword.

Although *Vaisakhi* normally falls on April 13th, the date when Guru Gobind Singh Ji first founded the *Khalsa*, this Sunday is actually April 17th. For the West Des Moines *Gurdwara*, *Vaisakhi* is celebrated when all members of the community can join together, with all holidays held on the closest Sunday, as that is the regular day of prayer for most Sikhs living abroad. Monikpal Singh, an undergraduate student at Iowa State University, drives down as many Sundays as he can to participate in prayer. Sikhs do not observe a Sabbath, Jumu'ah, or Sunday service day. Sikhism does not set aside any special day for a day of prayer. In fact Sikhs stay busy every day, actively worshiping and performing *seva*—selfless service—for the Sikh community. Over a hundred people have gathered for the festival, putting aside issues of distance and health to make the extra effort to celebrate with each other. The *Gurdwara*, which usually sees an average of sixty people on a regular Sunday, is bursting with its increased numbers. Many have brought dishes to share, so food is abundant.

The day is one of reconnection for the community, not only among people, but also with regard to the true meaning of the *Khalsa*—of what it means to be a Sikh. Dr. Harpal Singh Bal, a retired professor of veterinary medicine from Iowa State University, recalls the "dusty basement" days of the Sikh community when they were a small group and did not yet have a temple. Nowadays, due to health limitations, he only makes it to the *Gurdwara* on special occasions. His experience, which spans decades and continents, contrasts with that of the little boy watching the bathing and rewrapping of the flag and pole with his mother.

The Sikh community holds true to their history and tradition in all that they do, but

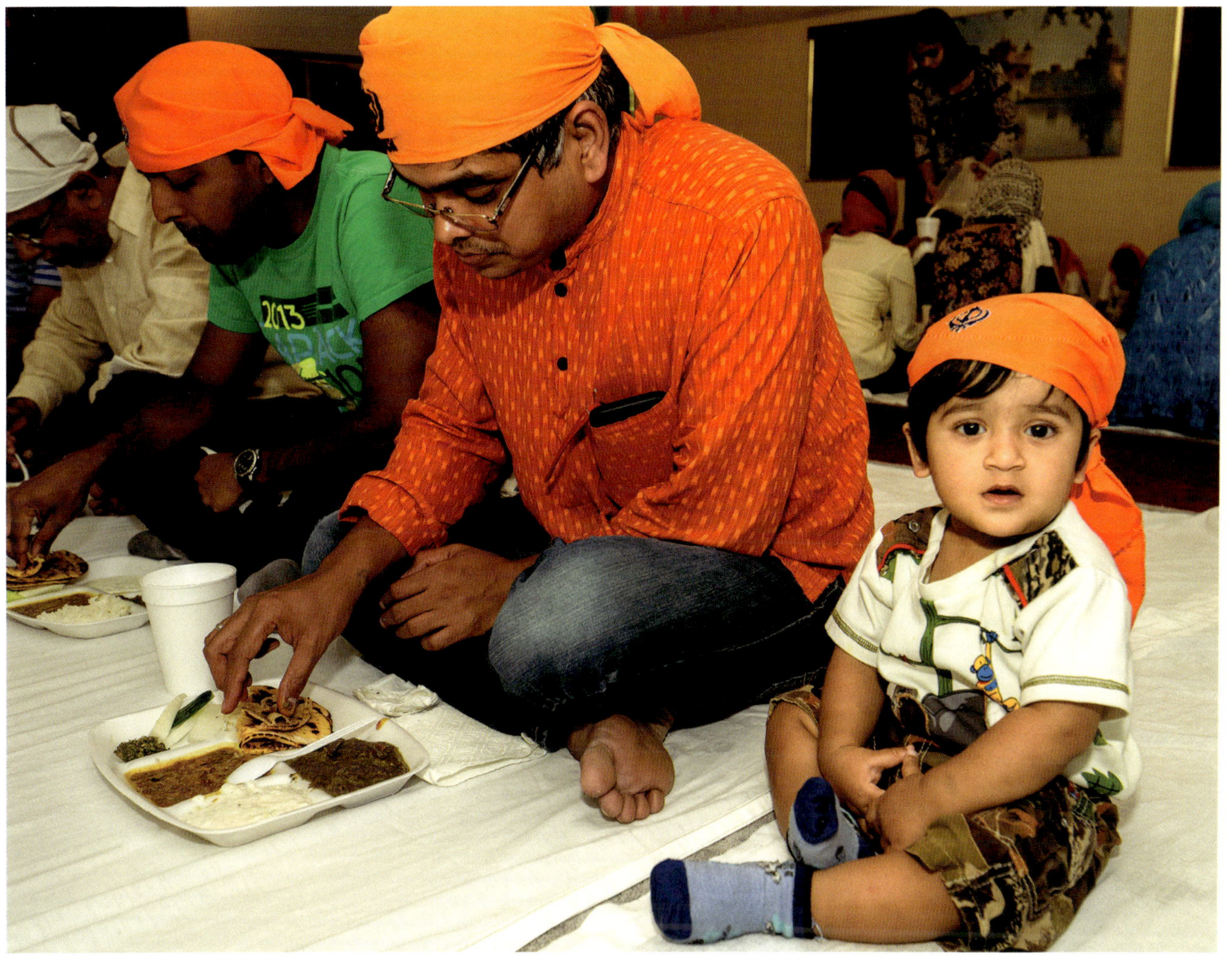

Members of the Iowa Sikh Association enjoy *langar*, while one of its youngest members, Rehan Iyer, the son of Gopi Iyer, poses

they have also adapted to their new home in the heartland of the United States. From the day of the week they have chosen for prayer to the necessity of abiding by flag height regulations, Sikhs have adapted their new environment. However, certain elements remain true despite the cultural divide. Covering one's head is a sign of respect, expected of both men and women. The *Gurdwara* provides head coverings for those who do not usually wear turbans.

In Sikhism, the turban is the traditional head covering of Sikhs who follow the "5 K's" and serves as a way to identify fellow believers. However, the choice to cut one's hair is a personal one, and not everyone at the West Des Moines *Gurdwara* practices this tradition. Individuals are treated no differently whether they uphold *kesh* or not.

In a post 9/11 world, growing up in America made some Sikhs re-evaluate these long-standing articles of faith. Monikpal is one such Sikh who cuts his hair and does not wear a turban. He explained that 9/11 "made my parents not want me to wear a turban. A lot of Americans saw turbans and thought 'terrorist.'" The turban is not the only distinctive feature of those who belong to the Sikh community. Sikhs choose to practice their faith in various ways, choosing when they will come to prayer and how they will raise their families.

Because Sikhism is comprised of diverse individuals and practices, these elements do not divide; they combine to create a unique religious community here in the heart of Iowa.

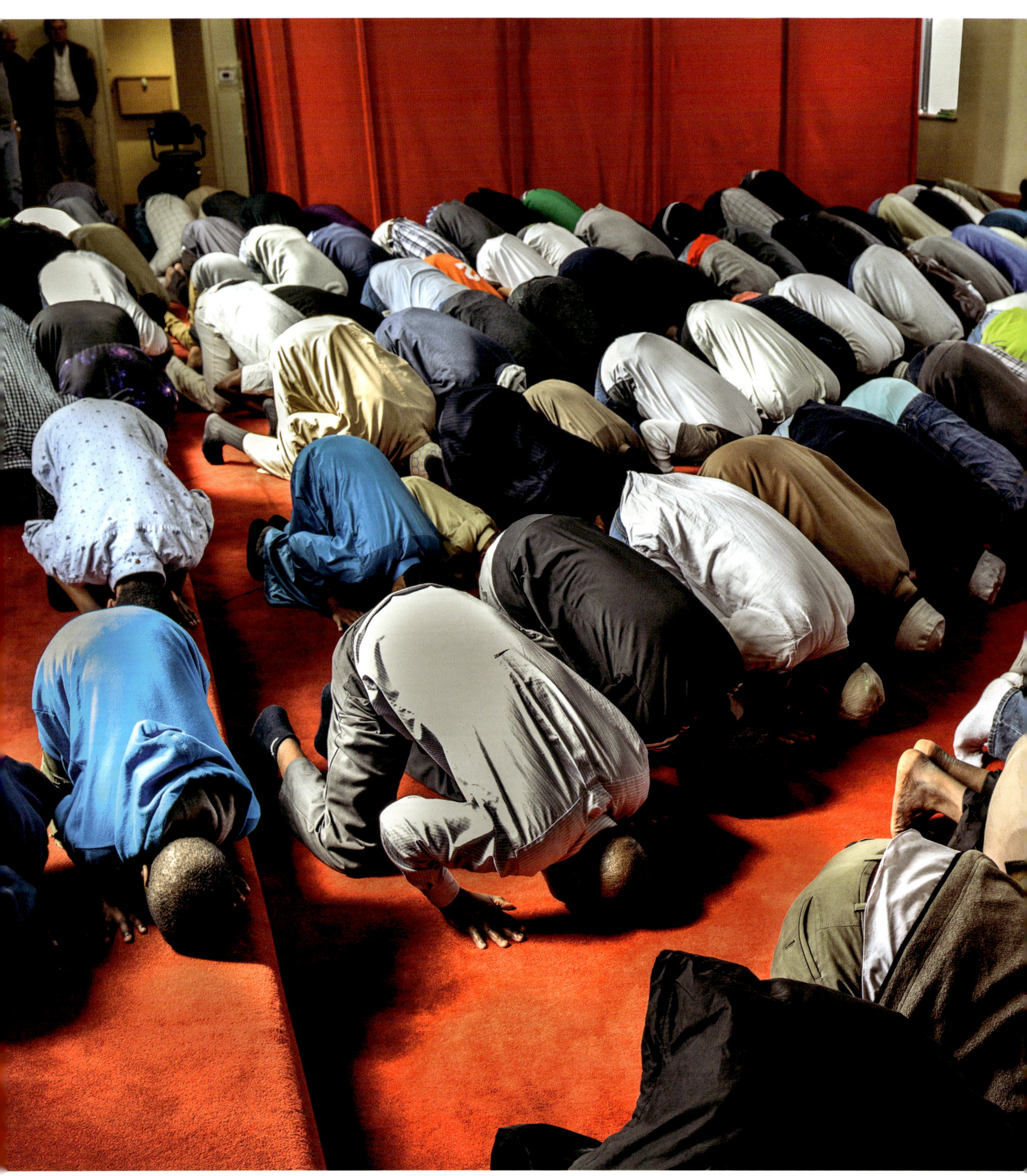

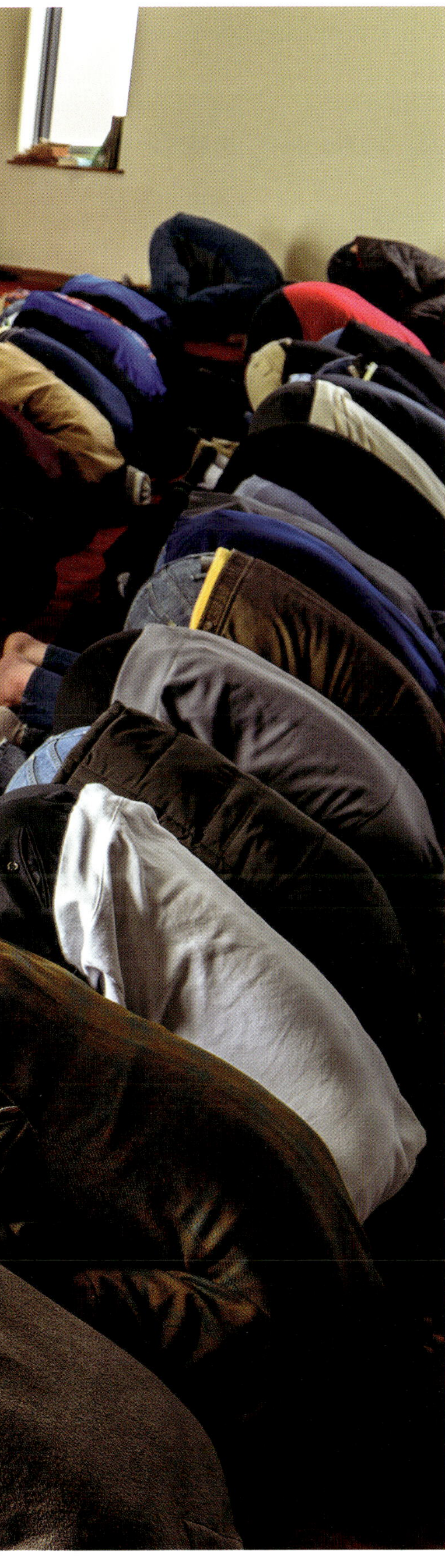

Masjid an-Noor

John Noble

IDENTITY At the bottom of the steps in the Masjid an-Noor mosque, Aisha Strain greets the men coming downstairs for the meal of meat and rice that she prepares for them after Friday prayers. *"As-salamu alaykum,"* she tells them. Peace of Allah be with you. The men respond with *"alaykum a-salaam,"* may the peace of Allah be upon you. Although Aisha only began attending the Muslim Community Organization (MCO) due to its proximity to her bus route, it was the welcoming atmosphere that made her stay. Having converted to Islam only six years ago, Aisha appreciates the egalitarian nature of the mosque because she once feared that they would not accept her. "Whether you're ten years old or a state legislator, it doesn't matter. I'm praying next to you," she says.

* * *

The imam, or religious leader, at Masjid an-Noor speaks highly of the practice of equality. Although this mosque is primarily made up of Sunni Muslims, all practitioners are welcome. This practice would be unheard of in some mosques, as attendance is usually restricted to one sect of Islam. In the United States, mosques often develop around ethnic identity, especially after

Male members of Masjid an-Noor perform the noontime prayer (*zuhr*) during the *jumu'ah* service

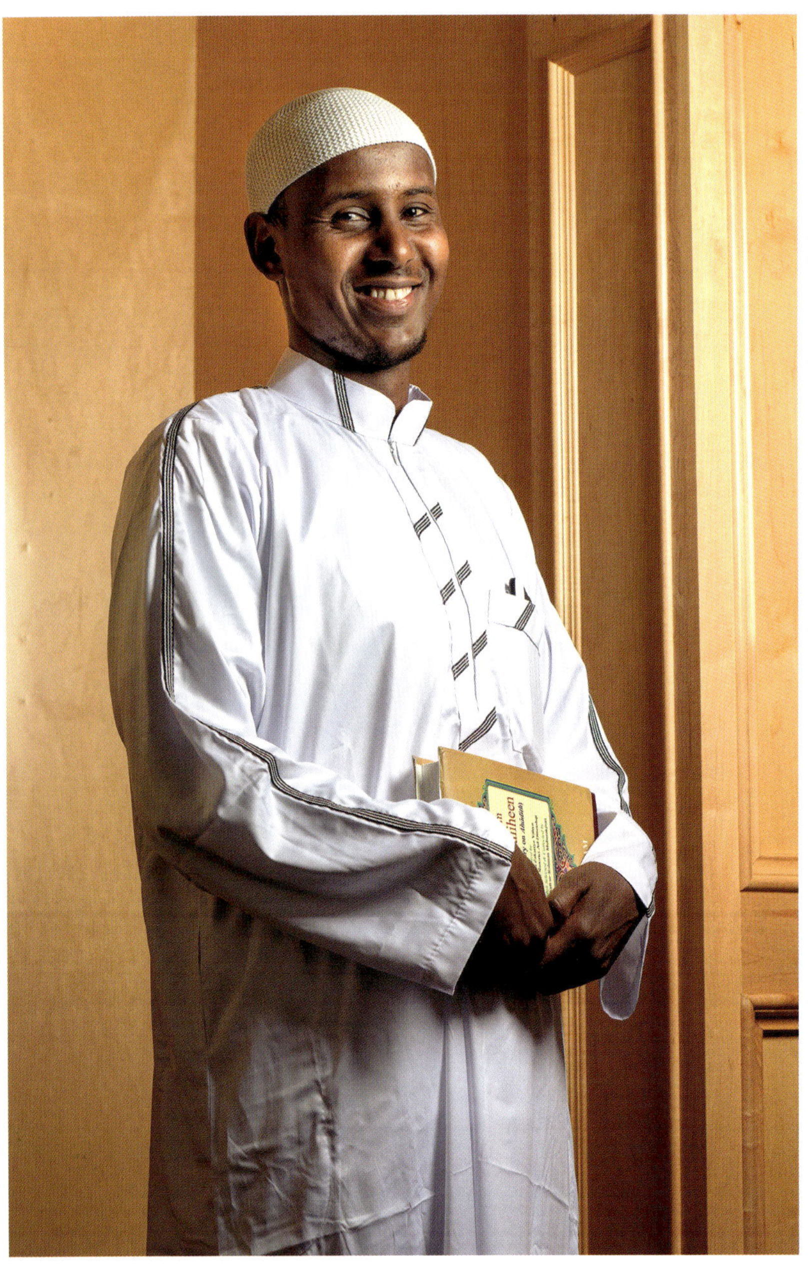

Imam Afrah Aden

mass migrations to the United States. Imam Afrah Aden, who presides at the mosque, recognizes the importance of these defined spaces but is excited about the possibility of diversity at MCO. "We can learn so much from each other," he shares.

The diversity of this community is truly astounding: students from Malaysia, businessmen who have lived in Des Moines for decades, and migrants from Somalia, Afghanistan, Pakistan, Sierra Leone, and Sudan. The theological differences of various sects provide challenges on an interpersonal, social, and global sphere. However, MCO readily takes on these challenges because the goal of a united Muslim community comes first.

Iqbal Rafi, a student at Drake University, admits that initially he found such diversity a challenge. Shia Islam is outlawed in the Sunni government of his native Malaysia, where most mosques are government-run. "Before this community, I only knew about one type of Islam." Now, Iqbal worships with those of varied beliefs and truly believes that he is better for it.

While prayers are given in the traditional Arabic, it's not uncommon to hear conversations going on in several different languages during mealtime. Many members know Arabic only through prayers; others speak it fluently. Since most members of the community speak conversational English, the Friday afternoon sermon, or *khutbah*, is given in both Arabic and English.

Imam Afrah's sermons draw from the Qur'an, the Muslim holy book, as well as the *Hadith*, the record of the Prophet's sayings and doings, and Islamic scholarship. He admits that finding teachings with cross-cultural application is difficult, especially in a community with so many cultures, ethnicities, and practices represented. However, he holds a deep belief that the message of the Qur'an is universal, a message for all people, regardless of their identities. He draws upon the Prophet Muhammad's final sermon where he tells his followers, "All mankind is from Adam and Eve—an Arab has no superiority over a non-Arab nor a non-Arab any superiority over an Arab; also, a white has no superiority over a black nor a black any superiority over a white except by piety and good action."

Faith, prayer, and humility before God unite this community across lines of class, race, ethnicity, and gender. Division is a human creation, many members will tell you, found outside the walls and security of this sacred space. In the holy space, the faithful are one.

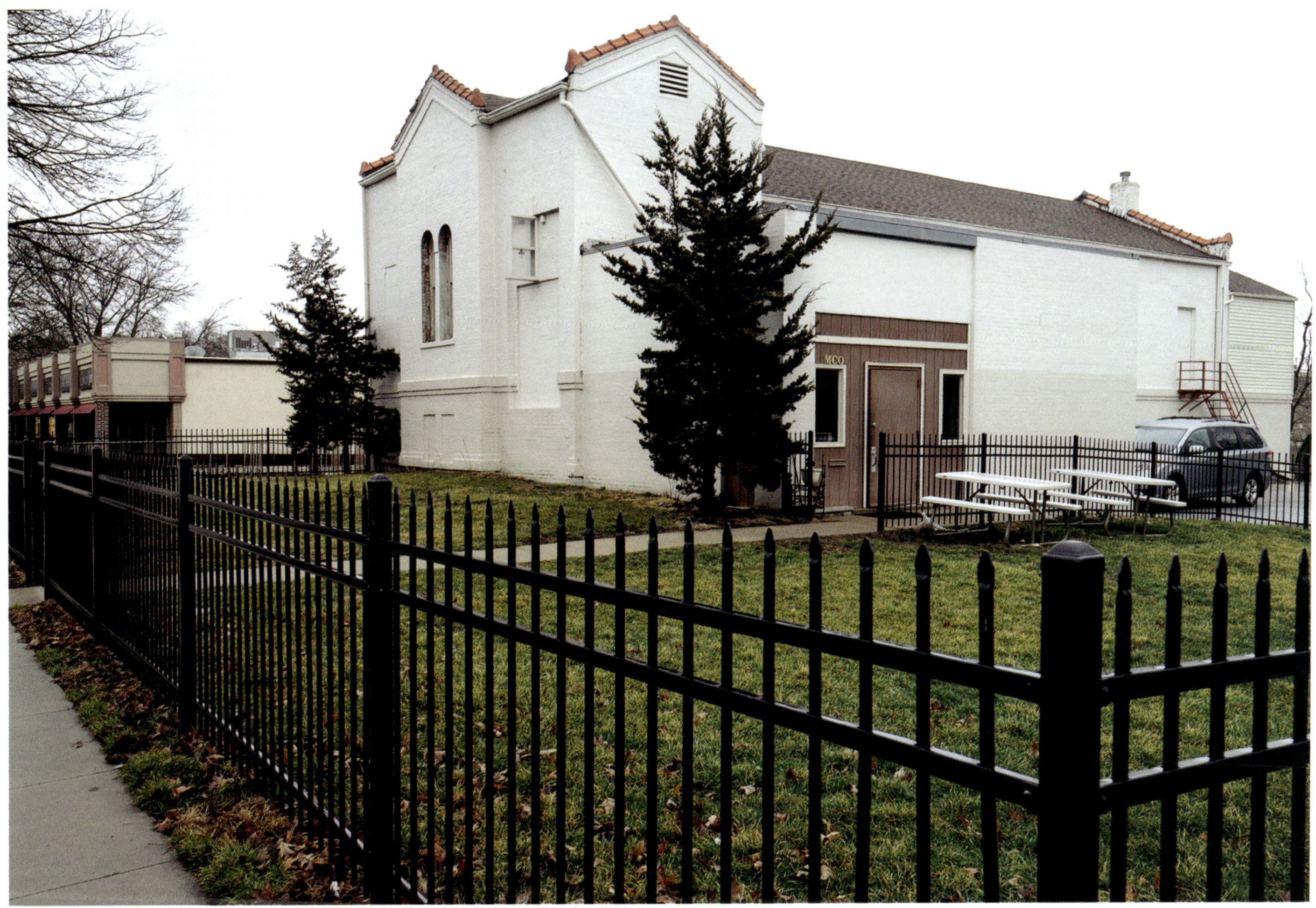

Masjid an-Noor

SPACE Imagine for a moment the Muslim call to prayer sounding over the rooftops of MCO's western Des Moines neighborhood: over the tree-lined streets of older homes, the coffee shop, the local pizza place, the nearby high school. "*Allahu Akbar*—God is the greatest." Christian churches in this same neighborhood sound their bells, some only on Sundays, others daily, on the hour. But in many nations around the world, it is the Muslim call that would sound locally. Here in Des Moines, the Muslim faithful, themselves, keep track of the prayer times.

Tucked behind a Hy-Vee Drug Store and strip mall on 42nd Street, Masjid an-Noor is barely recognizable as a mosque to passers-by. With its white tower, it looks vaguely like the Christian church it once was, but it's mostly an unremarkable two-story white building surrounded by a fenced-in grassy area. In addition to its former stint as a church, the building housed a number of organizations, including a Masonic Lodge.

A small group of men, women, and children attend the five Islamic prayer times throughout the day. For most of the day, though, there is little activity. Friday *jumu'ah* service is when the mosque fills up. President Khan reminds visitors to shut the gate as they enter this space since there is a busy street nearby and children play in the grassy areas.

The side entrance to the building opens into a foyer where entrants remove their shoes and put them on the racks surrounding the main floor. Posters have been hung, notifying members about local events sponsored by the Council on American-Islamic Relations, upcoming events

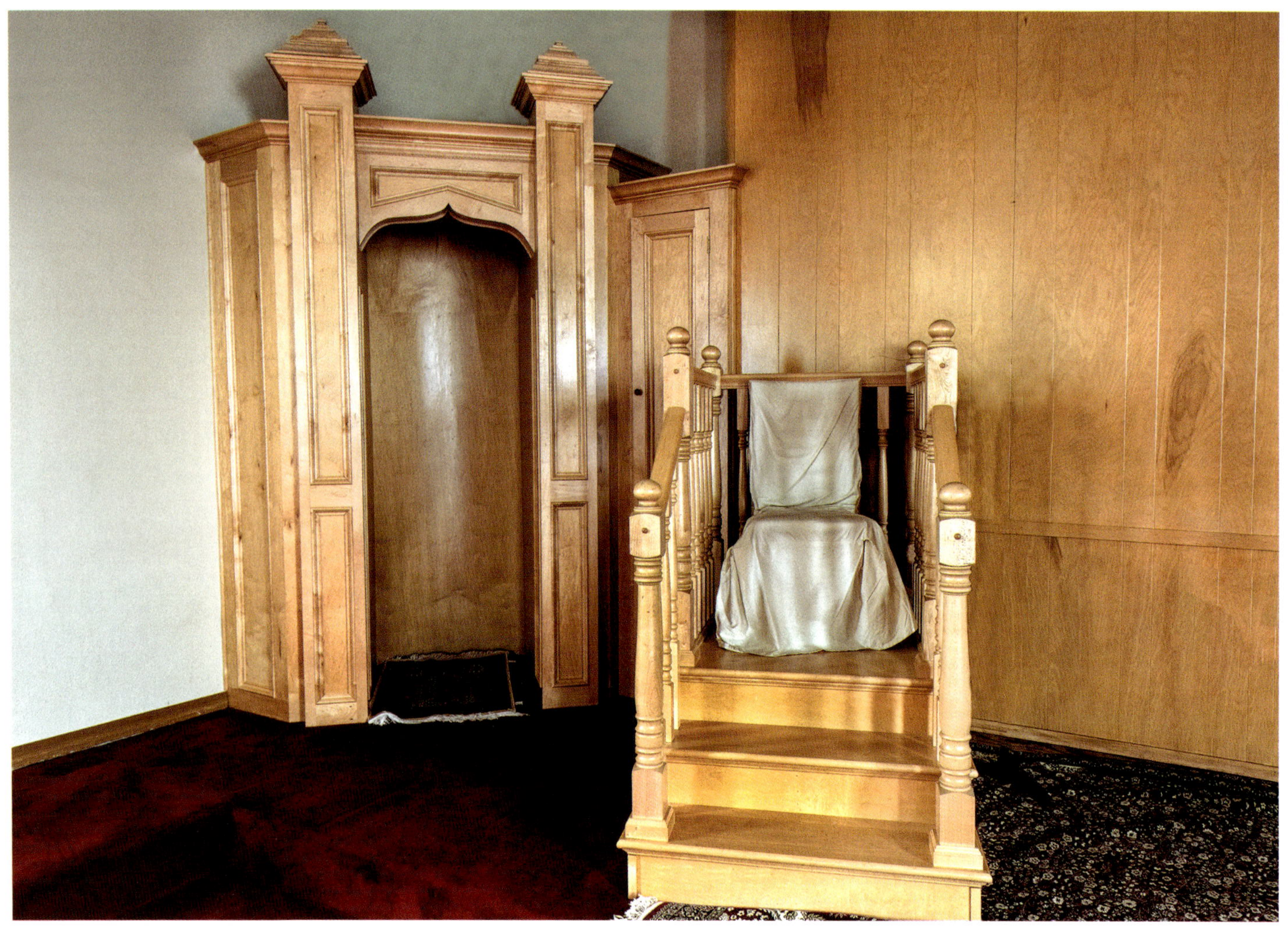

The masjid's *mihrab*, which points the direction to Mecca, and *minbar*, from which the imam delivers his *jumu'ah* sermon (*khutba*)

for the mosque, a chart of prayer times, and other general community announcements.

The MCO re-designed the interior to meet the sacred needs of its new community, sometimes in creative ways. For example, where some religious organizations might have the children's restrooms in the basement as first on their list for demolition, the knee-high faucets lining the walls now serve as a space for *wudu,* the ablution or ritual cleansing performed before prayer. Those multiple faucets once used by school children can accommodate a crowd.

After performing *wudu,* worshippers flow up the stairs to the prayer area where MCO president, Mohamad Khan, stands in the *mihrab.* The most important space in the mosque, this niche in the front left corner of the prayer room shows the *qibla,* or the direction of Mecca, the holy city of Islam, which is the direction Muslims face when they pray.

The prayer space is intentionally devoid of the kind of artwork one might find in a temple, synagogue, or church, as Muslims do not believe in depicting human beings through artwork. Where stained-glass windows might have once stood, translucent windows etched with beautiful Arabic calligraphy now filter light across the prayer space. Copies of the Qur'an and other prayer books are stacked neatly on each of the six windows, and people use them throughout the day. Red carpeting covers the floor of the space which is lined parallel with the *mihrab*. A raised step runs around the entire perimeter of the room.

The faithful enter in bare feet, each finding a spot in the room to kneel and begin their prayers. A divider covered in the same fabric as the carpet stands at the back of the room, separating men and women during prayer. President Khan explains that this practice is intended to discourage distraction during prayer.

A clock equipped with the day's five prayer times reminds the faithful when they are to return next. President Khan will be sure to vocalize that reminder as well, especially to the younger members of the community. Below the clock is a large display of the Five Pillars of Islam written in Arabic. These Pillars guide members through the foundational principles of their faith: the testimony of faith given by every Muslim, the guidelines of daily prayer, giving to the needy, fasting during Ramadan, and the pilgrimage to Mecca every Muslim able to make the journey is required to take.

Although the prayer room is sacred, life and vitality overflow in this public space where members of the mosque join together every Friday afternoon to share a meal. The men and women, separated by a divider in this space as well, share enthusiastic conversation about their lives. Here, engineers sit next to Drake students who are seated beside realtors. Egyptians sit next to Nigerians, and young next to old. All share in this experience; all treasure this space.

HISTORY Some members at MCO are used to informal prayer spaces—what some of the older members jokingly refer to as a "do-it-yourself" or "custom" mosque. Others, like the Malaysian students, come from a country where elaborate, massive mosques are the norm. But this place of worship is a mix of each.

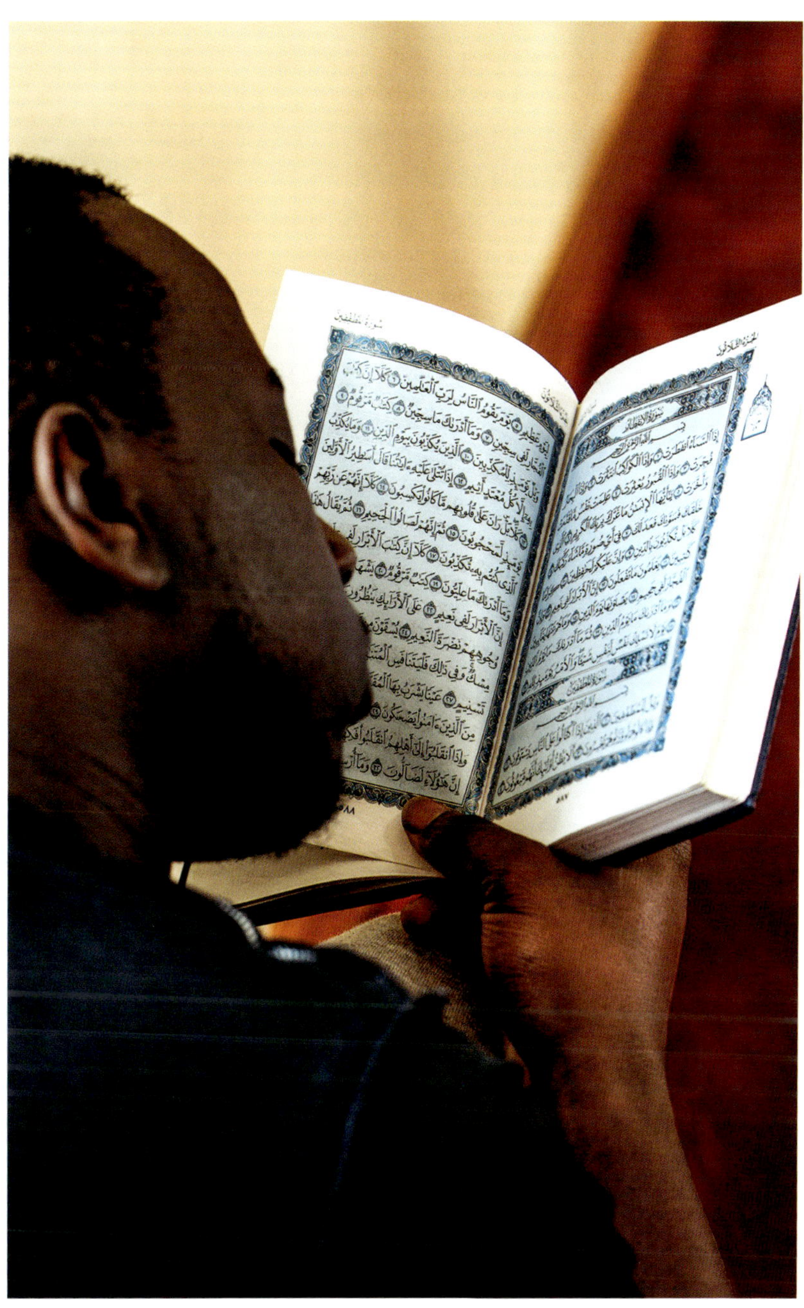

A member of Masjid an-Noor reads from the Qur'an

President Khan, who has lived in Des Moines with his family for four decades, worshipped in many different locations before beginning a "home mosque" where immigrants and other Muslims could worship together. Eventually, the need for a permanent spiritual home became clear. Members sought a place near their homes where they could practice their faith in comfort.

They also saw it as a valuable investment for Muslims in the community. In 2009, they found the building on 42nd Street and decided that it fit that very need.

The building's white church tower prompts a laugh from President Khan who tells of confused neighbors sometimes wandering in for Sunday services only to find a full-blown mosque inside.

Having this space, especially in Des Moines, comes with both opportunities and challenges. On one hand, Muslims from all over Des Moines can come here to worship, and many converts, like Aisha, have made MCO their spiritual home. On the other hand, a new challenge is presenting itself, as is clear from the packed prayer room that overflows down into the stairway. Since Des Moines boasts multiple mosques, the fact that MCO regularly draws over one hundred worshippers at a typical *jumu'ah* service is testament to the strong ties that have been built here, and to the growing community of Muslims in the metro area. Mosque leaders recognize that space is, once again, an issue.

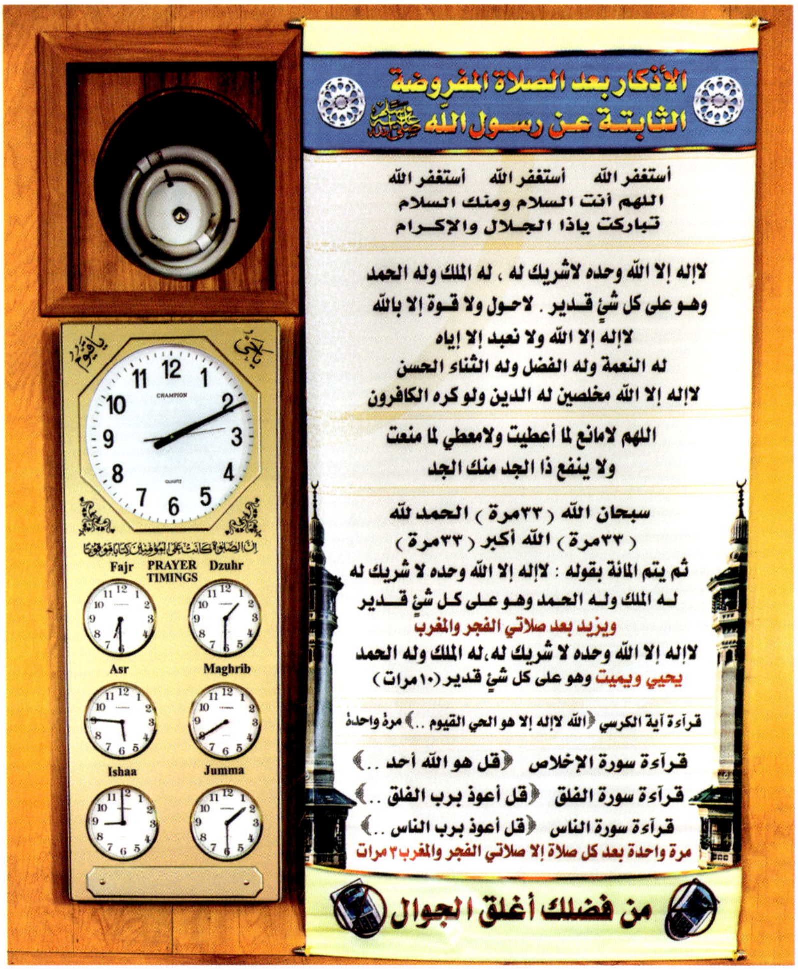

Most residents neighboring the mosque are non-Muslim. Imam Afrah reports that most members of the mosque have experienced at least some form of Islamophobia, although not necessarily in the neighborhood. Women who wear the *hijab*, a traditional covering for the head and chest, have been objects of fear or derision here in Des Moines. Understandably, then, they express fears about a political climate hostile to American Muslims. However, the leadership of the MCO views such misunderstandings as an opportunity rather than a threat. They are inspired to show non-Muslims in Des Moines what Islam is truly about. "When we are neighbors in the community," says Imam Afrah, "we can teach our neighbors that Islam is a religion of peace. We are part of this community."

The Muslim Community Organization demonstrates a balance between prayer and action—between the internal life of worship and the external life of service and outreach. From the beginning of its growth, Masjid an-Noor has served as both a gathering and worship space for Muslims as well as a center from which to show the city of Des Moines what Islam has to offer.

PRACTICE From young students to older imams, members cite prayer as the central act of their faith practice and of their personal devotion to Islam. Their devotion is strengthened by the knowledge that, locally and globally, a community of Muslims is centered on submission to Allah and the sacred act of prayer.

"We pray with our whole bodies, not just our voices or our hands," says Aisha. It is a powerful image: hundreds of members lying prostrate together participating in the service's call and

The mosque's clocks display the times of the daily prayers

response, in humility before God. "No matter who you are, no matter where you come from," says Iqbal, "you recite the same prayers." Even more powerful is the awareness that five times a day millions of Muslims around the globe are affirming the same belief in the same God and His message. "Since Muslims all over the world are praying these prayers throughout the day, I am part of a continuous wave of prayer being offered up to God," explains Aisha.

This frequency of prayer at designated hours is one of the Five Pillars of Islam, as established by the Prophet Muhammad. The position of the sun in the sky is what determines prayer times throughout the year, so a helpful chart at the entrance to the mosque explains the prayer times for the season.

Because, like most people, Muslims lead busy lives, attendance at daily prayer during the week can be sparse. Even though work may prevent them from attending, these prayer-goers know that praying alone at home or in the office is not the same as participating in daily prayer with other Muslims.

At a recent Friday sermon, Imam Afrah emphasizes the importance of outreach—of taking internal spiritual practice out into the neighborhood and the world. The faithful understand that, "In order to be a Muslim, one must live as a Muslim." Maintaining a regular prayer life matters, as does active community involvement, refraining from alcohol, and defending the faith to those around you. The imams encourage these practices, in part, because of the abundant negative perceptions of Islam in our culture. In this way, others witness the benefits of adherence to Islam. Community outreach need not look like direct preaching of the message of Islam; rather, the transformative effects of Islam in one's life speak for themselves.

Imam Afrah speaks proudly of MCO's efforts to reach young people, helping to curb violence and push back against neighborhood gangs. "We provide a safe and secure community grounded in faith for our young people. That is something they desperately need."

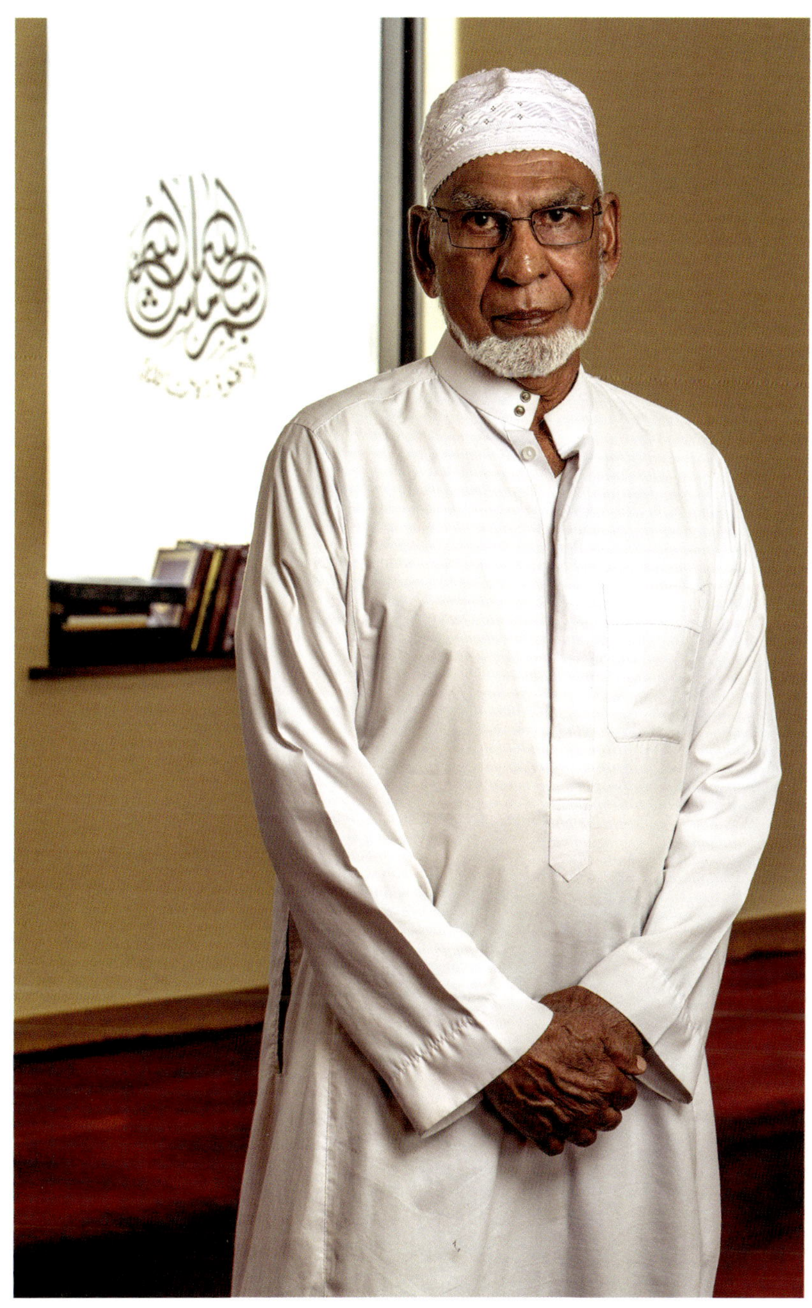

President Mohamad Khan

Whether it is through outreach to at-risk youth, or by encouraging members to live their faith even more deeply, the life of Muslims at MCO is grounded in a deep and powerful devotion to the tenets of Islam. They hope that this devotion will radiate out into the broader world, so that Muslims may continue living lives of piety and service.

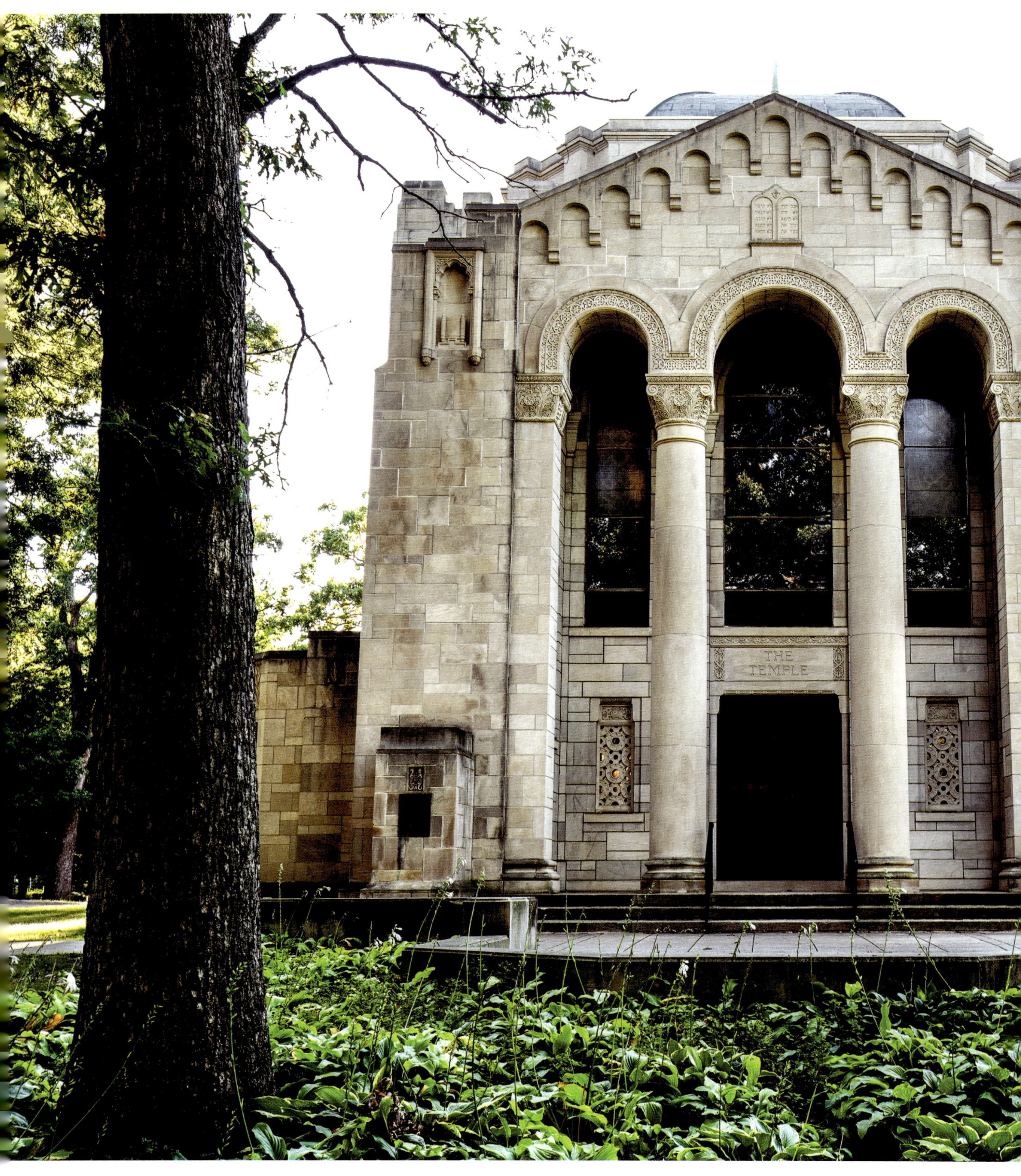
THE
TEMPLE

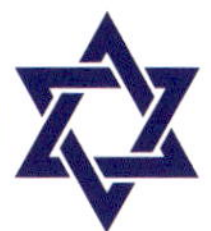

Temple B'nai Jeshurun

Nathan Jacobson

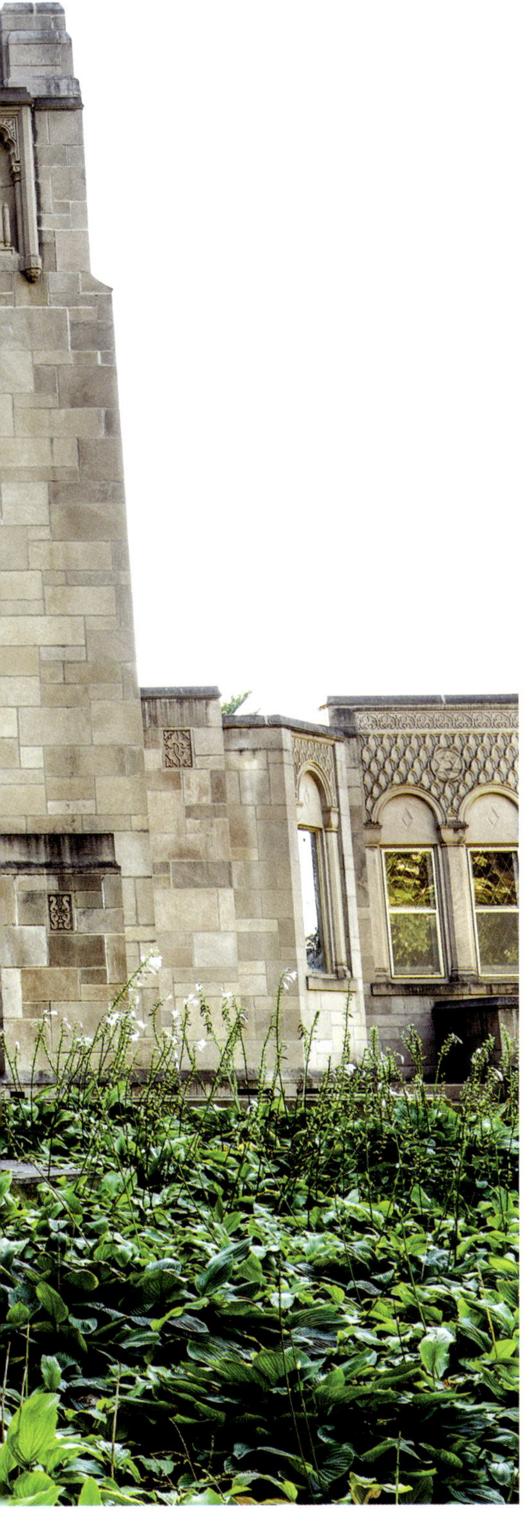

PRACTICE Chords strummed from a folksy guitar underscore the voices of cantors Ira and Laura singing "Hallelujah" from Psalm 150 of the Hebrew Bible for a packed Social Hall at Passover Seder. An English translation printed in the order of service assists those who may not know the meaning of every word. That way, all gathered can praise God through song, dance, and worship.

One of the most important of Jewish holidays, Passover commemorates the escape of the Jewish slaves from their Egyptian slaveholders through God's liberation. On this Friday evening marking the start of the seven-day holiday, hungry people fill the tables in the expansive Social Hall lined with tall windows, Jewish antiques, and a big stone fireplace, ready to indulge in the Passover meal. Scripture commands the faithful to read the story of Jewish Exodus from Egypt as part of the Seder. After the reading, children dart from table to table, laughing and playing, as adults enjoy conversation over sweet glasses of wine. Katie, a new member at the Temple, remarks that Passover is her favorite Jewish holiday because the physical act of eating Passover foods like the Jewish unleavened bread *matzah* gives contemporary religious significance to the stories and traditions of Judaism's past.

Temple B'nai Jeshurun

"It seems like they're moving pretty quickly tonight," I overhear someone remark to his table. In other Jewish denominations, the Seder service may incorporate many steps, ritual objects, and foods lasting until midnight or even later. Here at B'nai Jeshurun and many other Reform temples like it, briefer services feature more music, and the predominant use of English rather than Hebrew reflects the preferences of this modern and progressive congregation. By nine o'clock, festivities are done for the night.

Passover Seder attracts many more attenders than does a typical Shabbat service at Temple B'nai Jeshurun. In contrast with a Social Hall abuzz with lively congregants, a smaller number of faithful gather on a typical Friday at sunset to observe the start of Sabbath. However, the core of a Reform Temple lies neither in the smaller number gathered for regular Shabbat nor in the crowds filling the Social Hall at a Passover Seder. Rather, the words of Rabbi Kaufman of B'nai Jeshurun ring true: the Temple embraces the modern trends seen in the outside world. The Reform Movement proudly serves congregants in ways that are accessible to all. In addition to offering monthly children- and family-oriented services, this faith tradition adapts quickly to changes in culture by embracing LGBT people, for example, as well as women's ordination and by using gender-neutral language about God. Temple B'nai Jeshurun wants any and all people to feel comfortable walking through their doors.

In this respect, strict enforcement of practices or religious observance is not what's most important for attenders: it's the sense of belonging found at B'nai Jeshurun.

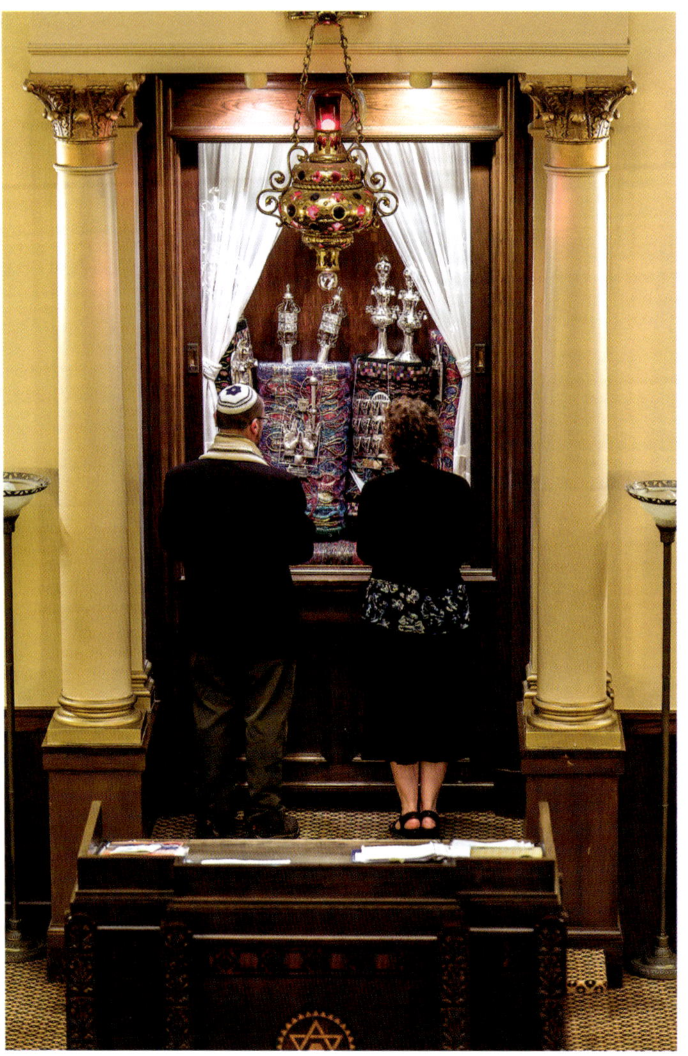

SPACE At 5:30 p.m. on a Friday night, a vibrant air of familiarity and connection fills the Social Hall as congregants gather for fellowship at tables filled with a variety of cheeses, crackers, and wine. Friends embrace, asking after children and pets or remarking on recent political developments. In a little while, someone looks up at the clock and calls people to the sanctuary for the Shabbat service. Relaxed and still conversing quietly, congregants file down the narrow hallway.

A holiness and reverence pervades the moment as people cross the sanctuary threshold, gazing up at the expansive dome and stained-glass chandelier. The dome appears to reach into the sky where a sun-like painting stretches to its peak. Outside, the actual sun sets, illuminating the stained glass lining the walls of the sanctuary in subtle hues that filter onto the wooden pews.

"The sanctuary is like God is talking to you," says attender Wendy Beckerman, who

Rabbi Kaufman and Cantorial Soloist Laura Sparks facing the Torah Scrolls in the Torah Ark (*Aron Kodesh*)

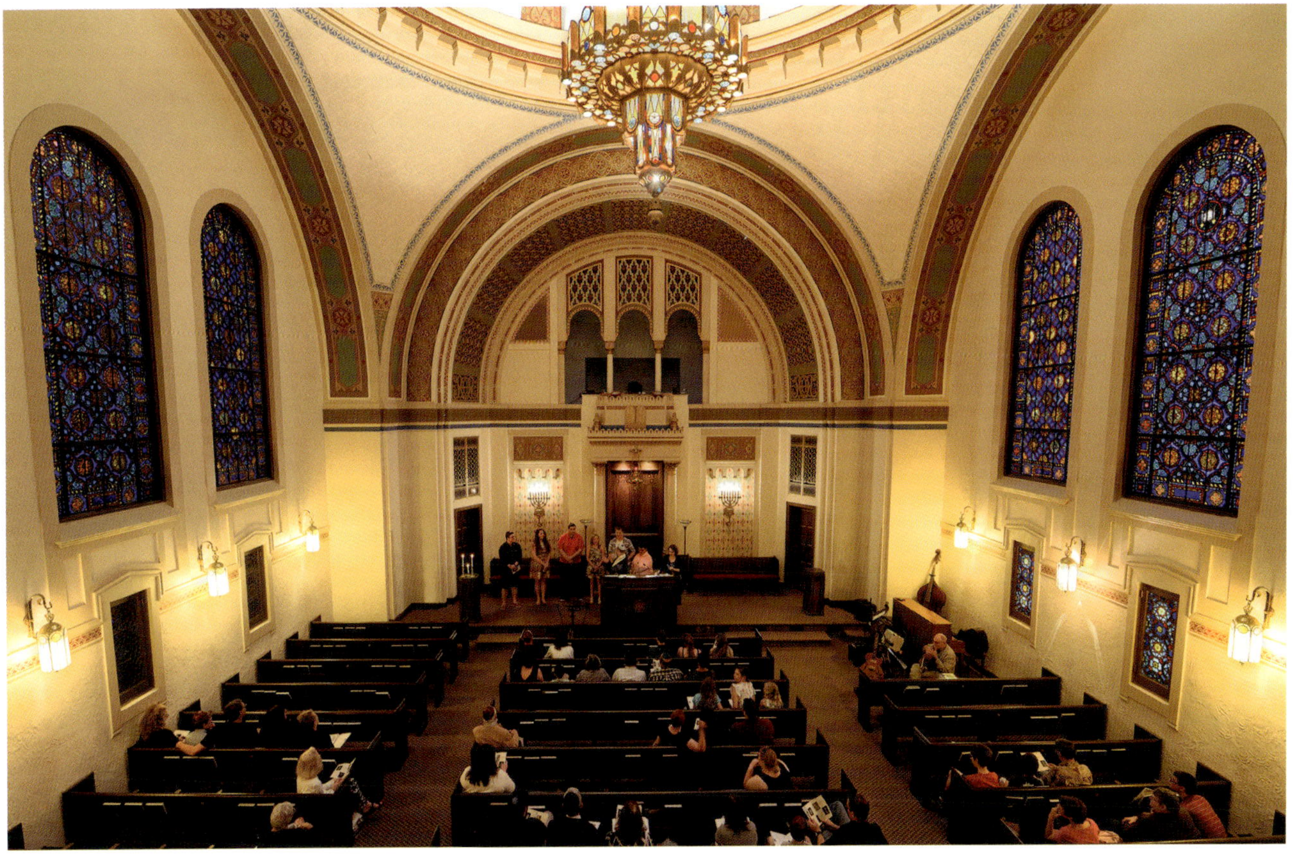

Sanctuary of Temple B'nai Jeshurun during a Friday evening Shabbat service

also leads educational programs at the Temple. Transformation occurs in this room, shifting the faithful from a focus on ordinary human affairs to one of transcendence and awe. People relax into the comforting atmosphere of this space. For Wendy, the sanctuary is "what keeps drawing people back" to B'nai Jeshurun. For long-time attender Elyse Weiss, being swept up in the reverence and holiness of the sanctuary brings her peace. With a warm smile, she describes how her thoughts wander and she loses track of time.

"The Sanctuary takes on a special quality that has sanctity in and of itself," explains Jake Jacobs. "It has meaning for everyone, the entire community. There's a quality of beauty that shapes your focus." Or, as Rabbi Kaufman puts it, "In the Jewish tradition, we have this idea of *Kadeish*, which means sanctified. Something that is sanctified is separated from the norm....The goal for the sanctuary is that things will take place in an environment that is not normal." This space is reserved for divine interaction. The dome transports the mind into the realm of the beyond. The windows shine God's colorful presence into the hearts of congregants. Communal prayers rise along the arching dome of the sanctuary, echoing upward and embracing the congregation with a sense of awe. In this space, God is distant, surpassing true human understanding; at the same time, intimacy characterizes the relationship, despite this distance.

"I think you can feel it," Holden Terpstra says of the Temple. "You can feel a presence—a presence of something not even necessarily divine, but of the heart that was put into building it." For Holden, meaning occurs in the vaulted stained-glass windows and Middle-Eastern architectural motifs. Jewish hands of the past have transformed this space into an abiding monument to Jewish belief.

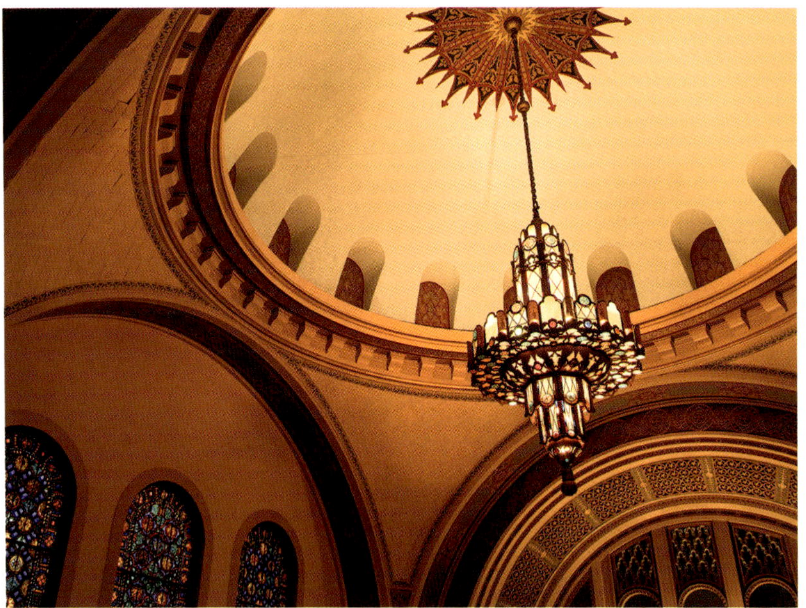

Ceiling and chandelier of Temple B'nai Jeshurun's sanctuary

In a world filled with technology and online connection, the sanctuary remains a haven of divinely personal communication that inspires and calms the soul.

HISTORY Founded in 1873, Temple B'nai Jeshurun was Des Moines' first Jewish congregation. Since that time, the Temple has served as a leader for the Jewish people of Des Moines and the larger metro area, hosting interfaith forums and partaking in service work around the metro area. The community's firm roots are built on Reform Jewish values.

At the same time, B'nai Jeshurun's history is largely shaped from its close relations with Des Moines' other Jewish congregations, Tifereth Israel and Beth El Jacob. While they differ in religious practice and theology, they come together in dialogue as Jewish people. The sense of connection across denominational lines runs deep among those who frequently attend one another's services and events. The camaraderie shared by these Jewish faith organizations traces back to their common identity, one shaped by the largely non-Jewish region in which they find themselves.

Like others, Jake studies Judaism's extensive history and complexity. He visits all Jewish congregations, finding that each offers its own perspective on Judaism and the ways it should be practiced and lived. For his own practice, he finds great meaning in the purely Orthodox prayers, yet loves the "warm and dedicated" group found at B'nai Jeshurun. The larger Jewish community of Des Moines is under the umbrella of the Jewish Federation, Jake explains. The Federation is the organizational body that attempts to capture the Jewish voices of Des Moines so that their collective identities and histories can be represented and celebrated together.

The Temple's history goes beyond its establishment as a prominent congregation in Jewish Des Moines, and it continues to shape the lives of the B'nai Jeshurun community today. For Elyse Weiss, it has been a space of Jewish connection in a city without many Jews. The relationships she has formed in this space could not have occurred outside these walls.

The Temple is "home" for Wendy Beckerman, as well—the place she keeps returning to and that nourishes her life. Her Jewish education began at the Temple years ago. It shaped who she is, and now, in turn, Wendy shapes the lives of the Jewish children in her classes. Life, faith, and learning are constantly coming full circle for her: students from years ago bring in their own children for a Temple education. These children shape the Temple's history and may, themselves, return with unique experiences and lives, a cycle of life and learning that enriches all.

The long-standing nature of community is important to those of the Jewish faith, explains Rabbi Kaufman. A connection to ancestors and to a sense of the past guides congregants as they balance the sometimes competing interests of tradition and modernity: "We are going in the direction that our past has led us. Because of the nature of Reform Judaism as an individual-based

Rabbi David Kaufman

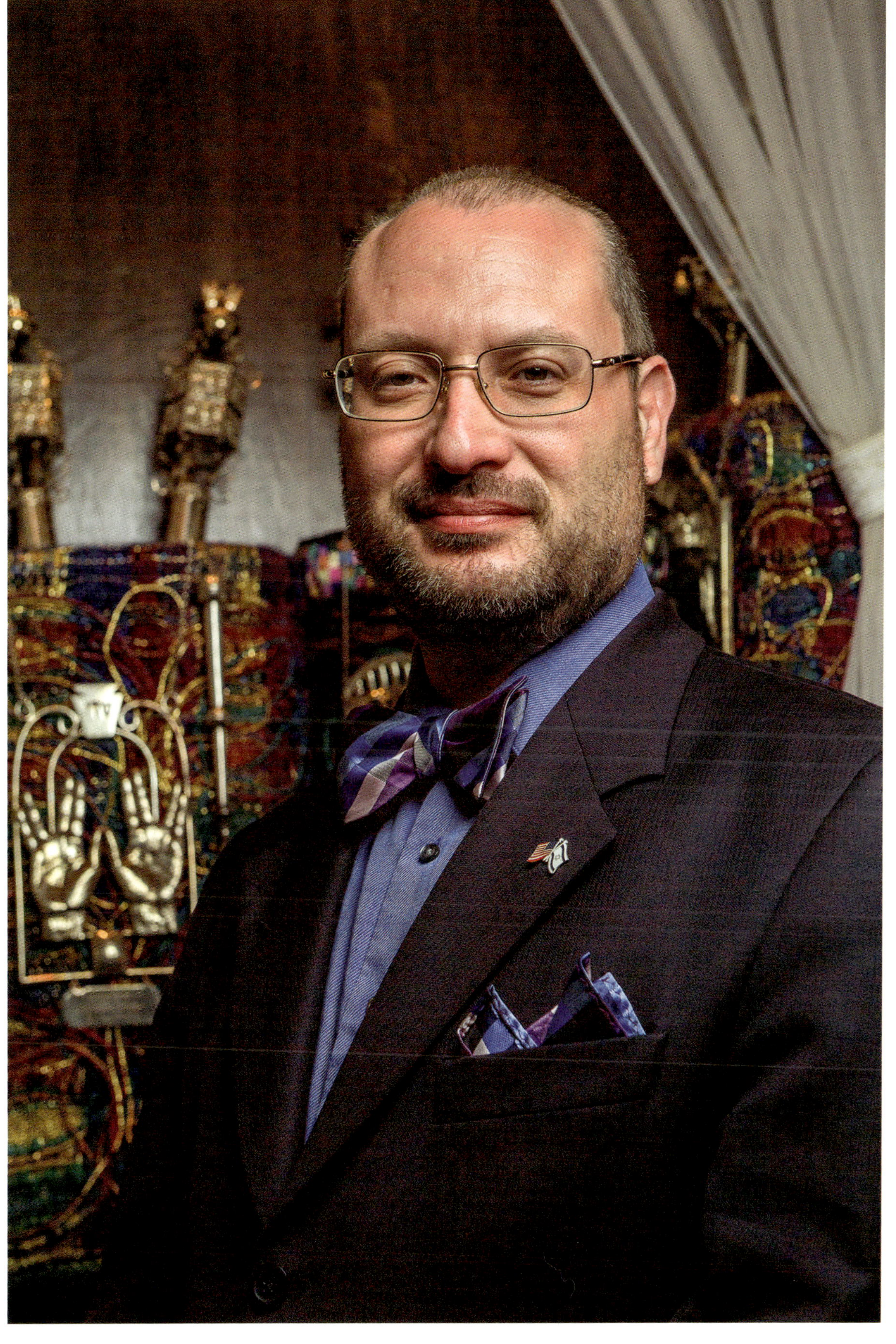

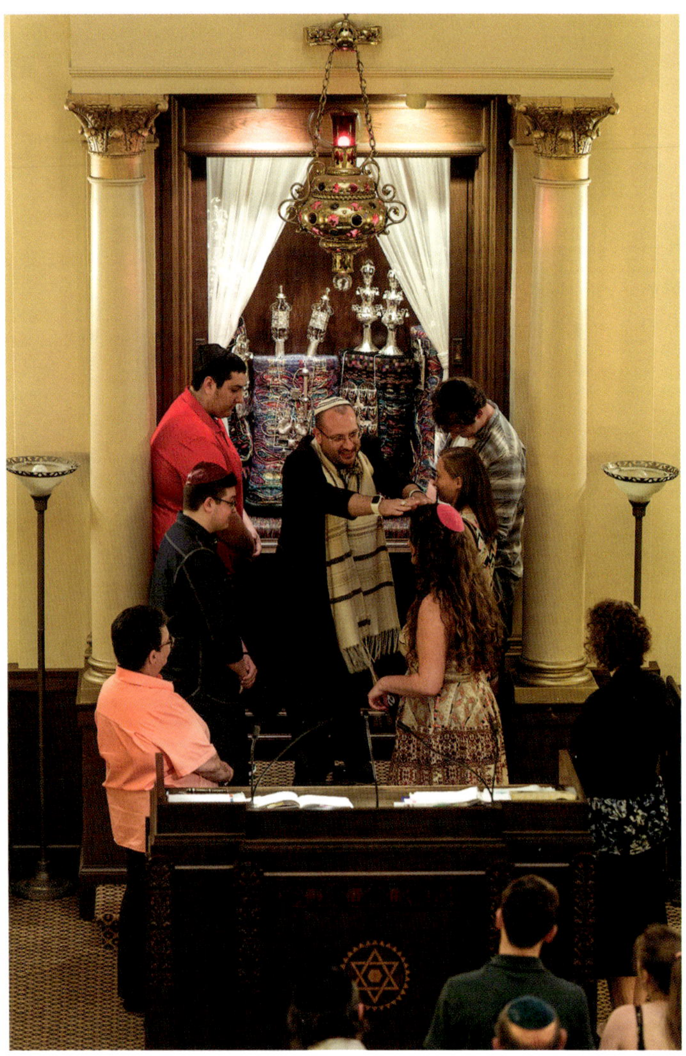

Rabbi Kaufman blessing Temple B'nai Jeshurun's graduating seniors

religion that can go in all kinds of directions, if you have that grounding in history and understanding of it, you're, in a sense, continuing what the people before you have done."

The Temple provides the congregation with a sense of belonging and rootedness to a faith tradition that has existed since long before their time. The faithful come and go where life takes them, yet they find meaning within the walls of B'nai Jeshurun.

IDENTITY The sight of children dashing around the room with chocolate from dessert smudged across their faces is common on first Fridays at Temple B'nai Jeshurun. One Friday each month, the Temple offers a kid-friendly service complete with skits, campfire songs, interactive games, and popcorn. As is typical, Ira and Laura lead services while a guitar and bass accompany them with upbeat Hebraic or Yiddish songs. Congregants talk and laugh together, attempting to wrangle their children. It is Rabbi Kaufman who manages to capture the children's attention when he holds up a picture book and reads in a variety of animated voices to the mesmerized young ones. In the background, parents and congregants relax at their tables.

Audrey, Jake, Gail, Elyse, and Holden sit together, sharing dessert. Holden, only 17, is studying a complicated Hebrew numeric system. He's about a year into his conversion process. Audrey and Jake converted at much later phases in their lives—Audrey after her children completed their Jewish education and Jake after the birth of his first daughter. In each case, their Jewish spouses inspired the belief system that has now become so meaningful to them. Gail and Elyse are the only Jews-by-birth at the table, Gail having grown up in an Orthodox home and Elyse having been raised a Conservative Jew.

At one point Jake discusses a Jewish mystical text he has recently studied. Not long after, Elyse adamantly expresses her love for Drake and local sports teams. Mention of the current political cycle arises, prompting many at the table to share their left-leaning ideals while holding true to their candidate of choice. They enjoy each other's company and learn from each other at the same time, whether that be Holden sharing his latest experiment with food or stories of Elyse's newly adopted dog.

A myriad of voices and identities comprise the people of B'nai Jeshurun. They represent different stages in their personal and religious lives, yet the Reform tradition and physical space of the Temple bring them together. For Jake and many others, Reform's roots created this congregation. With fewer theological requirements and a strong

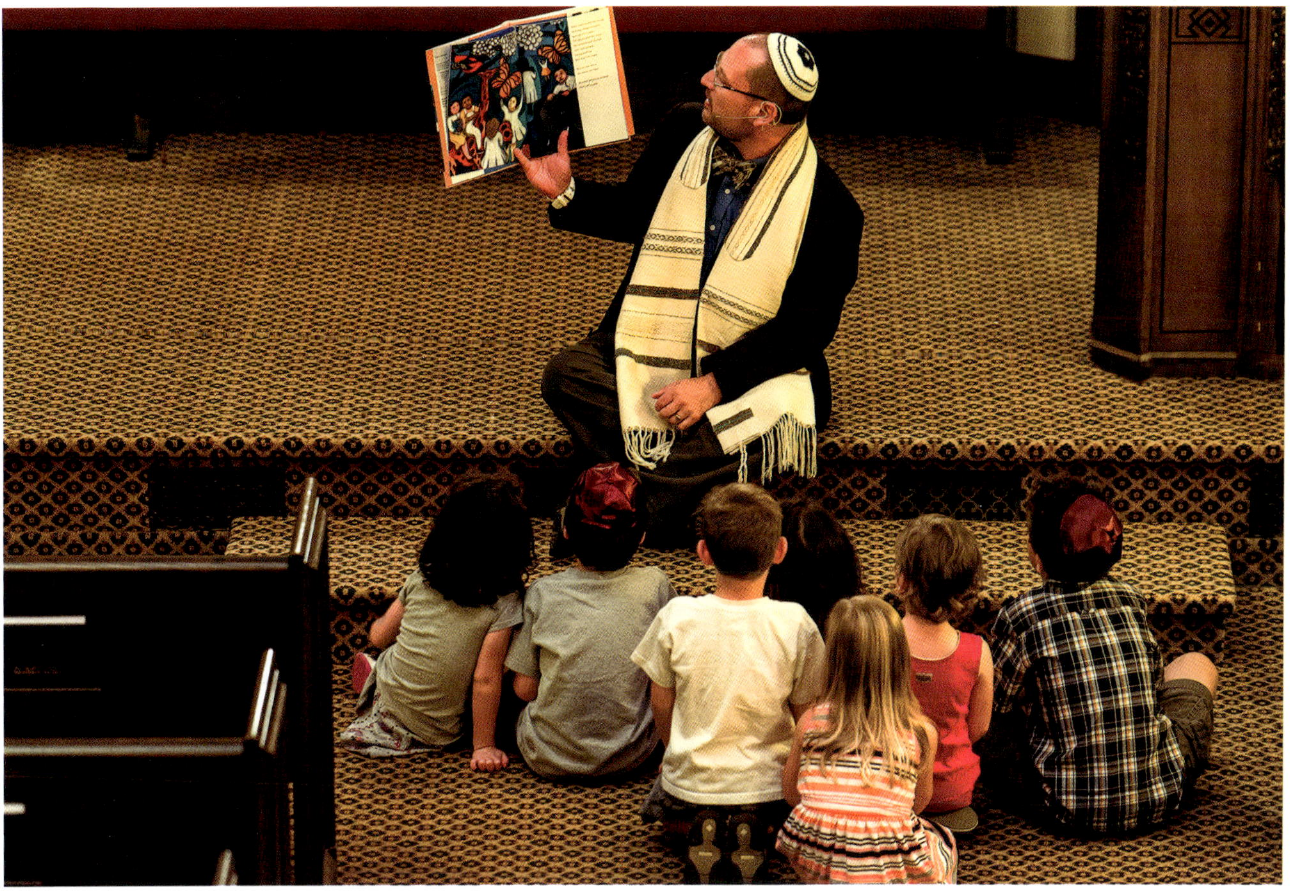

Rabbi Kaufman delivering the children's sermon

ethic of inclusiveness, the doors are opened wide, encouraging people from all walks of life to enter and search for meaning within a Jewish context.

For this Reform community, attendance at Friday Shabbat services is not mandatory, nor is partaking in every holiday celebration. People do what is right for them. Some hold Shabbat services in their own homes with other members of the Temple. Others may only attend family services in the Social Hall because they have young children. "You don't always know why you do it," says Wendy Beckerman. "You just do it." In other words, no cookie-cutter figure encapsulates the identity of a congregant of B'nai Jeshurun. All are welcome.

"When I look at my life, I've mostly socialized with non-Jewish people," says Elyse. That's one reason why the fellowship she finds at Friday night Shabbat services and during the conversations around a table in the Social Hall are so important. "I felt a need to get connected with the Jewish community because there are so few in Des Moines. I go to Temple to keep my Jewish life complete." For Elyse, the Temple provides a space to be Jewish in a way that isn't readily available in daily life. Holden comes to the Temple because, "it has shaped my morals, but it's done more than that. It has made me a more kind-hearted person." His mind, outlook, and actions continue to change because of the people he finds in this holy, yet relaxed, space.

The Temple is a place of transformation, refuge, and diversity. Differing theological, social, political, and personal beliefs coexist and flourish here. Under the Reform umbrella, Temple B'nai Jeshurun promotes individual choice and agency in living one's life within a supportive, religious setting. As Wendy put is, "this is just a very friendly, loving community of people...I keep coming for the people themselves."

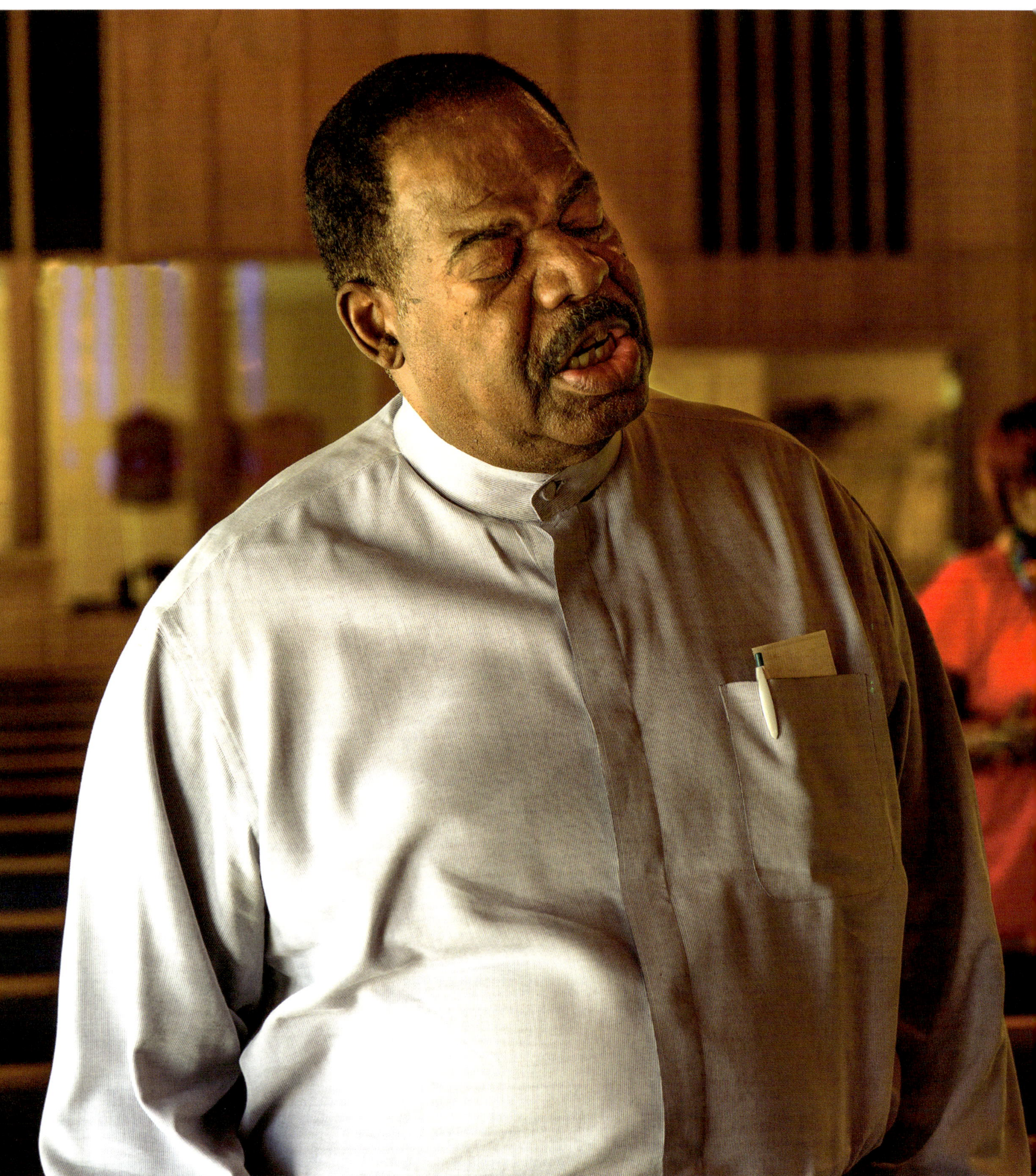

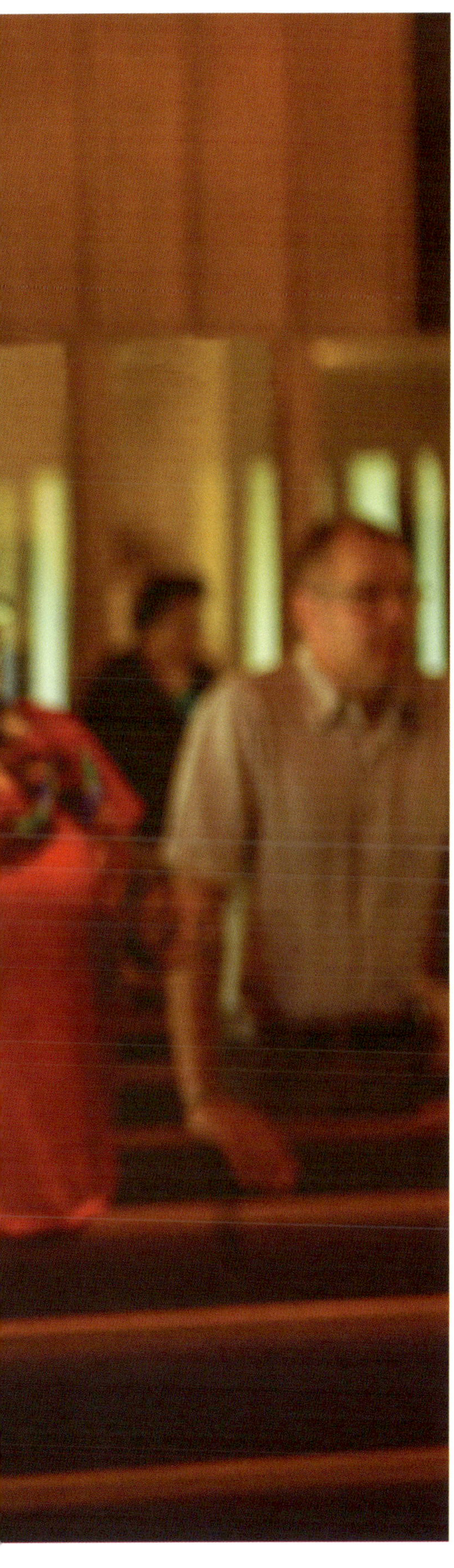

Burns United Methodist Church

Kayla Schween

IDENTITY Historically a predominantly African-American congregation, Burns United Methodist is a faith community where all are welcome and love and hugs abound. Many members have been attending Burns since their childhood, as several generations did before them.

Since the church's founding in 1866, African-Americans in Des Moines have had a place to worship freely within a tight-knit community of support. This tradition has continued to the present. Betty Jackson, who relocated to Des Moines from North Carolina, remembers how the older folks of the congregation welcomed her, helping her find a church home. For Joyce Wilks, Burns has been a "loving family" ever since the warm welcome she received in the late 1980s.

As part of the third largest Christian denomination in the United States, Methodists believe God is one Being, revealed in three distinct persons: Father, Son, and Holy Spirit. God came to the world through His son Jesus Christ, both true God and true man. To reconcile humankind to God, Jesus was crucified, but He will return one day to bring the Kingdom of God to Earth.

Harvey Andrews singing during a service at Burns United Methodist Church

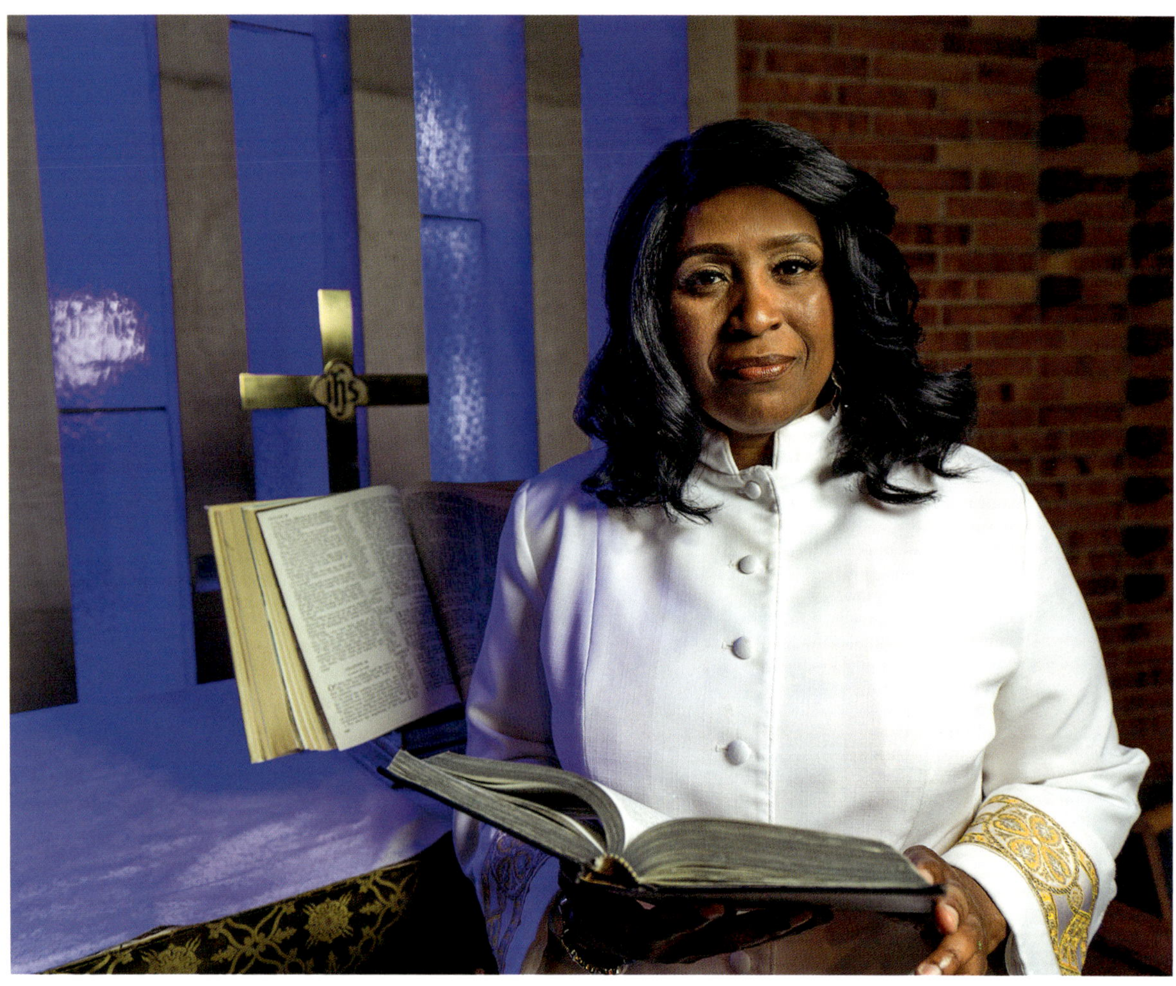

Pastor Angela Lewis

Methodism was founded in 18th century England by John Wesley, who sought reform in the Church of England. "Do all the good you can, by all the means you can, in all the ways you can, in all the places you can, at all the times you can, to all the people you can, as long as ever you can," is a famous Wesleyan aphorism.

Methodists are brothers and sisters in Christ and children of God who are made in His image. They regard their church as the body of Christ and each member as part of that body. The Bible, their sacred text, is believed to be God's Word and is used as a guidebook for life. Their mission is to make Disciples of Christ, transforming the world and supporting believers along their journey of faith.

"I practice Christianity through those I come across and my family," says member Harvey Andrews, who was raised within the Methodist church. For Mr. Andrews, becoming a member at Burns meant familiarity through practice. "Burns is like the church I went to as a teenager," he says. Tradition and consistent values endure among all Methodist churches. Members experience God's grace through love and faith in action, an experience vital to Methodism and to Christianity. Through the practices of ministry and service, members dedicate their lives to God.

Christianity is a religion of fellowship, and Burns United Methodist Church is a strong community of believers who have created a family in Christ committed to service, worship, and the glory of God. However, according to Joyce Wilks, "When you have family, you have disagreements."

Families aren't perfect, and members are not expected to be perfect, either. "Churches are diverse, and people are always going to be people," said Mr. Andrews. The congregants are true to themselves and honest about their lives, creating a safe community where people can be vulnerable and accepted. Congregants do not shy away from their opinions; they strive to create an atmosphere of open dialogue among members.

Members proudly identify as the oldest African-American congregation in Des Moines, one that is continuously transforming and yet always true to its foundation of family and community. The church provides a community of support through trying times and personal strife, delivering spiritual guidance for followers of Christ. "Burns being a smaller church makes it like a family," shares Steve Kitchen, a third generation member who has attended the church for almost 60 years. "Two church members actually got me a job pretty early on," he adds.

Burns is rooted in its people, and the people are rooted in Burns.

SPACE Azure light from stained glass windows bathes the sanctuary, illuminating walls lined with tapestries befitting the themes of the season. At once large and awe-inspiring, yet warm and personal, the interior, composed of warm woods and homey brick, encourages quiet reflection. Rows of straight-backed wooden pews facing the sanctuary keep church-goers comfortably seated while maintaining an atmosphere of solemnity. Up front, the pulpit leaves space for a choir and band complete with a set of drums occasionally played by Pastor Angela Lewis, who is, as it happens, a talented jazz drummer. In addition to Sunday morning worship and prayer meetings, the spacious church has plenty of room for community meetings and Sunday school classes.

During Easter and Pentecost, cream-colored tapestries depict the holy cross in one panel and Jesus Christ, with wounds and a crown of thorns, in another. "Christ is Risen" and "Alleluia" adorn the tapestries in celebration of the Resurrection. Below the few steps leading to the pulpit, a wooden altar area composed of

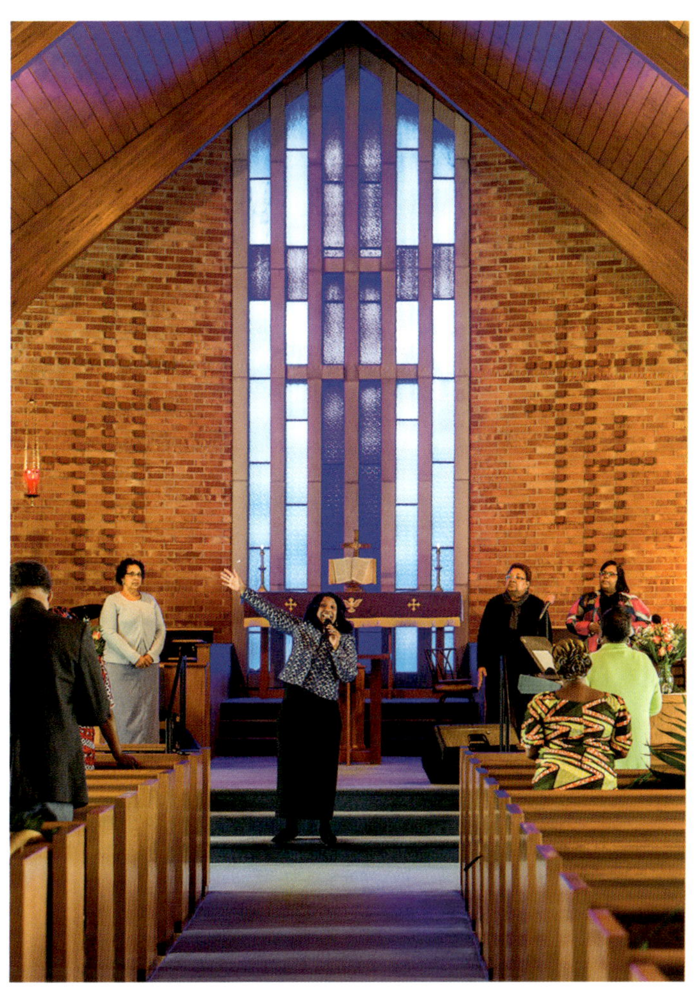

Pastor Lewis leading a service at Burns

wooden rails leaves space for congregants to come forward, kneel, and bring their petitions to God. This is sacred space.

The space that Burns calls sacred, however, has changed throughout its long history. At times, even tents and old factory buildings sufficed as their place of worship. However temporary or unconventional their place of worship has been throughout the decades, this body of believers has persevered.

Burns' prior location was a small building on Crocker Street, home to a Methodist Episcopal church until 1928, when Burns moved in. Burns flourished there, according to Mr. Kitchen, even though upkeep on the building had become more difficult. They later sold the Crocker Street property in order to raise money for outreach

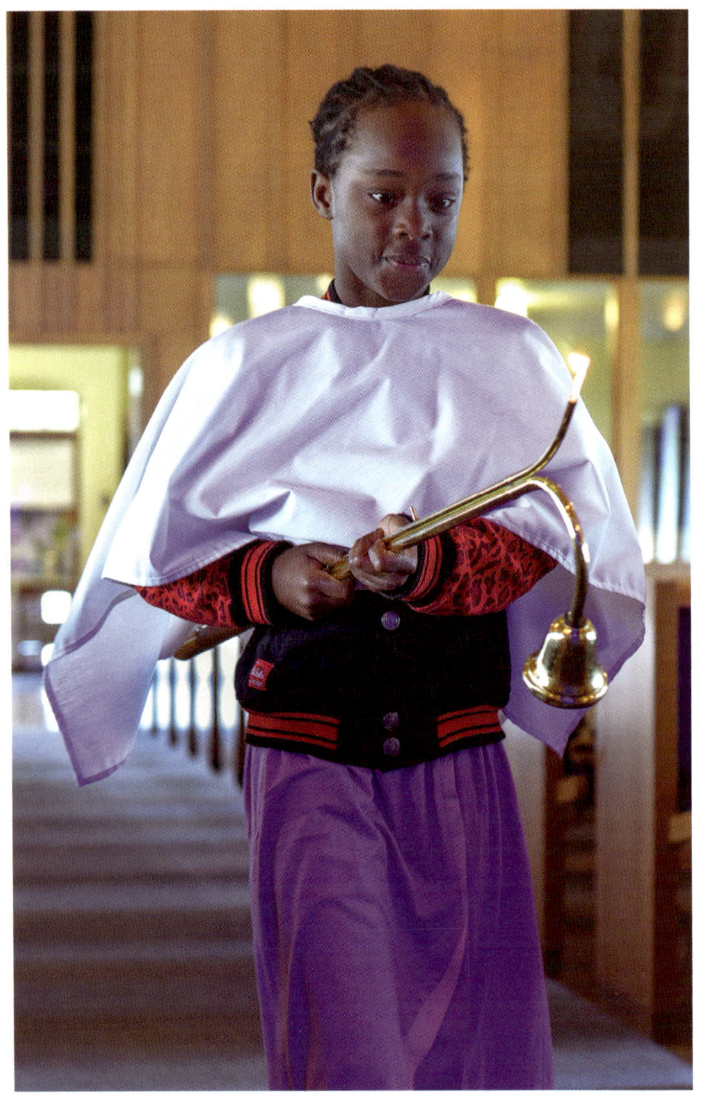

A young acolyte, Elizabeth Bukuru, processing down the aisle with candlelighter

and charity efforts. In early 2011, Gatchel United Methodist Church gifted Burns with its current location on Martin Luther King Jr. Parkway. With the help of Reverend Henry Bevel, and after much discussion and debate, the Burns congregation voted to accept the gift and moved to the space they now call home. As Mr. Kitchen puts it, "Gatchel was a blessing."

A former member of the Gatchel congregation, Gladys Alvarez, described the emotional ceremony during which her church's cross was handed to Burns. It felt like a funeral to her. But, while the ceremony marked an end for Gatchel, it was a new beginning for Burns and a new space to call home. Churchless for a few months after the congregation dissolved, Ms. Alvarez eventually gravitated back to the location that now houses Burns United Methodist. "My daughter thinks the physical space brought me back. You know, that's 'my church,' " she smiles. "Burns came to me."

HISTORY Joyce Wilks started compiling a history of Burns when the congregation began the process of selling the "old church" on Crocker Street. "The words 'In God We Trust' were true in the hearts of a small black congregation searching for a place to call home," she said.

Burns was an active, established congregation in a time before African-Americans could even own land in Iowa. Named after the first Black Bishop of Episcopal Methodism, Francis Burns, the so-named church became an official body in May of 1866. They began small, and, over the decades, have persevered through location changes, fire damage, economic hardship, and rebuilding. The words of Ms. Wilks ring true and pay homage to those who have come before them:

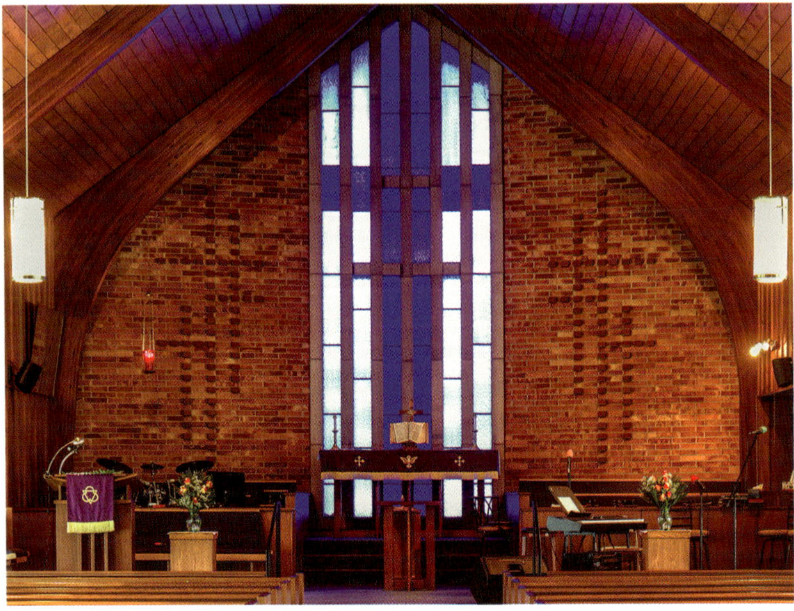

Sanctuary of Burns United Methodist Church

"Burns can never forget the struggles of those who have been a witness, those who have labored in the vineyard for our namesake. God has truly blessed Burns and we will continue to give to God all the praise and glory."

The 1960s brought the Civil Rights Movement and integration, an era when the South Iowa Annual Conference of the United Methodist Church recognized Burns as a member of the previously exclusively white Methodist Conference. On June 15, 1977, Burns United Methodist was placed on the National Register of Historic Places.

In the past five years, the demographics at Burns have changed. Recent refugees or immigrants, many from the Congo region, have brought youthfulness to the congregation and a distinct African flair to worship. Even though some don't yet speak English, the families attend services each week. The children participate in Sunday school and help light the candles during the service. This new generation has revitalized an aging congregation and will help to continue the traditions of Burns' ancestors.

One Sunday, Abia and one of her family members treat the congregation to a worship song. Originally from Burundi, Abia and her children have become part of the Burns family and appreciate the welcome of the community as they adjust to American life. Wearing the traditional clothing of her homeland, Abia stands in her bright green intricately designed dress and head covering. She and a family member slowly approach the front of the sanctuary, pulling out a conga drum and drumstick. A younger member of their troupe translates for them, explaining that their song celebrates the power and glory of God. The syncopated beat of the drum, combined with the two women's powerful vocals, transports listeners through exuberant movement, rhythm, and song to Abia's homeland.

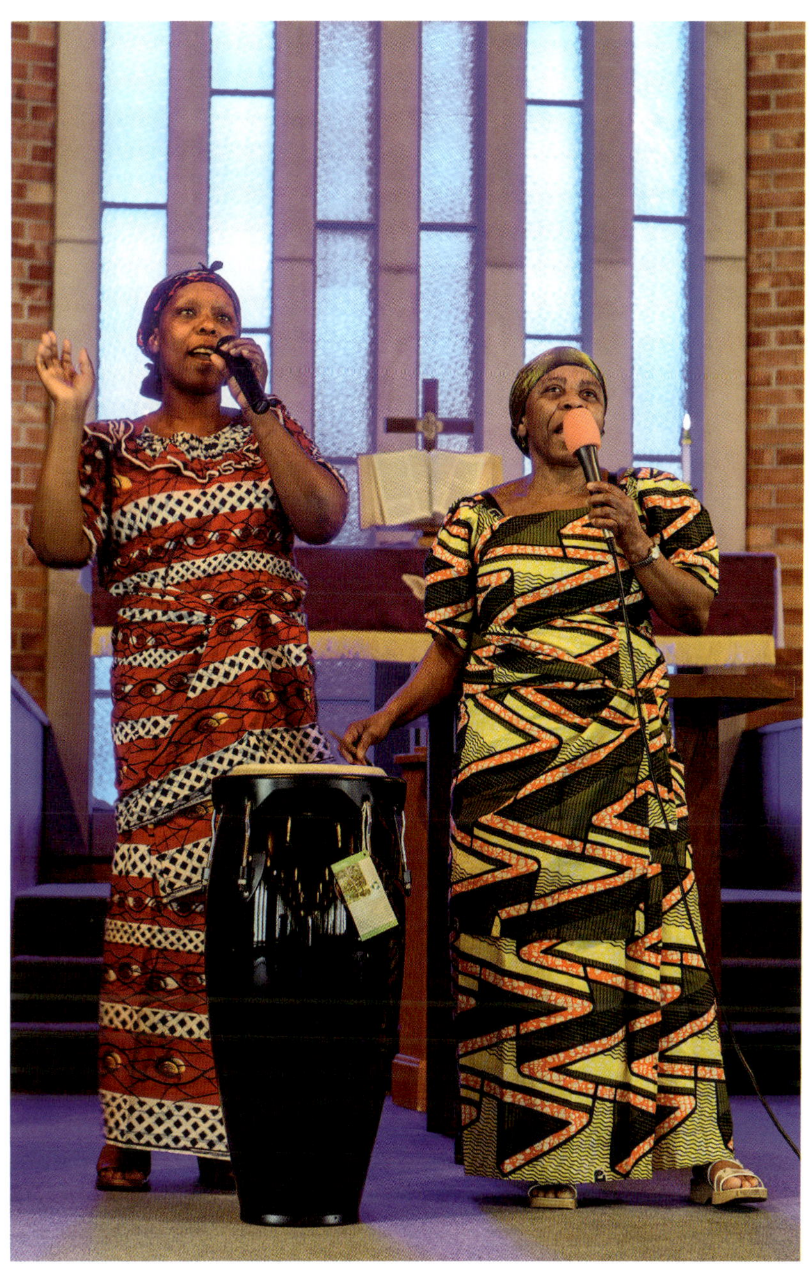

Parishioners from Burundi and the Congo (Abia Sindhaburu and Lwiza Naelendo, left to right) performing special music during a service at Burns

PRACTICE "There is nothing so big that God can't handle it," says Pastor Lewis, describing the work of prayer. A powerful tool for members of Burns, prayer is not always a private or quiet time. In fact, it is often quite vocal. "Yes, Jesus," "Amen," and "Hallelujah," charge the atmosphere with supplication and belief. The bulletin lists the names of individuals and families requesting support and prayer, but during prayer service, as well, members offer spontaneous shout-outs for additional loved ones.

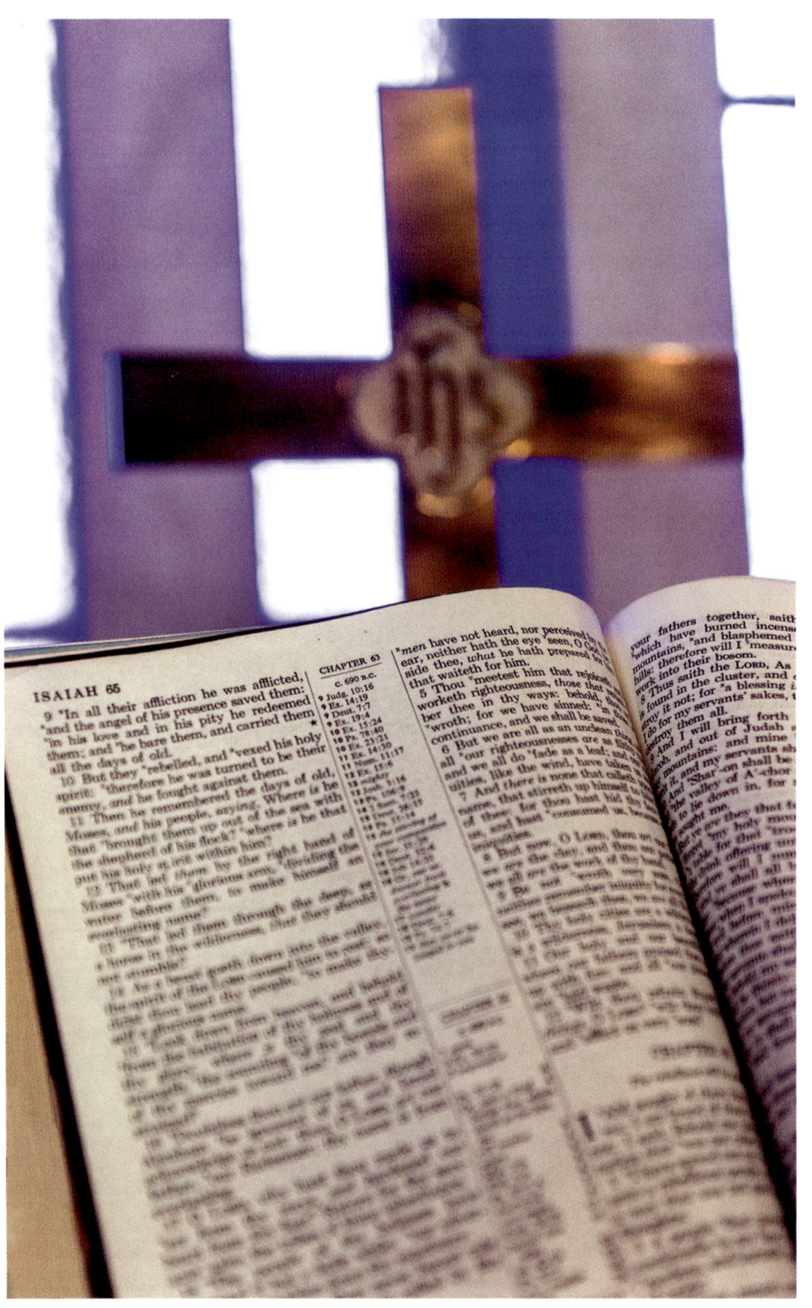

Bible and cross on main altar at Burns

The faithful at Burns value receptiveness to God's word and His interactions with them through prayer. This direct communication with God is a way to not just make requests but also to encounter His glory. Small groups gather, discussing the needs of those around them, their heads bent over prayers shared aloud. With prayer as the unifying force, warmth and love flow between all members of the congregation. Their lives, vulnerable once out in the open, become strong when intertwined with the stories and experiences of other followers of Christ.

Congregants will tell you that God has blessed Burns with a stream of dynamic leaders, each of whom brings his or her own flair to the congregation. Today, Pastor Lewis presides with passionate energy over services and in ministering to her congregation.

Service begins with a time of "bragging on God" called testimony, where sorrow and celebration occur together. From announcements of graduations to stories of joy and healing, congregants share how God moves within their lives. Mothers have recovered from hospital visits, brothers have found Christ in prison, and God's grace and goodness remain certain even through times of pain and difficulty. When Sunday school teacher Joyce Wilks recently announced her retirement, cheers and frenzied clapping filled the air as the congregation showed their appreciation for her years of hard work. After testimony, congregants chat, inquiring about each other's lives with genuine interest.

Music is another vital form of praise and worship. Even without a musician or large choir to lead them, the congregation at Burns becomes one voice, praising and worshipping their Creator. As Harvey Andrews puts it, "A song can take you there and bring you back." They sing traditional hymns, from the ever-popular "Blessed Assurance" to the more intimate "I Need Thee Every Hour."

Mr. Andrews brings his gift for song to the congregation, selecting and then leading the hymns many Sundays. "There is always a song in my head. You know, God speaks to me through music." Congregants old and young begin singing before they have even opened the hymnals, proof of the powerful combination of music and praise. The young, spirited soundman, Jerome, plays modern Gospel hits prior to and following the service, a reminder that contemporary music has a place, even in a historic congregation.

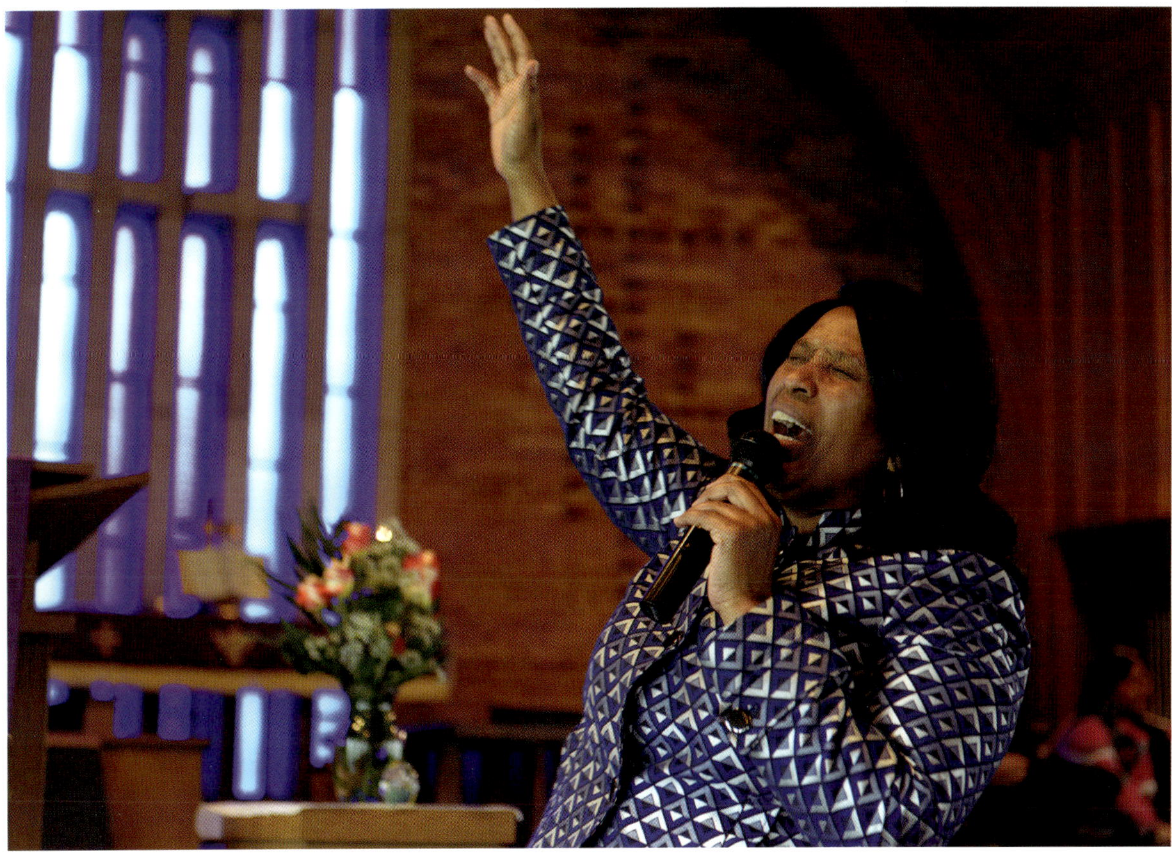

Pastor Lewis leading a service at Burns

Scriptural readings during services often come from the Psalms of the Bible—essentially songs of praise to God. The Psalms are reminders of God's steadfast love and the blessings He bestows upon those who follow Him. Many begin with tales of sorrow and hardship but end with God's glory and His promise to watch over His children. These eloquent verses lend support to the members of Burns whenever they need it. From the teachings of Jesus in the Gospels to the praise of the Psalms, the Bible gives congregants examples of ways to live life as followers of Christ. Dr. Dennis Zachary shared a verse he uses as a guide: "Love the Lord your God with all of your heart and with all of your soul and all of your mind and all of your strength."

Despite the living faith of congregants and the addition of recent immigrants and refugees, Burns still struggles to attract new members. As Ms. Jackson put it, "It's hard to get people to come. Young people just don't believe anymore." In hopes of attracting younger members, folks at Burns have taken steps to increase community mission work, offering neighbors a meal and, if needed, a change of clothes. Giving back is important to the culture of this congregation, namely by way of tithes—when one donates 10% of one's income to the church. These monetary gifts go to support the range of ministries the United Methodist Church is involved in, from Native American outreach to international trips. Even for those who cannot give financially or visit the elderly or ill, members of the congregation know a simple conversation and the act of reaching out can improve lives and situations.

Burns United Methodist Church is a strong faith community held together by love and adoration of God for 150 years. Now, adapting to the times, the church is entering a stage of revitalization where "every Sunday speaks to somebody." God is speaking to His people, and at Burns their hearts are open.

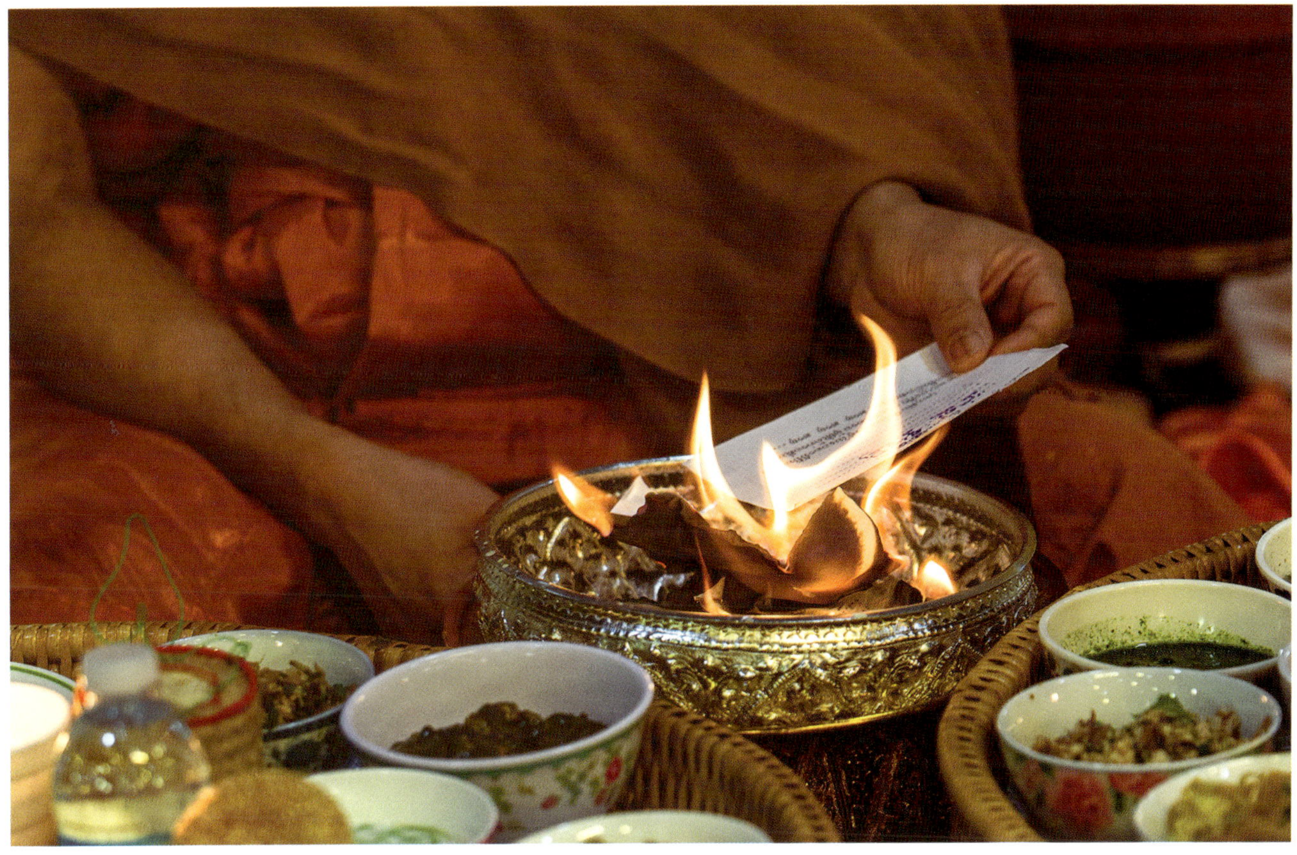

Ajahn Somphan burns prayers for the dead by members of Wat Phothisomphan

ABOUT THE COMPARISON PROJECT

The Comparison Project practices *global philosophy of religion* in the *local Des Moines community.*

Globally, The Comparison Project's *Lecture and Dialogue Series* enacts an innovative approach to religiously inclusive philosophy of religion, exploring common religious themes from different religious perspectives through scholar lectures, practitioner dialogues, and philosophical comparisons. Scholar lectures and philosophical comparisons are published at the end of every biennial programming cycle through a book-series contract with the international publisher, Springer.

Locally, The Comparison Project's *Religions of Des Moines Initiative* generates informational media about religious communities in the greater Des Moines area, collaborating with these communities to create narrative guides about them and digital stories by their members. Plans are in motion to expand this initiative to include interfaith summer camps, "meet my religious neighbor" open houses, and a centralized hub for the events and voices of local religion.

Our programming is currently supported by eight sources: the Drake University Center for the Humanities, Humanities Iowa, the Medbury Fund, the Drake University Principal Financial Group Center for Global Citizenship, the Des Moines Area Religious Council, Cultivating Compassion: The Dr. Richard Deming Foundation, the Slay Fund for Social Justice, and The Comparison Project's special series sponsor for its programming on death and dying, Iles Funeral Homes. We are grateful to them all.

Website: www.ComparisonProject.wordpress.drake.edu
Email: ComparisonProject@drake.edu
Facebook: @DrakeComparison
Instagram: @DrakeComparison
Twitter: @DrakeComparison

ABOUT THE DRAKE COMMUNITY PRESS

A unique small-press publisher since 2014, the Community Press is a two-year curriculum based publishing laboratory and community engagement experience that includes student and faculty collaborators from several academic disciplines, along with a selected non-profit partner with a story to tell about their work and mission. We are a 21st century publisher utilizing a variety of media platforms, related events, and supplemental publications to share our stories.

Our motto "Writing *With*" emphasizes the collaborative nature of our Press model, in which all campus and community stakeholders serve as contributors with a crucial voice in the production process from inspiration to content production to design and marketing. In our model, we are all students in some form and teachers in another, negotiating across boundaries of campus and community, academic role and discipline, and cultural background toward a common goal.

We share the purpose of producing beautifully researched, written, and designed publications that serve a community readership on issues of concern to Iowans. In addition, our books raise several thousands of dollars in support of the organizations with whom we partner.

Our first title, *The Ones I Bring With Me/Los Que Llevos Conmigo* (2014), features the journeys of Iowa Latina girls and their adult mentors as they navigate issues of identity, family, education, and achievement. This bi-lingual edition was produced for ¡Al Exito!—a Latino/Latina Central Iowa mentoring organization. Soon to be in its 2nd edition, the book is used in diversity training courses in college and corporate settings as well as in classrooms and libraries across the state. In 2016, it was selected as a featured title for the ¡Adelante! Book of the Month Club by the American Association of University Women.

Our funders include Drake University organizations that support initiatives in social justice and innovation in teaching and faculty development. In addition, we are generously supported by a variety of corporate and non-profit entities who share our goal of community betterment. If you are interested in supporting the Drake Community Press through involvement or with your donation, please find out more at:

Website: www.DrakeCommunityPress.org
Email: CommunityPress@drake.edu
Facebook: @DUCommPress
Instagram: @DUCommPress
Twitter: @DUCommPress

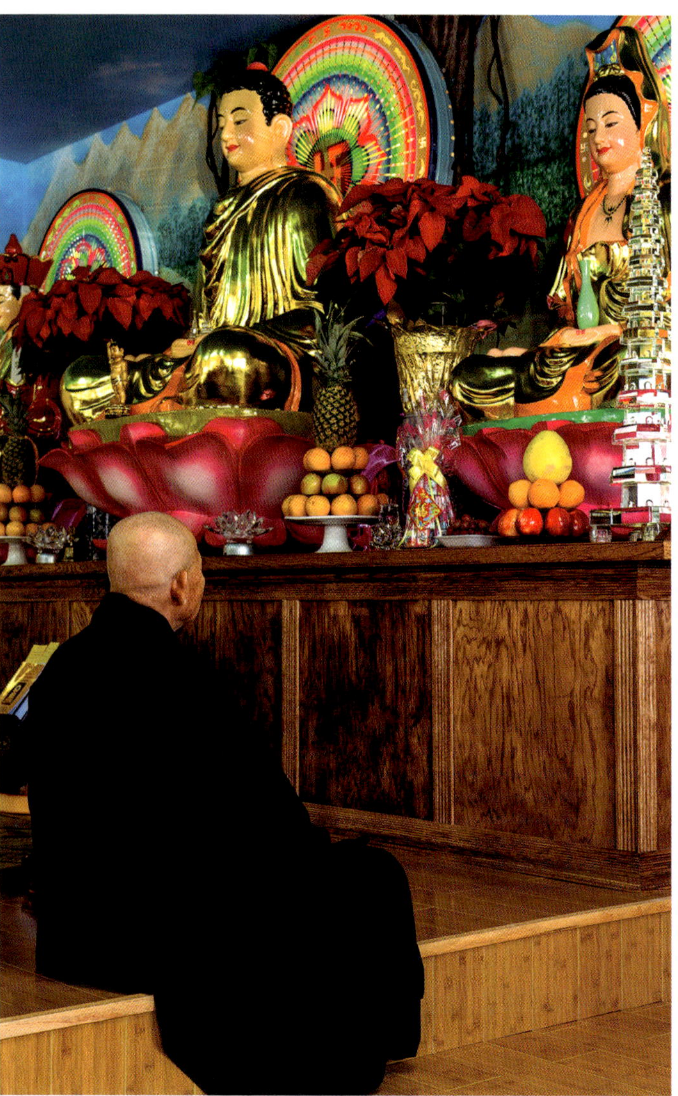

Thầy's father gazes up at a statue of Quan Âm on the altar at Tu Viện Hồng Đức

ABOUT THE DES MOINES AREA RELIGIOUS COUNCIL

The Des Moines Area Religious Council is a nonprofit, interfaith organization focused on a shared belief in helping low-income Central Iowans meet basic human needs. DMARC's core membership is built of over 130 congregations from four faith traditions: Christian, Jewish, Muslim, and Unitarian Universalist. DMARC has also formed interfaith relationships with members of the atheist, Bahá'í, Buddhist, Hindu, Jain, Native American, Pagan, and Sikh communities. DMARC provides interfaith dialogue and engagement through interfaith worship services, lectures, tours, and other learning activities. Learn more about the Des Moines Area Religious Council at:

Website: www.DMARCUnited.org
Email: info@DMARCUnited.org
Facebook: @DesMoinesARC
Twitter: @DMReligious
YouTube: @DMReligious

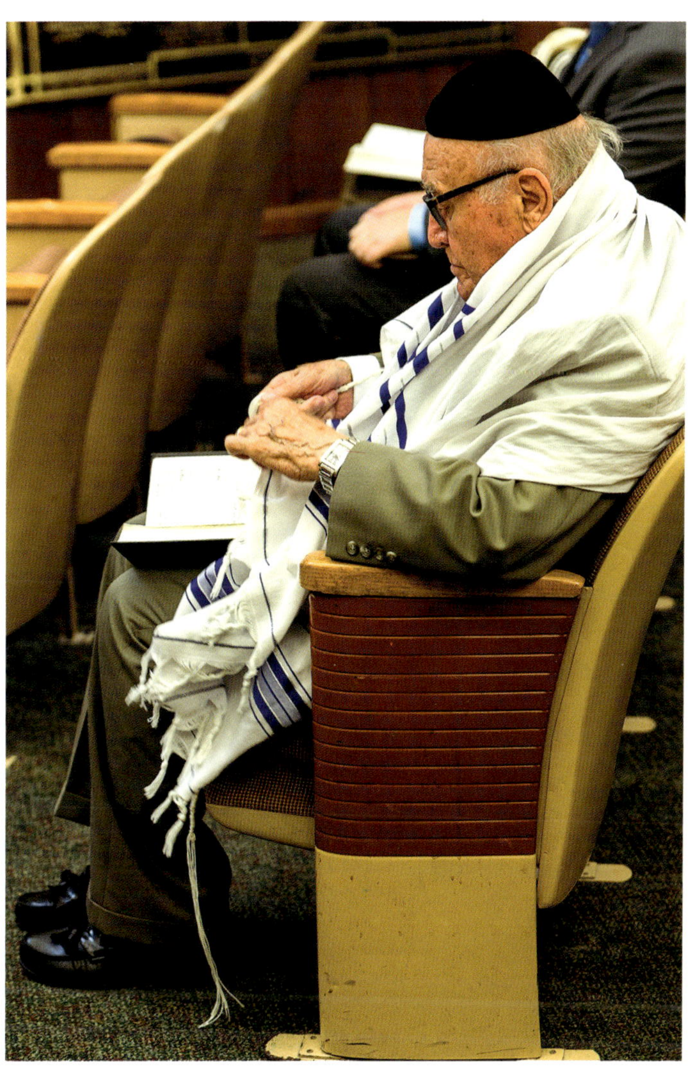

David Wolnerman reads from a prayer book in the sanctuary of Beth El Jacob Synagogue

CONTRIBUTORS

Carol Spaulding-Kruse
Director of the Drake Community Press
Tim Knepper
Director of The Comparison Project
Bob Blanchard, Photographer
(www.BobBlanchardPhotography.com)
John Fender, Director of Design
Carlyn Crowe, Director of Public Relations
Anna Steenson
Documentarian and Videographer
Morgan Cannata, DCP Web Design

EDITORIAL INTERNS

Abbey Maynard
Amanda O'Malley
Jack Davidson
Makena Schoene
Molly Adamson
Morgan Gstalter
Sarah Mondello
Stephanie Gaub
Tori Gedler

EDUCATIONAL SUPPLEMENT

Grace Boatman
Jonathan Lueth
Kate Havens

J-TERM 2017: BOOK PUBLISHING AND PROMOTION

Amanda O'Malley
Donny Hughes
Dustin Eubanks
Ellen Judge
Jack Davidson
Kate Havens
Kendal Owens
Michelle Stiles
Molly Adamson
Olivia Wasswen
Parker Klyn
Rachel Wermager
Sydney Schulte
Tierney Grisolano

SPRING 2016 RELIGION CAPSTONE COURSE (*STUDENT RESEARCHERS*)

Alliyah Greaver
Anoushe Seiff
Benjamin Weinberg
Dustin Eubanks
Hanna Howard
Isaiah Enockson
John Noble
Kayla Schween
Logan Potter
Matthew Becke
Meghan Plambeck
Nathan Jacobson
Taylor Donaldson
Tierney Grisolano
W. A. Chamindi Wijesinghe

2015-17 RELIGION UNDERGRADUATE ASSISTANTS

Anoushe Seiff
Grace Boatman
Isaiah Enockson
Matthew Becke
Nathan Jacobson
Taylor Donaldson
W. A. Chamindi Wijesinghe

FALL 2016 ADVANCED TYPOGRAPHY COURSE (*STUDENT GRAPHIC DESIGNERS*)

Adam Gray
Anna Shewmaker
Bailey Zander
Dustin Miller
Genna Clemen
Giuliana LaMantia
Kayla Marple
Kiana Anderson
Kylee Bateman
Madison Ottenbacher
Margot Stevens
Sarah Keppeler

SPRING 2016 COMMUNITY WRITING COURSE (*STUDENT EDITORS*)

Abbey Maynard
Ethan Turner
Giselle Gamez
Hailey Paulson
Mitchell Heacock
Molly Adamson
Sam McKinney
Sarah Mondello
Tori Gedler

ACKNOWLEDGEMENTS

SPECIAL THANKS

Darcie Vandegrift
Joan Faber McAlister
Renee Sedlacek

DCP ADVISORY BOARD

Barbara Boose
Carlyn Crowe
Chad Michael Cox
Hannah Wright
Ian Miller
Jan Kaiser
Judith Conlin
Justin Norman
Kay Smith
Kyle McCord
Lauren Oliver
Maureen Korte
Peter Caldbeck
Rachel Quinn
Renee Sedlacek
Sarah McCoy
Shawnna Stiver
Wini Moranville

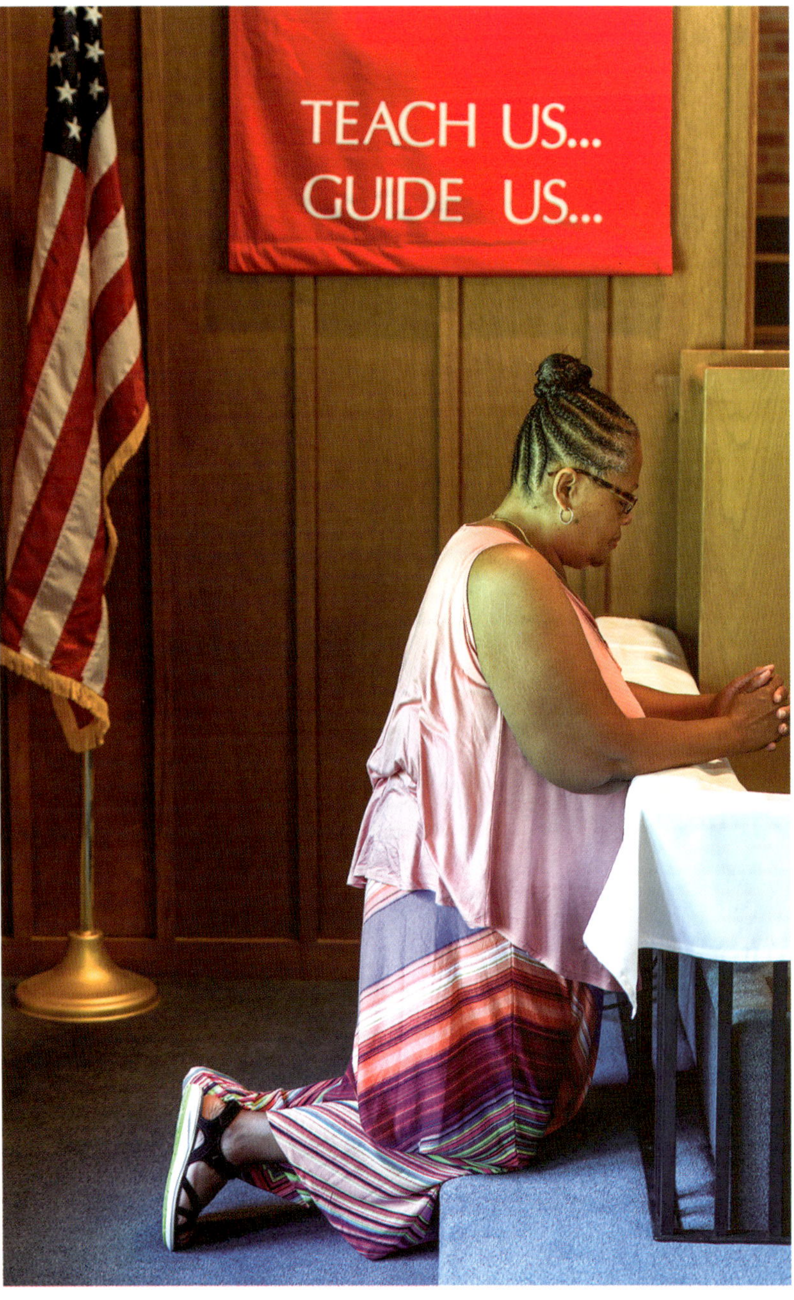

Pam Hamrick prays at the altar during a service at Burns United Methodist Church

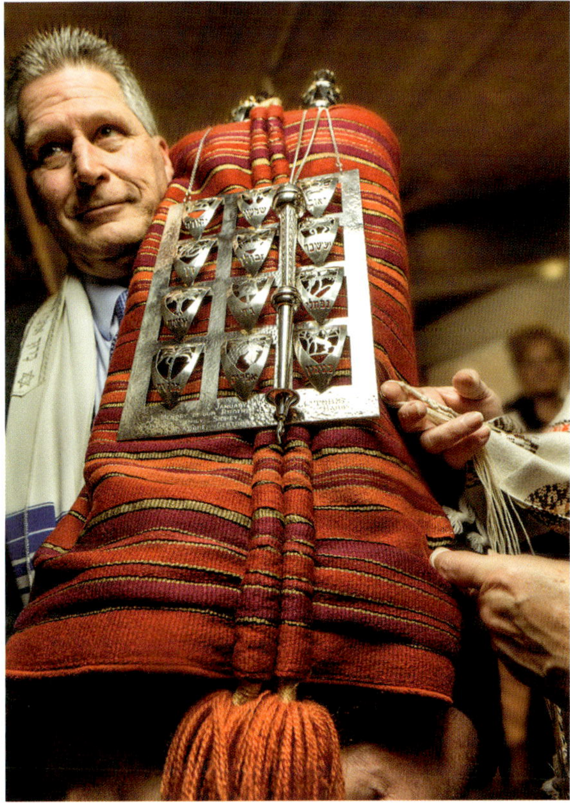

Ron Osby parades the Torah scroll during the festival of *Simchat Torah* at Tifereth Israel Synagogue

GENEROUS SUPPORTERS

College of Arts & Sciences
Cultivating Compassion:
The Dr. Richard Deming Foundation
Drake Center for the Humanities
Engaged Citizen Program Fund
Office of Community Engagement and
Service Learning
Office of the Provost
Principal Financial Group Center for
Global Citizenship
Ron and Jane Olson Fund
Slay Fund for Social Justice
Student Senate

We are especially grateful for significant donations from Dr. Richard Deming and Brent and Dianne Slay

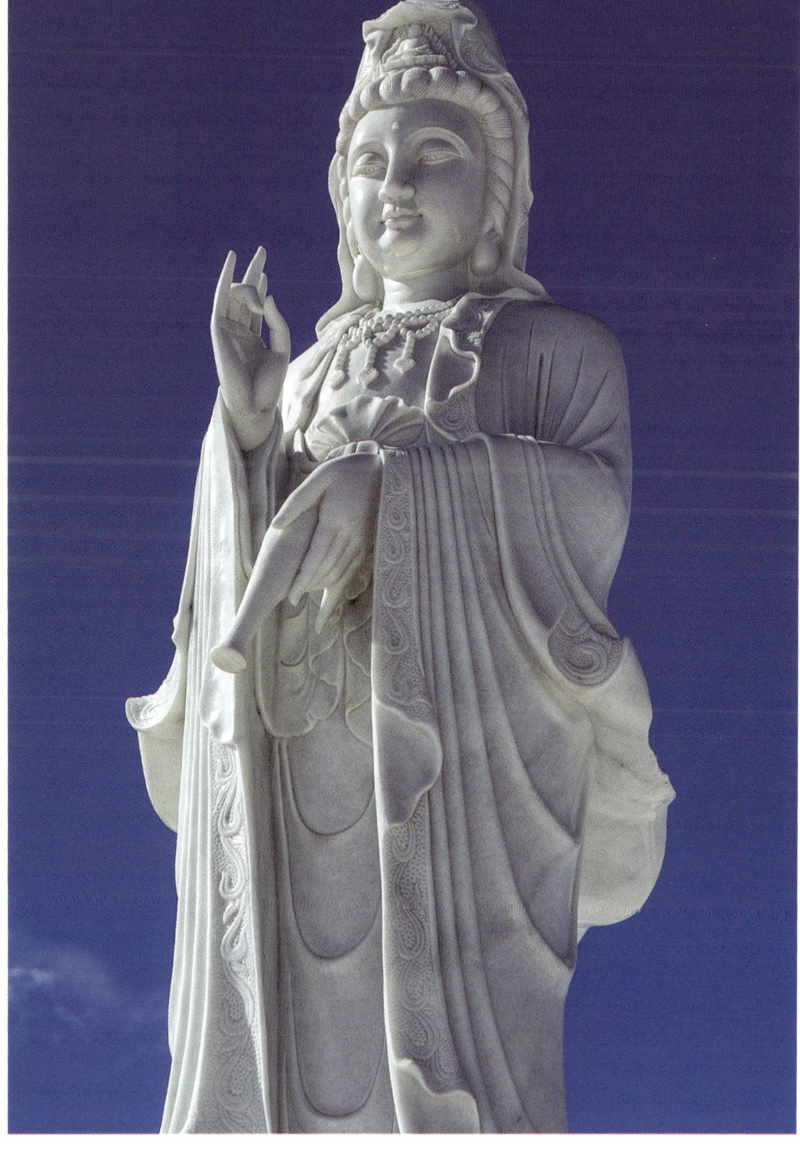

Quan Âm pours out her compassion in the sculpture park at Tu Viện Hồng Đức

COLOPHON
This book was designed by Advanced Typography students in Fall 2016 under the direction of John Fender. It is set in Crimson Text, a serif typeface designed by Sebastian Kosch, 2010 and Source Sans Pro, a sans serif typeface created by Paul D. Hunt for Adobe Systems, 2012. Printing on Endurance Printing Paper, Silk 80 lb. text and 100 lb. cover by Colorfx in Des Moines, Iowa

OTHER BOOKS BY THE DRAKE COMMUNITY PRESS
Zakery's Bridge: Children's Journeys From Around the World to Iowa (2011)
The Ones I Bring With Me/*Los que llevo conmigo* (2014)